Kathy's Real Story

Hermann Kelly.

Kathy's Real Story

A culture of false allegations exposed

Hermann Kelly

PREFECT PRESS

First published in 2007 by
Prefect Press Ltd,
An Teacht Bán, Dunleer, Co Louth,
Ireland.
www.prefectpress.com

Copyright © Hermann Kelly 2007

A catalogue record of this book is available from the British Library.
ISBN 978-1-906351-00-7
Printed by ColourBooks, Dublin 13, Ireland.

I dedicate this book to my father, Hugh Vincent Kelly.
Da, you gave me life and love,

Thank you

Acknowledgments

I would like to acknowledge and thank the following for use of material: *The Sunday Independent, The Irish Mail on Sunday, The Irish Independent, The Irish Times, The Sunday Business Post, The Sunday Mirror, The Sunday Times* (Irl), *The Irish Catholic, News of the World, The Mirror,* Mainstream Publishing, *The Smoking Gun,* Harpo Productions.

I would like to acknowledge and thank the following for use of material: members of the O'Beirne family, Margaret Power, Margaret Lacey, Valerie Murtagh, 'Maeve' in America, Tom Hayes (Alliance Victim Support), researcher Rory Connor, Claire McGettrick (Justice for Magdalenes group), Florence Horsman-Hogan (L.O.V.E.), Christine Buckley, (Aislin Centre), Tony Gavin / *Sunday Independent* for the Kathy O'Beirne pics, picture desk of *The Irish Mail on Sunday,* and Mary at Collins Photographs.

Many thanks to the kind people at F.A.C.T. UK and Pete Henshaw at SecEd. All those I interviewed or spoke to for this book, Kathy O'Beirne, Michael Sheridan, Bill Campbell of Mainstream, many thanks for your time and help. To all those who helped me in any way, I hope you now see it as a worthwhile project.

This work could not have been completed if it were not for the reporting of many journalists, especially: Dearbhail McDonald, Lara Bradley, Niall Donald, Daniel Boffey, Natalie Clarke, Breda O'Brien and *Liveline's* own, Joe Duffy. I would also like to thank Paul Drury for his support on my first approaching *The Irish Mail on Sunday*; and to John Burns at *The Sunday Times* for his help.

Thanks to Matthew Nugent who did the first subbing. All mistakes are my own. Thanks to Mr Garrett Cooney S.C. for doing the legals.

Contents:

Chapters

1 The Big Story of the Year

"There is a crack in everything. It's how the light gets in."
Leonard Cohen *'Anthem'* (1992)

*K*athy's Story is one of the best-selling books in Britain and other countries across the globe. It is the highest selling 'non-fiction' book by an Irish author in the history of publishing. Since it was launched in May 2005, by Mainstream Publishing in Edinburgh, the book has sold and sold, whetting the appetite of many for the growing genre of literature – memoirs of suffering, known as miserable literature, (mis. lit. for short). The book is perfectly scripted to feed the desire for books on clerical abuse which had been so publicly exposed in Ireland and America during the years preceding the book's publication.

In her book, ghostwritten with the help of co-author Michael Sheridan, Kathy O'Beirne makes truly sensational allegations against a large number of people.

Her book paints a dark picture of systematic abuse, both sexual, physical and psychological in a series of Dublin Magdalene laundries committed on a young girl called Kathy O'Beirne. It tells the disturbing story of a girl who suffered abuse within her own family before being committed into a residential school around 1970 at the age of eight. This was the first of six institutions which she claims she attended. She also claims to have been raped by two different priests, forced to take part in a regime of 'slave labour' and corralled into drug trials in a state mental hospital against her will.

Mainstream Publishing thought it was were on to a winner with *Kathy's Story* and pulled out all the stops to promote Kathy's book. She was ushered flawlessly onto a raft of morning talk show programmes in Britain. Treated royally, the hosts listened breathlessly as Kathy, with her charming Dublin accent and quickfire style regaled them with a horror story of an abusive Irish father who sent her off to institutions where she was beaten, abused and raped by a number of priests. The hosts, as they lapped up this story, never once thought to ask her for any proof. They just sat there, tut-tutting at the chain of endless horror. 'Poor girl, how could it ever happen in a civilised country?'

As her appearances increased, the sales of the book soared. By the summer of 2006, the book had sold almost 350,000 copies worldwide, the publishers said. It was estimated in the national press that the publisher had made profits of almost €2.2 million.

The publishers had sold foreign rights to the book as far and wide as Australia, America, Sweden and Poland.

Co-author Michael Sheridan later went so far as to say to this journalist, that the popularity of the book showed that the book was true and that people believed it.

By 2007, the book entitled 'Don't Ever Tell' in Britain was proudly marketed as a Sunday Times bestseller and had the ominous subheading: 'Kathy's Story: A True Tale of a Childhood Destroyed by Neglect and Fear'.

The publicity machine for the book rolled on relentlessly. It became serialised in a number of tabloid newspapers. It was splashed across two-page spreads with sensational headlines.

For instance, The News of the World on May 8, 2005 ran the banner headline: "MAGDALENE SURVIVOR KATHY O'BEIRNE TELLS OF HER NIGHTMARE CHILDHOOD"

The journalist, under the subtitle, "RAPED BY A PRIEST, WHIPPED BY NUNS" wrote that: "A MAGDALENE laundry survivor has revealed the horrifying abuse she suffered before and after she was locked in the institution.

"Kathy O'Beirne, who has scars on her body from years of beatings, has told the Irish News of the World of the nightmare she lived through as a child.

"Kathy, in her 40s, of Clondalkin, in Dublin, endured thrashings from her father as well as sexual abuse from two boys before being sent away. Then Kathy, aged only ten, was repeatedly RAPED by a priest and regularly WHIPPED by nuns."

But courageous Kathy would not rest until justice was done. Not for her, suffering in silence. If she could not get justice in Ireland, it was to Rome that she would have to go. In October 16, 2005, *The News of the World* ran with another headline, "KATHY IN QUEST TO SEE POPE" and below told of her Herculean efforts: "ABUSE survivor Kathy O'Beirne went to Rome this week to get the word 'penitents' removed from a monument for the Magdalene dead.

"Kathy, who was physically and sexually abused in institutions for 21 years, took a petition to the Pope demanding the sinners' stigma be removed from the monument in Dublin's Glasnevin cemetery. The 43-year-old has battled for 11 years to replace the memorial, but the Sisters of Our Lady of Charity have refused to let her."

Not to be outdone, a large-circulation newspaper, *The Mirror*, on Tuesday June 7, 2005, had the headline: "I'M NOT AFRAID OF ANY-ONE NOW. I'M READY TO DIE TO GET JUSTICE FOR THE VIC-TIMS; KATHY TELLS HORROR TALE OF SLAVERY & ABUSE IN MAGDALENE LAUNDRIES."

It reported that, "Kathy O'Beirne was only eight when a psychiatrist diagnosed her as a "child with a troublesome mind." She had suffered years of physical and mental torture at the hands of her cruel father.

"Kathy said: 'I feel my story had to be told. It was like a volcano inside me always ready to explode. So much evil was done there and there was a voice inside me shouting Justice.'"

Kathy told the newspaper that, "We were done wrong to. We were innocent people and the perpetrators are getting away Scot-free."

She added that "after a hard 11 years writing this book, and a second one I'm nearly finished called *The Aftermath: Who am I?*; I feel I've finally been set free."

She thanked the Lord for letting her survive, and let the paper know that her profits from the book were going to three charities – the Magdalene Graves, a children's hospital in Dublin and to Romanian children. The lucky recipients of Kathy's largesse are so unspecifically named as to be difficult to trace and confirm.

Yet, just around the corner, surely a tough journalist was waiting to ask her some hard and searching questions, to demand to see the evidence? And if the case was true, he or she would proclaim Kathy's horrific story to the world.

Vincent Browne is one of the best-known journalists and commentators in Ireland. He has a reputation as an aggressive questioner and relentless interviewer. After questioning an MEP with strong Christian values, former Eurovision contest winner Dana Scallan (nee Brown) during his radio programme, he had to apologise for his comments.

During the Irish General Election campaign of 2007, Vincent Browne hit the national headlines by grilling the Taoiseach (Prime minister) Bertie Ahern about his personal finances from the floor of the Mansion House hall during the launch of the Fianna Fáil party's election manifesto. Browne has shown he can grill anyone if he wants to.

When he still had his own RTÉ show, the RTÉ 1 national radio website put it that, "His controversial interviewing style is a sign of his determination to get at the facts and that makes the programme compelling listening."

During an interview on RTÉ radio's *Tonight with Vincent Browne Show* on Wednesday June 22, 2005 Kathy was asked how she came to be in a Magdalene Laundry. She told of her sexual abuse from the age of five, by three different people, one of whom was a priest. She said that eventually she went out of control.

"I was brought to a panel of psychiatrists in Dublin and they diagnosed me as a child with a troublesome mind, and a week later I was sent to an industrial school run by the nuns, I was there for just two years," Kathy said.

Vincent Browne asked her: "Where was this?"

Kathy O'Beirne responded: "I can't say because it is in the Enquiry [What enquiry? – would have be a good question here], so I can't mention the name of it, but it was in Dublin and like a training ground for the Magdalene Laundry, I think, I believe anyway, but I was there for just two years and I was sexually abused and raped by the visiting priest that came there and I told one of the nuns..."

Vincent Browne: "This was another priest, yet another priest?"

Kathy O'Beirne: "Yes, in the Industrial School, I wasn't the only girl, there were other girls raped there and sexually abused by the same priest and I did tell a nun about it and when I told her I was taken off again."

Vincent Browne: "You told a nun?"

Kathy O'Beirne: "I told a Nun that was looking after us and I was taken off again anyway to speak to this Doctor and he was going to help me and the whole lot, and I came back and a couple of days later I was sent to a childrens' mental institution in Dublin where I was for two years and I had electric shock treatment and drug trials. For the two years I was there, we were abused, horrible things went on in it."

Vincent Browne: "What sort of things?"

Kathy O'Beirne: "Abuse and drug trials and electric shock treatment."

Vincent Browne: "Can you say where this was?"

Kathy O'Beirne: "I can't no, because it is all in the Enquiry and you can't mention the name of the places until the Enquiry is over, it is all in the other book, I have another book coming out. *The Aftermath, Who Am I?*, is the name of it but until the Enquiry is over you can't mention the names. So I was transferred, after two years, we got up to mischief there and we came across this, it is in the book, this guy called Johnny, and he was just a breath of fresh air so we became friends, himself and another couple of girls, and our punishment was, when we done anything wrong, they used to send us down to the gate and at the gate there was a morgue and we would have to wash the dead bodies, people that died in the mental institution ..."

The interview went on like this for some time, where the lightest probing by the interviewer was met by a long stream of very serious allegations by O'Beirne. One question, "What happened ?" was replied to with almost 2,000 words, about three pages of transcript. Kathy did the great majority of talking as she regaled her interviewer with stories of innocent people disappearing to be quietly buried by nuns and clergy; about mass graves in the West of Ireland in institutions run by the Christian Brothers; about babies being sold by nuns for profit to America; about her witnessing a girl of 14 being gang-raped by five men in a girls' home, that they took liver and bowel biopsies from her without sedation.

She said, "So the Nuns and the clergy can bury innocent women and children, pick them up, pluck them up, bring them here, bring them there and burn them and do what they like with them and nobody knows why, where, who?"

Browne even momentarily broke from his very public and repetitive proclamation of his atheism to exclaim, "My God, what a story!" Indeed.

Yet O'Beirne easily fobbed off his questions.

And so the interview continued. Yet during it, and for the first time, a chink appeared in O'Beirne's armour. She stepped out from behind the facade of vague and sketchy allegations against anonymous people and institutions. O'Beirne mentioned High Park in North Dublin (near Collins Avenue), which was run by a female religious order, the Sisters of Our Lady of Charity.

In the author's note at the very beginning of her book, Kathy states: "For legal reasons, I have not been able to name any of the institutions in which I was incarcerated or any of the people who abused me."

It was a 'no-names' book, but when she became specific for the first time, it was then Kathy's Story began to come apart.

She also stated during the interview that, "I got my daughter's Birth Certificate after 30 years on Friday." Surely she would be able to produce it when asked by a journalist then?

The nuns intervene

Infuriated by this uncontested free publicity-ride for the book and the harm done to the name of the order during this interview, on June 24th 2005, the Sisters of our Lady of Charity of High Park and Sean McDermott Street issued a media statement saying:

"We can categorically state that Kathy O'Beirne did not spend any time in our laundries or related institutions. We met Kathy O'Beirne in the past year for the purposes of clarifying this with her.

"On a point of general information, we would like to state that although our order operated a number of residential homes for women and girls, our rules precluded us from accepting pregnant girls. As a result, no pregnant girls ever worked in the laundries operated by us and no child was ever born in any of our premises. We therefore never had anything to do with the adoption or placement of any child.

"We would also like to state that Kathy O'Beirne repeatedly refers to 'a mass grave for the female penitents' located at the Glasnevin cemetery. In fact, we have no grave at that location and the photographs produced by Kathy O'Beirne of a large stone cross in the Glasnevin cemetery actually depicts a monument rather than a headstone of a grave. This monument was erected by a member of the order in the first part of the last century as a memorial to women of the 'Monto' area and not to any women who was in our care. [Dublin was a British garrison town before Irish independence and the soldiers 'needs' were serviced during the first part of the twentieth century by the high number of prostitutes who occupied 'The Monto', an area in central Dublin]

"Regarding her allegations about women being buried without death certificates a full research has been done on those who died in the care or our order and names and death certificates have been identified. The history of our order in Ireland is being written and we hope to have it ready for publication next year.

"As the allegations being made by Kathy are so serious, we are now writing to the Minister for Justice to ask him to have Kathy's allegations investigated. We will fully co-operate with such an investigation and we trust Kathy will do likewise.

"Although Kathy's story is an horrific one, in the interest of fairness and justice to all, it is important that the facts of her story are clarified and verified."

Soon after this Kathy told journalist David Quinn of *The Irish Independent* newspaper that she had "all the records of having been in the institutions" adding she was not at liberty to name the institutions "because I would be sued." She also alleged to the paper that two clerics have paid her out-of-court settlements because of sexual abuse she says she suffered from them.

Next up, journalist Lara Bradley of *The Sunday Independent* on July 3rd 2005 squeezed out of Miss O'Beirne that she now explicitly claimed to have been in High Park and Sean McDermott Street Laundries:

"Ms O'Beirne told *The Sunday Independent* she had documentary proof that she was resident in High Park and Sean McDermott Street Magdalene Laundries, but refused to produce this. She said: 'Of course I have proof. I'm not one bit confused. I'm calling them liars. I never had an issue with people believing me. There are hundreds of people out there who know what happened to me. There had to be forms signed by psychiatrists. I was actually delivered by a nurse to High Park.

"Of course I have all the proof I need. The best wine is kept till last. I'm keeping it for the High Court. I'll sue them."

While the nuns of the relevant order showed journalist Lara Bradley relevant documents that Kathy had spent six weeks in one of their residential homes for children, they also explained that the records they had of the Magdalene Laundries of that time in question "are complete and so comprehensive that one woman's two-day admittance was recorded."

Responding to questions from the newspaper, the managing director of Mainstream Publishers, Mr Bill Campbell said: "We are satisfied Kathy's Story is 100 per cent true. It is an earth-shattering story. We have done our own investigations, which are very stringent. There is no question of us pulling this book."

The Sisters of Our Lady of Charity then wrote a letter to the then Minister for Justice, Michael McDowell asking him to initiate an investigation into the whole matter. In reaction to this, Garda Commissioner Noel Conroy, on July 6, appointed a Detective Superintendent to "examine the issues raised," in their letter.

Interview on her home patch

I first met Kathy O'Beirne at Bewley's Hotel in Newlands Cross, Dublin on the last Friday in June 2005. The hotel was directly opposite her house in Booth Road, Clondalkin. At the time, the book was standing at number 6 in Eason's best sellers list in Ireland. Kathy was on the crest of a wave, and talking of publishing a second book. When we first spoke, she was a bit agitated and spent the first ten minutes speaking to her publicist on the phone, raging on about "that bitch Lara Bradley". The upshot was, O'Beirne said: "Pass the word around the abuse groups in Dublin, that one (Bradley) will never get another interview again," she said. I sensed the conversation was for my benefit, as a warning not to ask any hard questions, rather than to just enlighten her publicist.

Kathy herself, is quite charming and very chatty. She likes to know all about you, asking where you are from and how did you end up as a journalist. She obviously knew a lot of people in the hotel restaurant, and greeted them casually but warmly as we made our way upstairs.

Having done a lot of research before interviewing Kathy, I approached her as I do most interviewees; softly at first, make them comfortable and at ease, start off with a few general questions which they will want to answer. I did this, telling her as we went that I used to be a teacher before I came to journalism. She suggested, at an early stage in the interview, that I was "too soft to be a teacher, and too soft to be a journalist." She was obviously feeling comfortable and so I switched to high questioning mode.

By the time I was finished the interview, one that was printed in *The Irish Catholic* newspaper on July 28, 2005, Kathy said, "You think you're a barrister don't you. Well, I'm not up in court!" What a difference a few hard questions make.

To cut it short, she admitted that yes, she had been under the care of The Sisters of our Lady of Charity in both High Park and Sean McDermott Street Laundries. She even suggested that in one of these laundries the nuns looked after her really well. You would never think this if you read her book.

Though claiming to have documentary evidence to show her stay in all the institutions, Kathy failed to show this journalist any documented evidence demonstrating that she had ever attended any of these institutions in the book. Neither the dates nor the full names of any living persons who worked along with her in the laundries are given either. When asked to name people who could prove to be corroborative witnesses of her time in the institutions, she declined to do so. Instead she said: "there are nuns who came to visit me, clergy who came to visit me, family who came to visit me, there are letters." She also said she had photographs of herself and other girls from the laundries. Again she refused to show me any of these photographs.

Questioned on whether she was taking all the institutions in which she claimed she was abused to court, she replied that "I'm not saying, what I'm doing or what I'm not doing." Asked if she had shown the documentary evidence to the gardai who have investigated the matter, Kathy replied, "Well, I'm not going to make any comment on that." Kathy told me she didn't receive an education during her time in these institutions: "I didn't get any education. I was in school for a couple of days and that was it. I certainly didn't get an education in any institution that I was in. Certainly not in the mental institution I was in because I was doped out of my brains all of the time." For a woman who claims she has had little education, Kathy has a very, very sharp mind. As a journalist, I have interviewed six Irish Government ministers, and numerous people of national renown and indeed international stature but the interview with Kathy is probably the most difficult interview I have ever done.

Stolen babies sold for profit

Kathy remained adamant, however, that she has all her files showing that she was there. I asked to see these files but again she declined. Amongst the most serious statements in Kathy's book (page 120) is the allegation that the nuns stole babies from their mothers and sold them to America. She claimed that various women she knew had seen ledgers with the babies' names and prices listed, that "beautiful babies were, as far as the nuns were concerned, human traffic to be sold for profit," she writes. Sr Sheila Murphy, regional leader of the Sisters of Our Lady of Charity, said this was totally untrue.

"We had nothing to do with the buying or selling or the adoption of babies. The laundries and related institutions of our specific order did not accept any girls who were pregnant at all," Sr Murphy told me. Kathy said that "the ledgers are there, they weren't burnt or washed away in floods. The babies' names and prices are there." Again sensational allegations were made but no ledgers or photocopies have been produced as proof.

Kathy later related that someone rang up a radio phone-in and claimed to be a driver who drove the children up to Belfast, but anybody, from Kathy's publicity agent, to the local Gardai, or this journalist could ring up the radio and get on air to make similar statements. An anonymous person ringing up a radio show does not amount to very solid evidence.

The publicity material in the 2005 catalogue of Mainstream Publishing for O'Beirne's book stated: "At 13, back in another Magdalene Laundry, Kathy was raped and became pregnant. Poorly from birth, her baby Kelly Anne, spent the rest of her short life in a home run by nuns and when she died she was interred in a mass grave. Kathy still doesn't know where her baby is buried." I asked Kathy about the burial of her child and she flatly contradicted the publisher's publicity: "Who was buried in a mass grave? Who told you that? You want to get your facts right." When I pointed out it was in the publishers' press release, she said they had "got their facts wrong. There is nothing about her being buried in a mass grave in the book." She added that her daughter, "was very well looked after by the nuns." Sr Sheila Murphy pointed out that only babies are buried in a Holy Angels plot, not 10 year old children, the age at which Kathy claimed her child died. Sr Sheila Murphy suggested that for a ten year old child buried in the mid-1980's surely there would be a birth certificate and death certificate? And what institution was the child put into?

Kathy told me that she had spent time in Magdalene Laundries with a woman called Maggie Bullen. "We spent a couple of years together. I knew Maggie very well. That's why I aired her story because I was so upset, the way she was buried." Maggie died in 2003 at the age of 52 and was buried in Glasnevin Cemetery, Dublin. For the first time, Kathy admitted it was she who spoke using the name 'Elizabeth' on the Joe Duffy *Liveline* radio programme on October 7, 2003 about Maggie Bullen's burial. Another breakthrough.

The *Liveline* programme is aired on national radio, RTÉ 1 every weekday at 1.45pm. The presenter, Joe Duffy is almost a national institution. Think Oprah Winfrey on radio rather than TV, with a soft voice, white skin, dark hair and male. Sounds delightful, no? Well, his show has a devoted following and huge listenership. It was on this two hour radio programme, under the assumed name 'Elizabeth', that Kathy together with other callers made a number of serious allegations.

Afterwards, a radio listener complained about the lack of accuracy and balance in the programme, following which the Broadcasting Complaints Commission of Ireland (BCC) upheld the complaint. In it's decision the BCC said: "This programme purported to be factually based. However, significant inaccurate claims made during the programme went unchallenged. The programme approached an emotive subject from a biased perspective and the Sisters of Our Lady of Charity were not afforded a fair right of reply."

'Elizabeth', or, as we now know, Kathy O'Beirne, claimed on the *Liveline* radio programme that Maggie Bullen's name was not put on the headstone, that the nuns were living like the "Queen Mother" while Maggie was in a "pauper's grave." She said on the national radio programme "The nuns killed her, the nuns destroyed her, they took her babies off her, they destroyed her..." She went on further to claim that "the babies were wrapped in sheets, and thrown into holes, unmarked graves, they weren't even buried in consecrated ground, so maybe she [Maggie] is lucky where she is."

These allegations by O'Beirne, of taking babies, wrapping them in sheets and throwing them into holes bears a sharp resemblance to the story of Maria Monk, a literary fraud of the 19th century which you can read about later on.

However, the BCC said that the significant inaccurate details included that Ms. Bullen was buried in a mass grave; that the nuns lived in the lap of luxury compared to the conditions they made Ms. Bullen live in; there was no eulogy given at Ms. Bullen's funeral mass; the Sisters of Our Lady of Charity was a 'mothers and baby's home'; and that the family was not informed of Ms Bullen's death. According to the BCC: "The programme contained many factual inaccuracies and the Commission is further of the view that the attempts made to contact the Sisters of Our Lady of Charity do not appear to have been sufficient. The complaint was upheld."

The Sisters of our Lady of Charity contradicted O'Beirne's allegations completely, and pointed out that Maggie Bullen had a well attended funeral assisted by three priests, religious sisters and many friends. A funeral homily was given by a priest who knew her, a special Mass booklet in her honour was prepared for the occasion and she was buried in a burial plot with her name inscribed on the headstone. Nuns from the order visited her regularly while in hospital and a very close nun friend visited her on the day before she died. In addition, one woman rang in during the show to say how, in her personal experience, the women in the nursing home were cared for very well by the nuns. This nursing home for women is still open and rests in High Park grounds today.

Kathy told this journalist that she had not attended Maggie Bullen's funeral; yet she felt justified in making these unfounded statements about how she was buried.

Kathy told this journalist that Maggie Bullen, "was buried in what the nun's called a communal grave, but any grave with more than six bodies in it is a mass grave. That's were she is buried." Kathy has made 'mass grave' allegations in other quarters.

During the previously-mentioned interview on the '*Tonight with Vincent Brown Show*' on June 22, Kathy claimed there were "hundreds and hundreds and hundreds of bodies buried on the lands of the Magdalene Laundries all around Dublin and around the country and in Letterfrack. [in Co Galway, Ireland] And they did not die from being undernourished. A lot of these children were murdered." Startling claims. Yet the question remains. Are they true? [we shall see in chapter 14].

So we could sum up Kathy's modus operandi, as making serious allegations but failing to bring forth any evidence to justify her claims. Indeed, much third party evidence contradicted what she had to say.

To add a bit of drama, to the already heady mix, Kathy widely proclaimed that she was going on hunger strike until the word 'penitent' was removed from a grave/monument in Glasnevin. However, after only a short space of time, she quietly called off her fast.

Baby no longer in mass grave

The immediate upshot of this interview was that after I contacted the publisher, Mainstream, to ask their response to what Kathy said -

that her child had not been buried in a mass grave - Sharon Atherton, a publicity director for Mainstream Publishing, said in October 2005 that this statement in their publicity material was false. Ms Atherton commented: "It was just very unfortunate that the ghost writer [Michael Sheridan] supplied us with the wrong information to put in our catalogue... If the book appears in any future catalogues that information will be amended." True to their word, the publicity material for *Kathy's Story* was amended the next time it was issued. The 2006 Mainstream Catalogue read as follows: "I feel my story had to be told. So much evil was done there was a voice inside me shouting 'Justice'.

"With no one to confide in, Kathy suffered in silence as she was battered and abused throughout her young childhood. Punched and kicked by her father and molested by local boys, she had nowhere to turn. At the age of eight, Kathy was torn from her family and incarcerated in a series of Catholic homes. When she was sent to a psychiatric unit, she suffered terrifying electric-shock therapy and further cruelty at the hands of her supposed carers.

"At the age of twelve, she was sent to a Magdalene laundry, where she fell victim to further sexual abuse. She gave birth to baby Annie just weeks before her 14th birthday, and it was that treasured little girl who would bring light and love into Kathy's otherwise blighted life."

There we go then, Kathy's baby was not buried in a mass grave after all. What was next? A reviewer for *She* Magazine commented that "Her story is so horrific, it's almost unbelievable." How prescient that magazine turned out to be.

Also in October 2005, the gardai interviewed a number of relevant parties and for the first time contacted the brothers and sisters of Kathy O'Beirne to interview them. The National Bureau of Criminal Investigation, the police unit which looked into the allegations contained within the book let it be known that they had carried out an investigation into them, a file had been sent to the DPP and the DPP had decided that there was insufficient evidence for a prosecution.

Life is all about L.O.V.E. many people believe. An energetic nurse, 43 year-old mother of three children and member of the Church of Ireland, Mrs Florence Horsman Hogan certainly thinks it is. This is a woman who was neglected at home but was taken in and looked after in a convent orphanage until the age of five. When the whole abuse and allegations fest erupted in the Irish media, she became upset and worried that many innocent religious were being treated unfairly, their reputations destroyed by the tarring with one brush.

In 2001 Mrs Horsman-Hogan began the charity organisation *Let Our Voices Emerge* (L.O.V.E.) to campaign on behalf of people who had been at the receiving end of false allegations of abuse. Up to this point in 2005, Mrs Horsman-Hogan has been moderately successful, while battling against the odds, in getting her message out – that innocent people were being falsely accused of abuse, and frequently for monetary gain. Yet, a bigger success awaited her. In June 2005, she heard of the publication of Kathy O'Beirne's book and the allegations that it contained.

In her first move against the book, Mrs Horsman-Hogan asked the Irish Conference of Religious (CORI) and the Bishops' Communication Office to investigate and verify or deny some claims made by Kathy: that as a young girl she had been raped by two priests and had received an out of court settlement for the same.

The L.O.V.E. charity, she wrote, is "insistent that where some of the people of the Church are guilty of wrongdoing the leaders must ensure they're held responsible. But where the Church is accused of wrongdoing and found to be innocent, it's the responsibility of the leaders to expose this fact to the public..."

Both organisations failed to answer properly. But she was to become a major mover in the demise of the book. Her drive to succeed, and serious networking skills were to prove incisive to the whole story.

After the initial bout of questioning in some sections of the media already outlined, things went relatively quiet from October 2005 'til August 2006. During this time, tabloid newspapers continued to serialise *Kathy's Story* and the book continued to sell well.

2 The O'Beirne Family raise their Voices

During this time, one of Kathy's brothers, Eamonn O'Beirne, contacted some newspapers to inform them that allegations in the book were false. Along with other members of the O'Beirne family, he was deeply unhappy about the portrayal of his father in the book.

However, when he rang up the newspapers there was no interest in his story. Eamonn O'Beirne said he found the newspapers did not want to know. "Kathy was a star and a big name, nobody wanted to contradict her."

After failing to have any success with the press, Eamonn contacted Wally Young, a communications advisor for the Sisters of Our Lady of Charity. It was Wally Young who put Eamonn O'Beirne and his other brothers and sisters in touch with Mrs Horsman-Hogan.

The L.O.V.E. charity made moves, encouraging other journalists to have a second look at *Kathy's Story*. Horsman-Hogan approached a few newspapers and from this, journalist Niall Donald of *The Sunday Mirror* gave the book a very close inspection.

By this time, *Kathy's Story* was republished in Britain under the title, '*Don't Ever Tell*' and was standing at number 3 in the non-fiction best-selling list. On the 20th of August 2006, under the headline, 'Family Wash their Hands of Laundry Rape Victim', Niall Donald broke the story that members of Kathy's family were going public for the first time to denounce her book as a collection of lies.

Kathy's sister Mary, 40, said the book had been very upsetting for the family. "Kathleen has done an awful lot of wrong to our family," she said, "but we haven't said anything over the years. But we want to set the record straight and say our father was a good man."

However, Kathy counterclaimed she had documents proving she stayed in a Magdalene home. She told *The Sunday Mirror*: "I have never lied before – and I don't intend to start now."

At this stage, the L.O.V.E. group launched an international campaign "to get the book *Kathy's Story* removed from sale until the publishers Mainstream can verify how they've authenticated the serious allegations of abuse made against the Irish medical profession, the author's father and a religious congregation."

At this time, my ears pricked up and I decided to look into the whole matter again. I started ringing around and made some contacts. I first tracked down Kathy's brother Brian, who at this stage did not want to become involved in the affair but he did give me another brother John's phone number, and I spoke to him.

I approached *The Sunday Times* with an idea of doing an article on the Kathy O'Beirne story and the Irish assistant editor, John Burns gave the go ahead and his full support.

The production team on the RTÉ *Liveline Show* hosted by Joe Duffy contacted Kathy O'Beirne to talk about her book. On Monday September 11, 2006, they had Kathy on board and made the usual pre-programme announcement on radio.

Eamonn O'Beirne takes up the story: "A friend of mine rang me up at 12.45 on Monday and said that Kathleen was going to be talking about her book on the *Joe Duffy Show*. Not being very happy about this I rang up the show number and told the call-taker that Kathy should not be allowed to make these claims, and that the whole matter was being investigated by the gardai. The show was not even aware of our family's existence, but once they did, they rang me back and asked me would I speak on their show. 'Of course,' I said, and had very little time to gather my thoughts. I didn't need much time, I just said what was true, that's all. I didn't need any preparation."

Kathy was introduced by presenter Joe Duffy who let her talk about her book and asked about her claims, and after she spoke, her brother Eamonn came on air to say that her story was completely untrue, that he never saw her with any baby, that her father had not been abusive and she had never been in a Magdalene laundry. This was the first time that listeners on the national radio had heard the story being called into question.

Seconds out. Round 1. Ding, Ding, and the contest's under way.

By pure chance, Eamonn O'Beirne was able to stage an ambush on air. It made for compelling listening. But once he spoke up, as he described it, "the floodgates opened. Many other people immediately rang in to question the story." One person, who did ring in to back up Kathy however, was her co-author Michael Sheridan.

Grilled sharply by presenter Joe Duffy on what documentation he had seen to prove that Kathy had stayed in a Magdalene laundry, Sheridan retorted: "I saw mounds of documentation that Kathy has. She is an extremely punctilious keeper of documentation."

Probing why the Sisters of Our Lady of Charity would say that Kathy O'Beirne was never in a Magdalene laundry, presenter Joe Duffy asked him: "Have you seen evidence that she was in a Magdalene laundry?" Sheridan replied: "I have seen. And I have seen evidence of interaction with Kathy and the Sisters of Our Lady of Charity in the Bishop's House." These few words would later return to haunt him.

Kathy came back on air, to voice her obvious discontent; as she had not been told that her brother was to be on the show as well. The presenter told her that people had the right to question her story as she had written a book.

One interesting woman did ring in to give her story some support, and that was a woman who found Kathy up a tree in her back garden. Kathy had run away from St Loman's Hospital in West Dublin. Maybe there were elements of truth in the book after all? Anyhow, every party got a fair chance to say their piece and it made for riveting listening. The national radio producers knew they were onto something, and for the next two days discussed the same issue at length. Many interesting matters were raised and comments made. Some of them quite amazing.

During this time I was interviewing people involved in order to write a news article. On that Saturday (16th September 2006) Dearbhail McDonald, legal affairs journalist for *The Irish Independent*, along with Ciaran Byrne wrote an article, "Publishers battle credibility crisis over book's veracity." She suggested that industry sources in Scotland and Dublin had estimated that Mainstream had already recouped a conservative estimate of stg £1.5m (€2.22m) on the book, while Kathy O'Beirne had an advance of €20,000 and still lived in a Clondalkin council house.

When Bill Campbell, the director of Mainstream Publishing was asked what investigation he had made into the veracity of the story, he told *The Irish Independent*: "We did everything we could to investigate the claims and even communicated certain passages to the religious orders concerned.

"We have strictures and checks that came into play. Our reaction is one of extreme surprise that one and a half years after its publication, this is the first we have heard of a problem and the allegations being made. We would question the agendas of those involved given that we even delayed publication to give the Archdiocese of Dublin an opportunity to respond, which they did, with no major changes."

Kathy O'Beirne herself broke a week-long silence to tell the paper: "I am above board, I have all my documentation. I don't care what people say about me. My comeback [to all the bad publicity] is that I have my proof, it's all above board. I dared to come out and tell the truth.

"My book has helped hundreds of people, I get letters from all over the world. I have helped people on the brink of suicide." O'Beirne asked: "Are we all liars?", referring to those who claim to have been abused, before bursting into tears.

Kathy did that with me as well. When I interviewed Kathy in June 2005, I asked her a hard question about herself and her relationship with Maggie Bullen. Perhaps knowing she was on a hard wicket and a lot depended on the way she answered the question, Kathy instead said nothing and turned on the waterworks instead. Then it was my go. On this occasion in *The Sunday Times* of September 17, 2006.

It was revealed that seven of Kathy's eight siblings denounced the main allegations in the book as false, and called for it to be reclassified as fiction.

Her older brother John O'Beirne, 51, said he was "absolutely sure that allegations in the book about sadistic abuse by my father are false".

He recalls visiting Kathy in St Anne's, a children's home in Kilmacud, and St Loman's in Dublin, a mental institution for troubled children. He said his sisters visited Kathy in Mountjoy when she was imprisoned for petty theft, and described the chronology of events in *Kathy's Story* as a "jigsaw puzzle and nothing fits".

Scottish publisher defends its book

Bill Campbell, managing director of Mainstream, told this journalist that the Scottish publishing house would stand by the story. "We have made every effort and are satisfied that the story is true," he said. Campbell said that he had interviewed Kathy in Dublin and had "other people go over the chronology in great detail," before signing a deal.

Campbell added that they made contact with the Dublin archdiocese inviting comments before publication of the book, but to date Mainstream had "received no substantive response." Asked whether he had seen documentary proof that Kathy ever had a child or was in a Magdalene laundry, Campbell refused to answer.

Most decisively for the whole story, and for the first time, three women came forward to describe their living with Kathy in a Dublin girls' hostel rather than a Magdalene laundry as she claimed. During the 1970s, the north inner city Sherrard Street Hostel was a voluntary hostel for girls who were homeless. Although never explicitly mentioned or alluded to in Kathy's book, three former residents of this refuge spoke up to confirm that Kathy spent over three years along with them.

Angela, a 48 year-old woman who lives in Blanchardstown said that she was in Sherrard House with Kathy for "at least three years." During this time (when they were both in their mid to late teens), Angela said: "Kathy never had any children, never spoke of having any children, never once spoke of being in a Magdalene laundry." Asked of her reaction to Kathy's book, Angela said: "This story is complete madness." She speculated that Kathy watched a film on the Magdalene laundries and now "seems to think she's her." Dubliner, Celine Dempsey, 47, remembers staying with Kathy for four years in the girls' hostel. During that time, she maintains that "Kathy never spoke of being in a

Magdalene Laundry, how could she be? She was in Sherrard Street. Kathy never spoke of having a baby or of ever being raped."

And yet another woman, Mary Lavin remembers that Kathy came to Sherrard House from St Loman's mental home. She distinctly recalls that Kathy used to ask the girls about their life stories and would write them down and keep them on record. "Kathy would ask the girls if she could write their stories down and she had loads of papers." Celine again is of the opinion that in the book, "These things did not happen to Kathy. Kathy took other peoples' stories, put them together and embellished them a lot."

Eamonn O'Beirne said that he had logged his phone calls and e-mails to Mainstream Publishers attempting to state that the allegations in the book were untrue. However, over the last year and a half, he says, he was "constantly ignored and brushed off."

However, amazed that a year and a half after the publication of the book people are questioning the veracity of the book Mr Campbell said "It's just a matter of media hype."

Standing by the book, they later released a statement saying that, "Mainstream took steps prior to the publication of *Don't Ever Tell* and were satisfied that the memoir was appropriate for publication. This included working closely with Kathy O'Beirne and providing the opportunity for comment or correction to the Archdiocese of Dublin by submitting relevant material to it. After correspondence of some six weeks, no material changes to the text were requested. *Don't Ever Tell* was put under considerable media scrutiny upon initial publication some eighteen months ago without any content being found to be untrue. Mainstream has no reason to believe that this position has changed. Further attention is now being drawn to the book as a result of a family dispute. Mainstream does not propose to comment on this."

3 A Press Conference is called

Our lives begin to end the day we become silent about things that matter.
Martin Luther King Jr.

The O'Beirne family announced and held a press conference in September 2006. On the day, a large spread appeared on page three of *The Daily Telegraph* (to which I had some input). It went under the headline "Author is accused of inventing story of childhood torture and rape." At the same time, *The Times* of London ran with a headline – "Author's family say abuse memoir is a cruel hoax." The end of the book's reputation was nigh.

Tuesday, 19th of September 2006 was a big day for the O'Beirne family; the day that seven of Kathy's siblings held a press conference telling their side of the story to the world's press. Journalists from Reuters and the Press Association turned up ensuring that their very words would be carried to the remotest parts of the globe.

Mary O'Beirne-O'Gorman, Kathy's sister, recalls the lead up to the event and the emotions that went through her: "My brother Eamonn called all the family together and we met in Clondalkin to discuss the statement we were to make at the press conference. The conference itself was arranged on our behalf by Florence Horsman-Hogan of the L.O.V.E. charity. We were very grateful for her help as we are complete amateurs and knew next to nothing on how the media works. L.O.V.E. didn't have much money either to rent a venue in a hotel, so the conference had to be held in a Dublin pub, in Baggott Street, as it was free.

"It was decided I would do the presentation, as I was a woman and presented a softer, more sympathetic face to the world. I don't know where I got the strength to do the speaking, because I was nervous.

When I started to read the statement I was then able to do it. I knew Kathy was telling lies, and I just wanted to clear Daddy's name really. It was very emotional and took a lot out of us to do it, and me personally."

It was Mary who read out the family statement; nervously at first, but she gained confidence as the event went on. The family's first purpose was to clear the name of their father who was accused of abuse by Kathy. Anything else about nuns and Magdalene Laundries etc. was very much secondary.

Mary read out: "We the brothers and sisters of Kathleen O'Beirne, co-author with Michael Sheridan, of the book, *Kathy's Story* have come together to speak out in defence of our family name, and that of our father, Oliver O'Beirne, and simply to tell the truth. In the book, our sister makes horrific allegations of abuse of child abuse against our father, a religious congregation, and a psychiatric hospital. We believe the vast majority of the allegations to be untrue, and we now wish to present the real story.

"Despite all of our efforts, Mr Bill Campbell of Mainstream publishers has refused to return our calls. Mr Bill Campbell is quoted in the Irish media over the weekend saying that he had checked the story with religious.... We noted as far back as 2004 that all religious with laundries and Magdalene homes confirmed to the Irish media that Kathleen never spent time in a laundry and this clear statement of fact was simply ignored. Mr Campbell is on record as far back as July '05 as there being no question of pulling this book despite the denials. At this time we thought this would be the end of this madness – but clearly there was too much money to be made.

"Our father was not an abuser, he worked extremely hard to feed, clothe and take care of us. Indeed, the suffering caused to our family due to Kathleen's psychological problems would have driven any other person to extremes of despair. Our sister Kathleen is not adopted as she has tried to claim, we have her birth certificate to prove it, and the family resemblance as you can see speaks for itself."

After going through a chronology of family events by which they could remember Kathy's whereabouts during the years 1967-1978, Mary stridently confirmed:

"Our sister did not have a child at the age of fourteen that she alleges died at the age of ten. Nor did she have the second child she claimed to have had, on the *Liveline* programme. Kathleen made this same claim as recently as five years ago, where she alleged to have been pregnant at 45 years old, but claimed the child was a stillbirth.

"Despite a very difficult relationship with Kathleen, from a very young age, we have always known her – and we were always in contact with her and knew where she was. We would certainly be very aware of the main events in her life.

"Our sister, to our knowledge, was not raped by two priests, and did not receive an out of court settlement for the same. There is not a shred of evidence to support such outlandish claims, and we believe our sister was uncooperative with the gardai when such was being investigated last year. Our sister has a self-admitted psychiatric and criminal history, and her perception of reality has always been flawed. This has presented great problems for us, her family, our neighbours, and friends. This woman has broken our hearts, especially the hearts of our now deceased parents, with her behaviour in the past.

"As with any family, we have our ups and downs, but thanks to the love and care our parents gave us, we have always cared for and supported one another. Any discipline carried out in our house was the same as for any family living in the 60's and 70's, no better, and no worse. Even at a stage when most families would have disowned Kathleen, we have visited her in these places, and tried to protect her from herself. It is absolutely untrue that we turned our backs on her when she made her allegations (in the book only), against our father.

"From this, it is clear that our sister is a disturbed and troubled woman. Yet Mr Sheridan took the utterances of our sister and transcribed them in book form to the world as true fact. He wrote the book, based on her alleged experiences. We are deeply sorry for all of the people who have bought this book believing it to be fact – and we can understand that many people will now feel hurt and conned – but we must tell the truth. Mainstream publishers did not speak to us as a family, and are callously refusing to listen to our appeals to remove this hoax publication from sales.

"Tragically our sister, who has been a major player in this farce herself, is also being abused for profit. We hold the publishers Mainstream, and the co-author, Michael Sheridan largely responsible, as it would have been perfectly clear to anyone who met our sister, that there were glaring flaws in her allegations. [We believe] Mainstream did not carry out the necessary rigorous checks; if they had, this book would never have been published."

The statement was signed: "Statement of Oliver, Eamonn, Mary, Margaret, John, Tommy and Brian O'Beirne".

Kathy had told journalists up to this point, that she was in her early forties, to some she said 44, to others 45. She also claimed to a number of people that she had been adopted.

The first line of the first chapter of Kathy's book states, "I am now in my 40's. I was the fifth child and the first daughter in what would eventually be a family of nine: six boys and three girls." This is untrue.

At the press conference, her brothers and sisters produced her birth certificate to prove that Kathy was born on October 18th, 1956 and was indeed 50 years of age.

Her parents are listed as Oliver and Anne O'Beirne. On top of this Mary pointed out humorously, "Look at me and Margaret. Kathy is the spitting image of us. She's not adopted, it's so ridiculous!"

Eamonn further elaborated on this, saying that Kathy was not the fifth child but the fourth child of the family. "From the very first page this book is lies. The second phrase says that she was the fifth child, but in fact, she is the fourth, and the lies go on from there." Kathy was born after Tommy, Oliver, John (51), and before Eamonn (48) , Brian, Joseph, Mary and Margaret." As Oliver would say, "just one more lie."

The effect of the press conference

Mary vividly recalls that, "At the conference, I said how I had problems eating and sleeping. I didn't say this at the time, but I had to ask the doctor for a prescription of sleeping tablets, I was finding it that hard to get to sleep. I never thought that I would feel this way, that anything would affect me so much.

"That day at the press conference it was absolutely great to do it. I was doing it for Daddy and Mammy. I had to do it for them.

"I was very nervous before the event and prayed to my Mammy and Daddy that I would be able to do it and I feel that they were there with me, helping me to do it properly without breaking down. It was for them, just trying to clear their name.

"Everyone said how well I did, and I must say, I was euphoric after it was over. Answering the questions wasn't difficult. It was only the truth I was saying. There was no need to prepare or think of making up an answer. That made it easy.

"When someone asks you a question, the truth comes easy enough.

"I felt on top of the world afterwards. I felt really good, I must say. I would do it again, I felt my Daddy would be proud of me."

The media impact of the press conference across the world was huge. In the next few days there were major articles on it in all the Irish and British papers. It appeared in *The Hindu*, and *The Daily India*, *The Malaysia Sun*, *The Age*, and *The Western Australian*, *The Scotsman*, *The Washington Times*, and *The Washington Post*, to begin with. Literary magazines and other publications took it up and discussed the fallout of the conference. TV news channels like Sky news and ABC News carried stories on the event across the world.

And how did Mary react to it being carried far and wide? "I was so happy that news of our statement went global. We have relations in California, in England and Australia. They may have heard about the book and the damage done to our family name, it was great that they could hear about the truth. And that Daddy was not the monster that Kathy makes him out to be. What she has done is make muck of our family name. She has taken away my confidence, she had made it difficult for me to go around in public. This must be made right. After the press conference I got Mass cards from parents in the school that my son goes to, people gave me bunches of flowers. But I still feel that there is something missing. Something is not yet right. It is still hanging there. I wonder will it ever be made right?"

The Ghost-writer stumbles, the story begins to fall

"I'm keeping the best wine to last," was a refrain Kathy often used when journalists asked to see some evidence, and ironically suitable for some comments made by Michael Sheridan to this author when I interviewed him for a *Sunday Times* news article a few days after the press conference (24/9/06).

For the very first time, Michael Sheridan admitted that there was no documented evidence to show central character, Kathy O'Beirne was ever in a Magdalene laundry or ever had a baby.

When I asked about the documentation he has seen showing Kathy O'Beirne's stay in a Magdalene Laundry, co-author Mr Sheridan said "I'll tell you the evidence we have. There are no documents. Those documents are either falsified or destroyed. There is no evidence or records of Kathy [O'Beirne] in the two Magdalene laundries. There never was any."

A startling admission, especially for someone who less than two weeks earlier on national radio said the very opposite. These few words starkly contradicted statements by Mr Sheridan on RTÉ's *Liveline* radio programme in which he said: "I saw mounds of documentation that Kathy has. She is an extremely punctilious keeper of documentation."

Probing why the Sisters of Our Lady of Charity would say that Kathy O'Beirne was never in a Magdalene laundry, presenter Joe Duffy asked him, "Have you seen evidence that she was in a Magdalene Laundry?" Sheridan replied: "I have seen. And I have seen evidence of interaction with Kathy and the Sisters of Our Lady of Charity in the Bishop's House."

When asked about this very stark contradiction, Mr Sheridan said that he was just thinking quickly on the spot and the evidence that he has seen and to which he was referring are documents of the interaction between Kathy and the nuns at the Bishop's House. He has, for instance, seen letters to Kathy from her mother which were sent when she was in St Anne's children home, Kilmacud, for six weeks. No-one disputes that Kathy was in St Anne's. But this is the only time that the Sisters of Our Lady of Charity said that Kathy stayed with them.

In the book it is also alleged that Kathy was raped and had a baby at the age of 14. However asked had he seen documentation about the baby's birth and death, Sheridan added that "the nuns did not register the birth of the baby Annie or get a birth certificate. Why would they? It would be holding their hands up and admitting girls got pregnant in the Laundry."

In the book, the alleged baby was sick for most of its life and died at the age of ten around 1980. Again asked whether there would be a death certificate for the baby, Sheridan replied, "No, not at all. This is part of the problem. They weren't getting death certificates. This was exposed in the '*States of Fear*' documentary." ['*States of Fear*' was an RTÉ TV documentary shown in April 1999 about allegations of abuse carried out by Catholic religious in Ireland. The programme was produced by Mary Raftery].

He claimed that "both the nuns and the Department of Education falsified and destroyed documentary evidence about the laundries." Previously, of course, Kathy O'Beirne claimed to have all her proof and all her documents.

Defending the book, Sheridan contended that the proof Kathy worked in a Laundry was that Mainstream Publishers in Edinburgh gave Dublin Archdiocese six weeks to come back at them about the contents of the book and there were no objections.

The Archdiocese of Dublin hits back

However, a spokesman for the Dublin Archdiocese countered that in March 2005, "The Archdiocese was invited to comment on the content of these pages which related to dealings Kathy had had with the Diocese during the previous two or three years. The Archdiocese subsequently pointed out to the publishers some errors in the account of matters concerning the Archdiocese and certain changes were made to the text to take account of these observations."

The spokesman stressed: "The Archdiocese only commented on those aspects of the book that related to issues that were within the direct knowledge and competence of officials of the Archdiocese. The response of the Archdiocese did not address other issues that are the principal subject matter of the book that was eventually published."

Michael Sheridan also pointed out to this author that Kathy had secretly taped a conversation between herself and a nun in which they allege the nun, Sr Lucy, casually acknowledged looking after Kathy in a Magdalene laundry; as well as the testimony of a now deceased woman, Ms Elizabeth Keegan who told Mr Sheridan she had stayed in a laundry with Kathy and had seen her baby. This recording has never been played in public by O'Beirne.

For the first time, both co-authors also admitted that Kathy stayed for some time in Sherrard House, a hostel for homeless girls in Dublin. Neither, however, would say if this place was explicitly alluded to in their book.

Defending the veracity of the book, Sheridan also said the "proof" that the story is true is that neither he, nor the Edinburgh-based publisher Mainstream Publishing have received a solicitor's letter from the nuns.

In the course of an interview for *The Sunday Times* article, Sheridan told this journalist: "It is extremely significant that, neither me, nor Kathy, nor Mainstream or any main news outlet which has carried this story has ever had a legal letter or a solicitor's letters from the Sisters of Our Lady of Charity. If they say she was not in that Magdalene laundry why don't they sue us. No-one has ever got a solicitor's letter from them. I have confirmed this with Mainstream. They have received no legal communication."

Directly contradicting this assertion however, a spokesperson for the Sisters of Our Lady of Charity said that on April 21, 2005, their solicitors, Walsh and Co. of Fitzwilliam Square, Dublin wrote both to Mainstream and Michael Sheridan. In this letter the Order stated categorically that the only time Kathy O'Beirne was with the nuns was for a 6-week period in a reformatory school. This was intended to clarify matters, as they were aware Mainstream were about to publish the book about Kathy. The nuns later said: "We received a curt response to this letter from Mr Bill Campbell of Mainstream dated, 11th May 2005. We also wish to point out again that after allegations by Kathy O'Beirne in 2004 all four religious congregations who ran laundries confirmed to *The Irish Independent* newspaper that Kathy O'Beirne never spent time in a laundry or Magdalene Home." [Statement on September 19th, 2006]

The main assertion of her story, that she was abused while in Magdalene Laundries in Dublin has been completely dismissed by the four religious orders that ran the now closed laundry service in Dublin. They have all countered that they have no record of Ms O'Beirne having been one of their residents. In fact, the Sisters of Our Lady of Charity, in their letter to co-author Michael Sheridan and Mainstream Publishing, pointed out that they had done strenuous checks, hiring a professional archivist to carry out an exhaustive trawl of their records to be certain that no trace of Kathy can be found as ever having attended their laundries or adjoining accommodation. Mainstream still went ahead and published the book.

But the dog wasn't going into the corner to lie down and die just yet; Michael Sheridan and Kathy O'Beirne went on the offensive making new allegations against her family. Rachetting up their campaign to vilify the names of Kathy's seven siblings who rejected the veracity of her claims in the book, Sheridan made serious intimations of sexual impropriety in the O'Beirne household while Kathy was growing up there.

Not against her father, mind you. These allegations were completely libellous and no paper would publish them. However, when I asked about them, the O'Beirne brothers rejected the claims outright. Kathy's brother, Brian O'Beirne responded: "Me and my friends at work have laughed at how ridiculous their claims have become in the last few days. Their book and their accusations are absolute codswallop."

Sheridan also claimed that Brian had been sexually assaulted (though not by his father). When I put this to Brian, he denied it completely. Saying first, don't be so sick and then, laughing at how ridiculous the claim was, he said: "I wasn't raped and I think I would remember if I was. I obviously wasn't pretty enough!"

Showing that the death sting can be the most dangerous, Kathy rolled out her youngest brother Joseph (42) to make some noises in support of her. He told the local newspaper that he too was to write a book describing his experiences growing up. Among these was a claim that his father made the boys walk through a nearby field wrapped in a blanket.

His other siblings just had a laugh at this. "How ridiculous," was the response. "Just where did he get that from," Eamonn said.

Kathy then suggested that the family are only disagreeing with the book because of a legal disagreement about her father's house, and its disposal as left in his will. There was a court case in early 2006 which had to do with the disposal of the house. The family home was to be sold and the proceeds divided equally between the nine siblings. However, Kathy, who still lives in the family home, refused to vacate the house. She produced her book and told the judge of her alleged life of woe. The circuit judge allowed her to stay in the house. Her siblings said in response, that the court case was something Kathy kept holding over their heads to keep them quiet about the book.

The photos and school records tell a different tale

Kathy's Story reads as a grim tale of sexual abuse and physical beating of a vulnerable child and young girl. You can understand that people would feel compassion for such a poor put-upon young girl. If her story was true, you could reasonably expect Kathy's demeanour to reflect her bitter upbringing, her sad and malnourished state.

But look again at the pictures of Kathy. Even in her own book, the photos which she presented to the world to back up her story of abuse, show her smiling radiantly in almost every one. Look at the pictures and ask, is this the face of a dejected and remorselessly beaten girl or someone who is enjoying her life?

Her brother Oliver, said he remembers her, "always jolly and in good form, never depressed." The photos which she presents in her own book back up that assessment. The family album would then prove to be a rich seam from which to mine evidence of Kathy's childhood.

Then it was the turn of *The Irish Mail on Sunday* to give *Kathy's Story* a close examination and thorough work-out. Journalists Daniel Boffey and Catherine Murphy did a colourful and eye-opening two-page spread in the newspaper (24/9/06) unpicking the story using pictures supplied by the family.

"These are the pictures that could be from any happy family album. A little girl smiling proudly beside her older brother's bride. In other snaps, the same girl, now grown up, plays with her little nieces and poses at her younger sister's wedding.

"There are no signs of anything much wrong. Few would conclude that the smiling girl at the centre of these images is in any way remarkable. Yet this is Kathy O'Beirne, the author whose searing account of her violent childhood and incarceration in Dublin's notorious Magdalene laundries has shocked and appalled millions around the world," *The Irish Mail on Sunday* said.

Opening up the family album and asking where was the victim of rape and serial abuse, Eamonn told the newspaper, "We want people to see these pictures and see the truth. Look at Kathleen smiling next to her brother's bride on her wedding day. She is 11 years old in that picture and according to her book she had already been beaten to within an inch of her life, raped by a young boy and been sent to a children's home and psychiatric hospital.

"Does this look like a girl who has been through that? We have also got pictures of her when she was 17 with us at Mary's First Communion, with our dad standing by us. Yet there is no sign of the baby she claims to have had after being raped at the laundries. And there she is with our dad, who she claims would not have her staying at the house. We are speaking out because our family has suffered enough. We can't let these lies go on."

Interviewing Mary O'Beirne in September 2006, I asked did she know where Kathy spent her school days and if she knew anybody who was at school with Kathy. 'Yes', was the answer to both questions and thus began a hunt for an old classmate of Kathy which was eventually to lead the family to the unearthing of Kathy's school attendance records.

I was able to track down a classmate of Kathy's, who remembers being at school with her until the age of roughly 12-and-a-half. This person was afraid that going public might make her job in Clondalkin difficult but instead pointed to somebody else who would help the family access the school records.

Making the proper contacts led to three of the siblings, Eamonn, Mary and Margaret sitting round a table in Kathy's old school going through old attendance record books looking for the correct ones.

There was a very large number and these were totally disorganised so it took some time to find the correct books.

Mary describes the high tension she felt as she feverishly searched: "We were sitting in this small office, with jumbles and jumbles of old attendance books in a heap and we were scanning them all to see could we find the correct ones. My blood was racing because I felt that at any moment, Kathy and a load of heavies would burst through the door and grab all the records off us before we found the evidence. When I found the correct books, we immediately got them copied, and just in case, Eamonn also took a few photos. Not until I got the copies back home and locked up, did I feel safe. I felt a huge sense of relief at finding them and knowing we had some hard evidence that would show Kathy's story to be untrue. I rested a bit easier that night, but even then I knew we had to get word about these records out to the public. There was still a long way to go."

The executive editor of *The Irish Mail on Sunday*, Paul Drury, expressed an interest in the story when I floated it to him, and he rigorously checked all the documented material that I now had. Having checked it a second time again, in great detail, he ran the story as an exclusive on October 15 under the headline, "Proof that Kathy's story is tissue of lies." You couldn't shout it out any louder!

"The photograph of the school records finally prove that Kathy's story is a tissue of lies. They show that Kathy spent the years 1961 to June 1969 in Scoil Mhuire, her local national school in Clondalkin which she left at age 12 and a half years.

"They starkly contradict Miss O'Beirne's claim that she spent two years in a reformatory school (from age 8), two years in a public psychiatric hospital (from age 10) and finally a Magdalene laundry in High Park, Dublin (aged twelve).

The only significant period of time that Kathy was not in Scoil Mhuire was a brief six week period at the age of 11 which she spent instead, in St Anne's Reformatory School in Kilmadcud in 1967 – which is fully accounted for in her school records."

Kathy reacted quite angrily when I rang her up to ask for her response to the unearthing of her school records, even threatening legal action, in case I was feeling nervous. Reacting to news of the school attendance records, Kathy O'Beirne said: "I don't really know anything about the records. I haven't heard anything about it. I have my own. It is in the hands of the solicitors now. I am in the middle of suing people and taking them to court, so I have no comment on it."

Asked about the apparent contradiction of the school records and claims in the book, Kathy added, "I have court documents. I suppose they are up and above legal. You would have to consult my legal team because if they [the school records] were got, they were got without my permission. They would have to be obtained under the Freedom of Information Act and I haven't signed anything. Contact my solicitor about that." She concluded: "Ok, I will get my solicitor to get on to your editor. Bye."

Taking the two school record books together, Kathy's school attendance records show that she was present at Scoil Mhuire, Clondalkin in the school years below:

'61/62.......169 days
'62/63.......158 days
'63/64.......188 days
'64/65.......164 days
'65/66.......175 days
'66/67........60 days *Recorded she went to another school for a while*
'68/69.......141 days

Kathy's Confirmation certificate reveals that she received the Sacrament of Confirmation in Clondalkin Parish church on the 15th of May, 1968.

Within a few weeks of *Kathy's Story* being called into question, 21 women approached Christine Buckley of the Aislinn Counselling Centre in Dublin to say that they are certain that Kathy O'Beirne did not attend a Magdalene laundry. [Magdalene Laundries began as places of refuge for woman who were poor and homeless].

Christine Buckley told this journalist: "I have had a number of former 'Magdalenes' [a woman who has attended a Magdalene Laundry] say that Kathy O'Beirne's claims in her book are untrue. They were very upset, because it does not help genuine people who were there."

The publishers, she said, "are the ones whom I would have a grievance with. They should have [better] checked their sources and any evidence before publishing."

"It is," Ms Buckley said, "an awful thing to use survivors for monetary gain. Indeed, it is shocking given what they have gone through. Kathy O'Beirne and others should not profit from other people's pain."

4 In the Name of our father

"This is an account of my early life. I decided it was safer to trash my parents than a lot of television executives."
Actor Griff Rhys Jones in his memoirs, '*Semi-Detached*'

In her book, Kathy O'Beirne accuses her father of being a domineering and emotionally frigid man who gave his wife and children not love and a good life but a home culture of fear, violence, brutality and hunger. His other children now paint a very different picture of the man that Kathy castigated in her book as "cruel and evil."

On behalf of the seven O'Beirne siblings, Mary O'Beirne (40) said: "the anger and frustration that we feel at seeing our father branded world-wide as a horrific abuser is indescribable."

At their press conference in September 2006, they pleaded with the journalists present: "We hope that in the name of our father and mother, Oliver and Anne O'Beirne and the O'Beirne family, you will now be able to bring our story to the public and help us right a horrific miscarriage of justice, where an innocent man can be branded an abuser, and given no right to his good name in the interest of financial gain."

Not an abuser

Quite contrary to the description which Kathy gave of her father, her 49 year-old brother, Eamonn said: "I know my father did not abuse or torture me. The stuff as alleged in this book, simply did not happen in our house."

In her book (p22), Kathy alleges that the father Oliver used to squash the hands of his children in a door jam until they passed out with the pain. No medical records have ever been produced by Kathy to show this is the case, nor X-rays to show that the O'Beirne children all had broken bones in their hands and fingers.

Her brother Johnny (51) is a driver based in Dublin. He is "absolutely sure that allegations in the book about sadistic abuse by my father are false." He is adamant that, "My father worked night and day to provide for his family, and I never saw him lay a hand on Kathy. He worked so hard, he hardly had either the time or energy to beat his children."

According to brother Tommy (60, also a driver): "I never saw the girls getting hit by my father ever. They may have got roared at, but that was it. I never heard any of the girls say that Dad hit them or anything like that."

Kathy has alleged that her father held her hand in a pan of boiling grease long enough for her skin to peel off (p23); an action which, you would think, would leave a lasting scar and possibly even a 'claw' hand but when you meet Kathy, she isn't disfigured like this at all.

Her brother Eamonn doesn't, "believe for a second that my father ever abused her like she claimed in the book, and that she was in a laundry – it is just lies. I also know my father did not abuse or torture me."

But someone who loved us all

John continued: "My father was a good man, a loving man, who worked very very hard to provide for his family. Now, Kathy has hurt a lot of people, and it's now time for the truth to be told." The publisher, he said, "probably thought that the nuns were a soft touch; they expected the clergy to accept it and move on. Our family won't. It's a matter of justice, of my father's good name."

For Mary, her father Oliver, was "a loving and affectionate man whom I loved to bits and idolised. Even today, nine years after his passing, I miss him terribly.

"Yes, he was strict and you had to do what you were told, but I also felt absolutely comfortable with him. If I had problem, I could go to him and talk to him. And he would help me. But what man is Kathy talking about? It is not my father she is talking about. That's certain.

The whole world is reading about this 'evil monster.' I can't believe it. I can hold my head up because I know what kind of a man he was. And I will not stop until we clear his name. He did so much for us and the rest of us feel the same."

Who was strict on discipline but fair

Oliver Snr, the father, was born and brought up in the countryside, near Roosky, in County Roscommon, in the Irish midlands. The original homestead is still there, nestled in close to the banks of what Shane MacGowan sang of: 'the broad majestic Shannon.' Even today, almost 80 years after he was born and 60 years after he left his home in the country, the picture of the Sacred Heart of Jesus is still sitting above the mantelpiece. Where once his family gathered for family prayer, a local farmer now keeps a few calves. In the other room, opposite the fire place, the same farmer uses it to store two ton of turf, compressed peat used to light a fire. Up the road, the old school house where he first walked to school each day is newly done up and modernised into a fine dormer bungalow; testament to Ireland's ten year building boom.

Oliver Snr married his wife Nancy at the age of 19. This early age of marriage was successfully replicated by his eldest son Tommy, who today is 61 years of age. According to Tommy: "My father was a fair man. The same as other fathers at that time. If you didn't tow the line, he was a stern man. He was this way because he had to rear a family and try to keep them on the straight and narrow. Wherever this 'monster thing' that Kathy came up with – no-one knows about that. My father hit me once I think. I got a few clatters for doing something he told me not to do. That was the generation we came from. That was the norm.

"I can honestly say that I kind of grew up with my father. He was married at 19 years of age. I was born when he was twenty. We went and did work together. We worked on the plot together. We would have been very, very close. I can sum him up as being a fair man with everybody. A considerate man in his own way but stern. You have to remember the background which he came from. He never got anything for free. He had to work for it. If you wanted something you got it, but you had to work for it. You weren't going to get something for free. You wouldn't be spoilt."

Eamonn recalls: "Our father wasn't a saint. The boys would get a clout – and we probably deserved it. But he would never dream of hitting the girls. My father never abused or raised his hand to my mother ever. He never abused her in any way, or raised his voice to her."

Oliver Jnr remembers that his father mellowed with time as the children grew up: "My father would not impose on you. He would listen to you and then he would tell you what he thought. He would listen to you and it was then up to yourself if you took what he said on board or not. Things happened later, and he would be proven right. One time we were cutting wood in Roscommon and something dangerous happened, something he warned me about; and really once nobody was hurt, he laughed about it with me as well. He was easy going enough, with his pipe and that. He has been totally misrepresented in Kathy's book."

One local woman in Clondalkin, who knew both parents, came up to Eamonn, saying "I read your sister's book, and I laughed when I read the bit about your father ruling the family with an iron fist. The only thing your father ever ruled was the shed at the end of the garden."

However, quite contrary to all this, Kathy writes in her book: "To the outside world, my father Oliver presented an image of respectability. He was a handsome man, well-built at 15 stone, who dressed immaculately. A builder's labourer, he went to Mass every day and, to the people on our estate, he appeared to be a highly religious pillar of the community. But inside our home he became a cruel and violent man who subjected his family to a terrible life of mental and physical abuse. He regularly beat my eight brothers and sisters and me with his belt. The buckle would cut into my legs and the flesh wounds often turned septic.

"He would put our hands in the crack of the kitchen door and press it with his foot until we passed out with pain. One night, when he was in a particularly bad rage, he held my hand in a pan of hot grease. The pain was unbearable. I closed my eyes and screamed, so he threw me outside the back door while he ate his dinner."

Mary's recollection of family life in the O'Beirne household is so different from that of Kathy's that they are either from a different planet or one of them is telling lies. On the area of logic, there is a maxim that two contradictory statements cannot be true at the same time. Mary says their father was strict but kind: "My father never once lifted his hand to us. Never," she says. "Yes, of course we were chastised if we had played up, but he never hit us. It was a normal, happy childhood. We would go for days out in the mountains and had such fun up there. He was a very proud, good man and it breaks my heart to see the terrible lies Kathy has written about him."

And worked hard to provide for his family

Tommy could see from the way Kathy's book was written that "there was a lot of venom in it. Even calling my father a builder's labourer. He did not have a trade, but I would like to think he was more than a builder's labourer, not that there is anything wrong with that. He was very good with his hands and could turn his hand to anything, and make a good job of it. Electrics was the only thing he never dabbled in."

Their father Oliver was a very hard working man and had to bring up his family during the 1950's and 60's, a very tough time when many Irish people were experiencing poverty. Tommy would be asked to till turnips first thing in the morning, before he went to school and joined with his father before he went to work. As Tommy said, "The work had to be done because there was a large family and they had to be provided for. We had what we needed, he worked hard and provided for us."

Oliver used to do different shifts at work. Sometimes 5am to 12.30pm or 8am to 4pm. He would come in from work and go to bed. He would then get up when Oliver and John would come in from school. They would have their dinner, 'and then go to the garden shed, get all their tools, put them in a wheel barrow and go and build Mickey Laughlin's wall or someone else's. "We built walls all over Clondalkin, up the Commons Road and further afield," brother Johnny said.

On top of this, the O'Beirne Family had a large garden plot. As part of former Taoiseach (Prime Minister) Eamon De Valera's vision of Ireland, many families were given a garden plot, which they could work for themselves and in some way, strive to provide for themselves and not be reliant on the State. It was also a nod to the rural ideal beloved of

Irish nationalists at the time.

The plot comprised about half to three-quarters of an acre; and was situated opposite the family home, exactly where the Bewley's Hotel at Newlands Cross is today. It was to this plot, that Oliver Snr and some of the older boys, Tommy, Oliver and John would come every Tuesday and Thursday to tend carrots, onions, potatoes, cabbage and other varieties of vegetable. They also kept chickens. It took four of them to weed the plot, as it was quite large.

"You name it, we sowed it." Johnny explains, "and at the end of the year, my father would dig a big pit and fill it with potatoes and straw. He would dig them out during the winter when he'd want them, so they'd keep. My father was so proud of being self-sufficient, he even made a potato grater out of aluminium, punching the holes one by one, with a six inch nail."

Both parents were also very proud people. During the 1960's when there was a depression and a lot of people were out of work, the schools would come up with free dinners for the children. At the time, John says, "my father was on short time hours at work. We were the only ones who didn't go for the free dinner. We went home for our dinner: soup and sandwiches and tapioca rice. We never wanted for anything."

This contradicts Kathy's assertion that they got very little to eat and their father rationed the food (p27). John was aghast at what Kathy wrote in her book: "Where she got that idea in the book that he would lay out two slices of bread, two eggs and a tea bag for his wife and five children is beyond me." The rest of the family laughed at the suggestion.

Who cooked all the family's bread and the Sunday Dinner

How many Irish men today would cook the Sunday dinner and bake the bread for the house? Very few, wouldn't you say? Without fail, Oliver O'Beirne Snr used to make the Sunday dinner and also bake the bread and scones.

John has very fond memories of his father cooking bread and the Sunday dinner for the whole family and especially the appealing aroma that used to fill the family home. In addition to this, "On Saturday he used to cook up 'boxty', a potato dish from Roscommon. With egg on top and butter. It was gorgeous."

"In the later years of his life, even when he was on a crutch, he would still cook the dinner on Sunday. It was just something he loved to do."

Our father only drank in his later years and then only in moderation

In Kathy's book, [page 23] she makes allegations that Oliver Snr was a very heavy drinker who,, when he got loosened up, was even more mindlessly cruel than normal. But even that was not strong enough for her. She also said his cruelty was mindless, and alleges that he would roll in drunk from the pub and out of malice make the O'Beirne children stand out in the hall, all night in the freezing cold. But Brian (45) totally refutes that any incidents like this ever happened. He also added: "It was only in later years, when we were all grown up, that he would go down to the pub for a pint at night-time. It would be after the nine o'clock news. I would often go down with him. He would have four pints of Guinness. That is all he would have. And sometimes, he would have a whiskey and water, a single Power's whiskey. I would go down with him, and I was married at this stage."

And helped all his children get set up in life

During the family press conference they revealed the anguish they had to endure, suffering under a false allegation of abuse:

"We, as a family are testimony to the fact that false and exaggerated allegations of child abuse can be made, and we can also testify that when they are made, the embarrassment, shock, and isolation involved are horrific."

According to daughter Mary: "My father worked every day and seldom took a day off. People who worked with him thought very highly of him. He was great with his hands, and helped a lot of people out. He helped all of us out. He helped set up Oliver in a shop, he helped set up Eamonn in his joinery business, he helped us all. He paid for my wedding, helped us put in gas heating. He also helped Kathy. He helped build a chalet out the back to help the boys save for a house. He took me to Irish dancing competitions, and to Mass every evening during Lent."

Unlike in Kathy's book, where it says he was a daily Mass-going pillar of respectability, Oliver was working every day, doing shift work and didn't have time to go to Mass every day. He went to Mass on a Sunday with the rest of the family. As Oliver Jr commented: "That's just one more lie in Kathy's book. One of many."

Tommy agrees with that assessment: "My father tried to help everybody. He gave money to all of us to set us up in what we were doing. To either get a trade or set up a shop. As a family we would help each other out and we're still like that."

On her father, Kathy's past actions contradict the sentiments of her book

Mary is quick to point out the stark contrast between the words of Kathy in her book and her actions when her father died. Oliver Snr died of a heart attack 10 years ago (in July 1997 at the age of 70) outside St James' Hospital in south central Dublin. "He could not have been all bad because Kathleen put up a notice in his memory at the spot where he died. Indeed, Kathy's last will and testament which she handed to Brian in September 2006, states that she wanted to be buried in the same grave as her father. This is alongside her mother in Sleeping Meadows cemetery, Palmerstown."

Mary highlighted that, "He died on his own outside St James hospital and Kathleen put flowers and a type of plaque outside in his memory. For the man she hates! In the hospital when he was dying, Kathleen was the one who was at his bedside saying repeatedly, 'I'm sorry Da for what I did, I'm sorry, I'm sorry, I'm really sorry.' I said, 'So you bloody should be, you gave him such a hard life.'"

"Then we had to tell her to shut up. But I can tell you this, if I hated a man for what he did to me, I wouldn't be saying sorry for what I did to him or putting plaques up for him where he died or anything like that. I wouldn't be going to his funeral and living with him in the house into my forties as Kathy did. But Kathy has done all these things. Can't you see the contradiction? If he was so cruel, why was she living with this same man in the same house into her forties? Even her own fabricated story doesn't add up."

In addition, Oliver Jnr used to meet up with Kathy in Bewley's Hotel and have a chat, even up to recently, before her book came out. He recalls, "There was never any talk of my father the 'monster' ever to me. Nothing like that. To me she was my sister. All the way growing up, Kathleen was jolly and happy. She would never be one to be depressed or down very much. She's a person who was well looked after."

Sleeping outside Kathy's door but for a very different reason

There is a reference in Kathy's book, that on occasion her father used to lock her bedroom and sleep outside her door (p24). According to her siblings, this in part is correct. This event did happen but the reason why it happened is completely different from that given by Kathy. The reason for this is that the boys were up in arms, because Kathleen would creep at night into their bedroom on her belly, crawl under their beds and rifle their trouser pockets for any money.

Three of the brothers used to sleep in a double bed. It came to such a stage that Johnny and Oliver used to sleep with their socks on and their money in the socks. According to Oliver Snr, "She used to go round the house at night like that, stealing all the money. Because we told our father what she was doing, he slept outside her room for a time to catch her doing it. In her book she switched it round to suit herself. That she was the victim rather than the perpetrator."

Despite the brothers best efforts, their belongings were never safe. They were forced to resort to the tactic of hiding their money in their socks while they slept at night, but this was was uncovered by their sister. On one occasion, she even cut the toes off Oliver's socks and took the money as he was asleep. They laughed and laughed at remembering the the ingenuity of the actions, but the actions were still disturbing and their efforts to stop her failed.

On another occasion, Oliver Jnr hid two and six pence under the plug in the bath at night: it was gone the next morning, stolen by Kathy. There were no hiding places for money when Kathy was about. "We eventually ran out of places to hide our stuff," Oliver recalls, "Kathy would always find them. Nowhere and nothing was safe when Kathy was about."

He literally bailed Kathy out on many occasions and even then, she would take advantage

Margaret recalls a time when: "Kathy spent time in Mountjoy prison for painting Tom Cronan's house and car, and threatening him because he refused to let her into the local Gaelic Football club. My sister in law, Jean and I went up to visit her in Mountjoy. At the time, I was pregnant with my daughter, and what happened but Kathy asked me to give in a urine sample, so she could say she was pregnant. I responded, 'I'm not doing that. I'll get into serious trouble."

"At the same time, putting aside the great shame and embarrassment that he would have felt, my Da went down and paid £450 bail money to get her out. This was the man who was supposed to have done nothing for her. He had to go back a few weeks later to get the bail money. But what did Kathy do? She had gone in and forged his signature, taking the bail money out and put it in the Irish Permanent Bank. He couldn't get his money back. That's what you call getting well and truly fleeced."

While their father Oliver stuck by Kathy and helped her out of her many troubles, one can see now why the family suggested, "the suffering caused to our family due to Kathleen's psychological problems would have driven any other person to extremes of despair." As her brother Eamonn said, their father always rose above this and always tried to help his daughter: "Certainly, I can remember my father having to bail her out a few times. He always did. He would never let her down."

At about the age of 16, Kathy herself chose to go into the girls' hostel in Dublin, known as Sherrard House. Eamonn remembers that his parents pleaded with her to come back but she refused. "But, she was always welcome back, as you can see from the pictures when she was 17, and my Da never turned his back on her, as you can see from Margaret's wedding pictures in 1991. He loved her.

"It would have broken my parents' hearts to see what is being said today. What is hard for us to deal with is the fact that our father was a good man and he cannot defend his good name."

Margaret O'Beirne is very straightforward in her approach: "How dare Michael Sheridan speak about our family like that. How dare he speak of my father the way he has. The cheek of him. I would not like to meet the man because I don't know what I would do to him. I'm that angry about it."

Mary, with her eyes burning, is adamant, "My father did so much, working his fingers to the bone for his family. I can tell you this, I will not stop until I clear my Daddy's name and the rest of my brothers and sisters feel the same."

5 Kathy's Youth: The pride and joy... who went off the rails

"**K**athy's real story is quite simple really," says her brother Eamonn. "It's the story of a girl who was spoilt and went off the rails. Kathy was a wild one."

"Even at a young age, she was always getting into fights," Oliver recalls, "getting sent home from school, being disruptive, threatening to burn down the premises of shop owner Joe Ledwidge, as well as stealing from him. She would steal from shops in Clondalkin Village and was constantly in trouble like that. And you're talking from a very early age.

"The police were at the house door frequently. You could go on all day about what she did and got up to."

According to Tommy, Kathy was given free rein of the house and would run rings around her brothers. She frequently got into trouble. "If there was an open window, she would be out of it. She was here, there and everywhere."

"But eventually the neighbours had enough of it and started to complain of her stealing their stuff. Kathy chose to go into Sherrard House, but she was out every second day on the Booth Road.

"Sherrard House was somewhere to stay at night and stay out when she wanted. It was a handy base for stealing in town. My parents pleaded with her to come back, but she refused them. Kathy was still hanging around Sherrard House when she was 18."

Where was she, growing up?

At the family Press Conference, Mary said that: "Our sister was not in a Magdalene laundry, or Magdalene Home, she was in St Anne's Children's Home, Kilmacud, St Loman's psychiatric hospital, Mountjoy Prison, and Sherrard House for homeless people. Our parents placed her in St Anne's for a brief period when she was eleven, because of ongoing behavioural difficulties.

"Kathleen stated she was in a Magdalene home from when she was 12 to fourteen, and became pregnant as a result of rape there when she was thirteen. These are the years 1968 to 1970. As with any allegations that only emerge years later we have had to use the best method we could think of to remember. We chose family activities.

1967:	She was in St Anne's Children's Home, Kilmacud for 6 weeks.
1968:	She was at a cousin's wedding, she still lived at home with us at this stage.
1968:	Kathleen dressed our sister Mary, for our mother's return from hospital after having our sister Margaret. She still lived at home with us at this stage.
1969:	Used to take Patsy's new baby out for walks. She still lived at home with us at this stage.
1969/70	Brian and Kathy were in hospital together having their tonsils out.
1970:	Made her confirmation with our brother Eamonn, she was 14. Still lived at home with us at this stage and did not have a child.
1968/69/70:	Eamonn and Kathleen went to quarry playing with friends after school, and Saturdays. At this stage she lived at home. We also went swimming in a local swimming spot, the 'sandy hole.'
1968/69/70:	During the summer months, went swimming with Eamonn and friends at the 'sandy hole'.
1972	She was at Mary's Holy Communion, as far as we can remember, she was still living at home. She would have been 16 years old.
1974:	Eamonn met Ann, now his wife, Kathleen was living at home most of this time.
1975:	Eamonn and Ann went to visit Kathy in Sherrard house. She would have been 19 years old.
1978,	Mary, Margaret, Mam & Dad went to see her in Mountjoy.

As the first girl in the family, Kathy was spoiled and had certain privileges. According to Eamonn, she was looked after better than the boys. As the first and oldest girl, she got away with a lot more than the boys in the family. John recounts the boys being grounded at one stage because they didn't do what Kathleen wanted to do.

Far from being beaten and abused as a vulnerable child as per her book, the family say that Kathy was treated as the favourite from the day she was born. For instance, Eamonn recalls: "She was the eldest daughter, of course she was the pride and joy. She would get to stay up that bit later, be seen as the responsible one, get the biggest bed in the girls room."

Kathy's sister Margaret used to hear Kathy laughing with her parents downstairs as Margaret lay in bed. "She was allowed to stay up with them that bit more." Margaret added, "and this was despite her behaviour which was always a bit off. She would dare some of the boys to do silly things, and get them in trouble, that sort of thing.

"At one time, Kathy asked her father to go out to the garden and look towards the house while cajoling Brian, who was very young, to stand up on the window board with no clothes on. A big laugh for sure. But always getting into trouble and bringing others with her when she could. I think she was spoiled actually," comments Margaret, "she had everything and started teasing other children in the area and stealing."

Kathy also created many problems at school. According to John, "She would regularly beat up other children while in Scoil Mhuire. On one occasion she cut a girl, Carmel Foran's long plait off, and then relentlessly teased her when the girl began to cry.

"On another occasion a very upset mother called to our house with her daughter and holding a handful of hair. Her poor daughter had lumps out of her. What could my mother say?" When interviewed in Bewley's Hotel, John agreed that, "Kathleen had no fear. She was afraid of nothing, afraid of no consequences."

In her book, Kathy had a miserable life of abuse and beatings, of humiliation and malnourishment in her home. But to Oliver, Kathy "was always jolly and in good form. She is a person who was well looked after." And why wouldn't she be, she ran rings around her parents and siblings. But her parents realised pretty early that Kathy's behaviour was not just unacceptable but also abnormal.

Because of her violence, other children were afraid to play with her. However, Nancy, her mother used to confide in John: "At one stage, my mother told me, before Kathleen went into St Loman's, the psychiatric institution, that Kathleen had been classed as 'mentally retarded', as they used to say in those days. She used to give me 2/6 in old money to play with her for one hour every day after school.

"I used to entice Oliver into it. I had to give him six pence, but I had to, so he would play with me, that I could play with her. But we never got a full hour out of it. Because she would flare up. Something would go wrong. She would say you're not doing it my way and the whole thing would blow up and come to an end." Oliver laughed raucously when reminded of being paid to play with Kathy along with Johnny, "because everyone else was terrified to play with her."

After she was put into St Anne's Reformatory School at the age of twelve, John used to visit her every week and Oliver every second week. John said you would have noticed a difference. "She was very well presented in her school uniform and black leather shoes and seemed to be much calmer. She wasn't running round pulling people's hair out and beating lumps out of them. She was calm and we used to walk around the grounds. Everything was all right. It was only when she didn't go back there that problems started again."

"The reason that Kathy was put in St Loman's [Psychiatric Hospital] was that the neighbours were getting a petition up to put her away." Oliver remembers that, "Father took her to the doctor, and she was referred to St Anne's and then later to St Loman's."

Telling stories and seeking attention

In her book, Kathy alleges that she has a bowel complaint. This is true. According to her brother Tommy: "She actually has some bowel complaint, something like a twisted gut and she knows what to eat to trigger it off to get attention, so she would be in hospital and everyone would be in to visit her.

"Kathy has always been a great one working for attention; for getting into trouble and also telling you stories, seeing you believe them and chase them up and her sitting back and enjoying herself as you got into trouble. She once told me a Garda took money off her as she came out of a bank, ripped the money in two and tucked it in his back pocket. Stupidly I followed it up, as if it was true.

"To meet Kathy is to come face to face with a talented and engaging storyteller. Everyone who knows her or met her has said how convincing she can be. She will make you believe what she is saying. Don't delude yourself about that, but when you ask for details or proof - that is when she runs into trouble."

All her siblings are agreed that Kathy is very streetwise. "She is very cute. And she can well talk for herself," observes Margaret. According to her sister Mary, Kathy is, and always has been, a compulsive liar. "Kathy is lying about all this – just like she has lied about things all her life," says Mary. "She is very convincing, though, and that is what makes her so dangerous."

Eamonn says that, "Kathleen has always lied. If you did not agree with her, you would be beaten up or threatened. If you did not do what she wants, you are no good to her. That is the type of girl she is. She is a very cute girl. She does this all for money. She will do anything for money. Kathleen will run you into the ground until you have no energy left to oppose her. She will best you. She will wear you down until you cannot do anything about it."

Mary too attests that, "Kathy saps every bit of energy out of you. If you go up against Kathleen, she makes your life a living hell. She will do everything in her power to make your life a misery. Really, we let her away with things for too long. We turned the blind eye, but she is not doing it any more."

As in many homes with children of that age, there was plenty of childhood fun during the summer in the O'Beirne household. Contrary to her insistence in her book that she can't swim (pages 98 and 99) because some social worker supposedly tried to molest her in the water, Eamonn and his brothers often enjoyed carefree days swimming in a nearby stream. According to Eamonn, "contrary to what she says in her book Kathleen was well able to swim."

After a six week stint in St Anne's boarding school, Kathy was soon after admitted to St Loman's Psychiatric Hospital. John and Oliver together visited Kathy In St Loman's quite often, "getting the bus up on a Sunday afternoon to see her at 2 o'clock. We would come back at six," says John. "There was no restriction within her unit. They obviously did not mix her with the other 'heads', like she says they did.

"We had tea or coke, whatever we wanted and we would be out walking around. We didn't sit around for four hours, we were playing, we had to do something. But, for sure, she wasn't drugged or doped up to her eyeballs. She was normal. She was in St Loman's for a number of months, and went there shortly after going to St Anne's school."

Kathy wasn't in St Loman's just for the fun, she was there for a reason, and this reason remains apparent even after she got out and was back in her Clondalkin home. In her book she admits to a criminal record of petty theft and this was something she developed and practised from an early age. If you were to ask what Kathy did in her youth, you would be pointed in the right direction by her book. According to her brother John, she spent a lot of time, hanging around street corners in Clondalkin and stealing from shops:

"In her teens, hanging round Ledwidge's shop in the village was her top trick. Shame to say, I was there if anything went wrong. Because there could be a gang of 10 to 12 lads hanging around outside on the scran (tapping passers-by for a few pence). It would be a Saturday evening and she had it timed to a tee. Mr Ledwidge, the shop owner, came back with a sack of change for the tills. A bag of half-crowns, the old money. He would take out some of it, give it to the girls at the tills and put the rest of the bag under the counter.

"Kathleen would be at the window looking in, and see exactly were it was. Kathleen would look in, then time it, and watch it. And then, just at the right moment, she would go in and ask the woman to get something small from around the corner. Of course, once the woman went round the corner, Kathleen got down on the ground, and hid the sack under her coat. Get up and pay the woman for what she got, perhaps a packet of aspirins or something. That was it. I was there and I wouldn't let any of the other lads touch her.

"They would just be standing round the shop tapping people for a few bob. That is how she got her money. She did it a lot and until this day, I don't know how the shop owner didn't cop on to it. She would be about 16 at this time. She was living at home, in between living at Sherrard House. Although Kathleen doesn't have a huge education, she is very cute, and very cunning. Whatever Kathleen learned, she learned very fast."

Indeed, Margaret recalls Kathy coming shopping with her and asking to push her child's buggy. Kathy would come out of the shop and pull stolen goods out of the back of the child's pram and Margaret would be mortified.

In and out of Sherrard House Hostel

Sherrard House was a hostel set up to help young women who were homeless. In her late teens Kathy decided that she wanted to go and stay there, which she did intermittently.

Kathy would return home for frequent long-term visits and even when she slept in Sherrard House she would be out in Clondalkin during the day. The elder O'Beirne boys viewed it as a place which Kathy could use as a base for shoplifting. She was freer to do whatever she pleased within the basic and comparatively lax restraints of the hostel.

Mary visited Kathy there frequently, along with her parents: "I don't believe she was ever in a Magdalene laundry, she was in and out of Sherrard House and she was coming and going home at the same time. I visited her in Sherrard House with my sister, Margaret as well as my niece, and mother and father. We saw her bedroom where she slept. A lot of our time was taken up visiting Kathy in Sherrard House and all the other places.

"We visited her in Sherrard House at the same time she now claims to have been in the laundries. Our visits to Kathy virtually took over our lives, and I don't know how my parents did it. It would have driven most people demented. I don't know how they didn't just wash their hands of Kathleen some day and just walk out. She saps every bit of energy out of you."

Kathy's Tactic: Divide and Conquer

As the eldest son, Tommy (60) has experienced all sides of Kathy's personality and how she has interacted with the rest of the family. "I think," he says, "Kathy has tried to break up every marriage in the family including that of my mother and father. She would try it by telling stories about this or that. By poisoning one person against another by telling stories. By trying to turn people against each other. Kathy tried this repeatedly.

"She tried it on my mum and dad, against myself and [my wife] Jean. From listening to others, I can say she has had a go at almost everybody; in trying to split them up. She once got it to the stage where my mother and father were in different rooms. She would play one person off against another and try to separate them. Divide and conquer was always Kathy's motto.

"Kathy once suggested to me, 'Do you know, I think you should leave Jean.' This was because Jean disagreed with her when Kathy wrote the very first article in the *Irish Crime* magazine [a magazine edited by Michael Sheridan]. Jean read the magazine and said to Kathy, 'That's all lies, that's not true.' Jean immediately stopped having lunch with her, and Kathy turned against her.

"You can't know Kathy very well. You only think you do. But she is very believable and convincing when she tells a story. She would have you in tears very easy."

Kathy's propensity for spreading vicious rumours has also had an effect on Mary who thinks that, "Kathy will attempt to destroy you. She's a very cold person and she doesn't care what she does on anybody else.

"To give you an example, years ago, when I first moved into a flat in Clondalkin, Margaret moved in with me. At the time, I was going out with my husband and Margaret was going out with her husband. To cut to the chase, Kathy once went home to my parents and said the four of us were sleeping together in the flat!

"I just laughed at this story but Kathy also told this fantasy to Joseph to get him riled up and set against us. Kathy loves to plant evil little seeds like this and to watch what happens. She is very convincing but she doesn't convince me. Kathy always tried to poison the relationship between my mother and father by making up stories and lying to them."

John remembers that, for years Kathy tried to break up her parents. He recalls being in the house on a Saturday: "my father would be cooking the boxty, and perhaps steaming a bit of fish. He would shout in from the kitchen, 'Will I put yours on now Nancy or do you want to wait?' My mother was a bit deaf in one ear, and Kathy would be sitting beside her in the lounge room. My mother would say, 'What?' And Kathy would say to her, 'He said you can make your effing own dinner.'

"That is how she would try to split them. I was sitting beside her, and I tell you, if Jennifer had not been there, I would have decked Kathy. But all I could do was say to my mother, 'Do you want your food now Ma, father is going to make it?' She said, 'No, No. I'll have it later.'"

Their father Oliver died in July 1997 at the age of 70 after a massive heart attack. "While all the family," Tommy says, "were in the room with the doctor discussing what to do, the doctor had recommended that the life support machine be turned off. Kathy turned around and said to him, 'I'm a trained nurse'. Now no one said anything because they were so used to her telling ridiculous stories that they would not even bother. No one would believe her anyway. She would be telling stories all the time, you wouldn't take them seriously. You would become so used to hearing these things you wouldn't even comment on them.

"It sounds ridiculous, but that's the way it was. We have had a lifetime of listening to her ridiculous stories. You close off to it. But now what she has written about our father is a tissue of lies. And she is totally wrong.

"An awful lot of things she got away with over the years, and we turned a blind eye, but when you sit back on reflection, and take into account everything that has gone on in those years, Kathy got away with murder. She has treated our mother and our father like dirt. Not alone did she do it while they were alive, but she is treating them like dirt now they are dead. I don't agree with that. No member of this family agrees with that.

"This girl does not care because it is disruption that she is into.

Disruption and displacement of families and she doesn't care who she hurts or what she does. With all the new evidence now coming out her back is up against the wall. She is lashing out in all directions now and we are worried that she will hurt somebody, even our children and grandchildren. She is dangerous and there can't be one law for her and another for the rest of the world. We are now worried. And she has a brother of mine in tow." (Joseph, the youngest at 43)

In her book, Kathy's mother is betrayed like a perfect saint and Kathy as her true adoring admirer. But Kathy's relationship with her mother was not as she portrayed it. Indeed, according to her siblings, Kathy could on occasion be very nasty to her, not only when Kathy was a youth but even into her forties. "It was not that long ago," Eamonn says, "that Kathleen, in front of us, wished our mother dead, and wished her dead with cancer of the face. She cursed and damned the woman into the ground. And she did it in front of people."

According to Margaret: "My Mam was taking something out of the oven and I was standing at the sink, I don't know what happened. Mammy said something to her. But Kathleen said, 'I hope cancer walks out of your face.' My Mam said, 'May God forgive you.' She was crying but I said, 'Don't mind her.'"

Tommy's wife Jean remembers on another occasion, that Kathy once left her mother down in the village in the wheelchair.

The seven siblings are agreed that Kathy is very streetwise. For John: "Kathy will do anything for money. I remember coming down the stairs one day, my father was out, but my mother was there. I looked out the window of the house to see Kathleen hanging out the window of the chalet right beside the house. She was after sneaking in to steal Oliver's honeymoon money."

Oliver elaborates further on this story: "Kathy got into the chalet or maisonette at the back of the house, and she stole the old style watch which I had for my wedding, and had it pawned off at the pawnbrokers. I had to go and get it back before the wedding as well as the envelopes of money made ready for the photographer and other people involved in the wedding but which she had stolen.

"These are things that we let her get away with at the time because she was our sister. They were brushed aside for the sake of family. That's what we did.

"I remember at the time, there was a worry that she would not be at our wedding because of a court appearance at the time. We married on March 26, 1977."

As far as Oliver and Jean can remember, Kathy worked for Urney's chocolate factory in Tallaght for a few weeks in her twenties. She could never hold a job.

Eamonn said: "At one stage she got a bungalow off the council in Bornogue in Clondalkin. About 12 years ago, she was there a few months. She also had a two storey house off the Council in Bawnogue for a short while using papers belonging to Oliver. I believe she went with false papers to the Council. She used other people's documents but the local people ran her when they found she had no children and was there by telling lies while genuine people in need of a house were left without one. She got the house under an assumed name. She is very able to get what she wants."

"Apart from these short times," Eamonn continued, "she lived in the apartment / chalet out the back of the house in her thirties and forties. She had electricity, running water and she ate in the house."

Kathy: adopted at first but then a natural child again.

A few years ago, Kathy started to say that she had been adopted as a child from another family. This was the reason Kathy gave for her claim that she found it hard to bond with her father. She told Mary that she was adopted from the country. "Kathleen started saying this when she started to write her book after her mother died. She told this to both Margaret and me. I said 'Don't be ridiculous, you're the image of us.' I had to leave the house that night. It was totally ridiculous.

"This adoption thing came up in court, discussing her birth certificate, her barrister said, 'This is under investigation.' Why would her birth certificate be under investigation? Surely he should be investigating her silly story of adoption."

When Kathy learned that her family had procured a copy of her birth certificate, she changed tack again. Later admitting she was not adopted, but the natural child of Oliver and Nancy O'Beirne as plainly stated on her birth certificate.

Kathy's Extensive Criminal Record

You don't expect criminals to be so upfront about their criminal record, but Kathy isn't shy about hers. In her book, she speaks about it freely. One of the captions for one of her photos as a youth with a beaming smiles reads, "This was the day I stole a mac from Penneys. I ended up spending three months in Mountjoy Prison."

She and a friend stole coats out of a well-known clothes store, for which she ended up before the Children's Court in Dublin where they were charged with shoplifting. Kathy says she stole from shops and picked the locks of phone boxes to rob the money inside. In her book she claims she was given three months in Mountjoy Prison.

The members of her family have already spoken of going to visit Kathy there on a regular basis and the shame their father felt when he had to go and bail her out at court.

After months of tracking down her records, I was able to obtain, from a source close to the Gardai, confirmation that Kathy had a sizeable criminal record.

The source was able to confirm the memories of Kathy's family of her being up in court, being convicted and then spending time in Mountjoy Prison.

The nine dates on which Kathy O'Beirne was convicted and the courts in which she appeared are listed below. Almost all of the convictions involve petty theft. These show that Kathy engaged in petty crime for a long period of her life.

27th February 1976	District Court 4, Dublin.
29th July 1976	Smithfield Children's Court.
13th January 1977	District Court 4.
25th May 1979	District Court 4.
13th December 1979	Kilmainham District Court.
23rd July 1981	Kilmainham District Court – Probation Act.
22nd September 1981	Smithfield Children's Court.
1st June 1982	Kilmainham District Court.
22nd February 1989	Kilmainham District Court.

As Kathy was born on October 18, 1956, the last conviction listed above means that she was found guilty of crime at the age of 32. The list above is certain and guaranteed as accurate by an impeccable source. However, it is not complete. The source also confirmed that there were at least two more convictions in court.

Kathy's sister Margaret also says she remembers going to visit Kathy in Mountjoy Prison around November 1992, when she was pregnant with her daughter.

Kathy's arguments in her book are like Mountjoy prison in Dublin: Full of pros and cons. Indeed Kathy herself spent some time in Mountjoy as a petty thief, a con, rather than a pro.

Now a neighbour contradicts another part of Kathy's book

While virtually all those mentioned in Kathy's book are dead or unnamed, a neighbour, Nancy Buggy is mentioned in the book as one who allowed Kathy to stay in her house at night and feed her up. (acknowledgement page II) Kathy also alleged that Nancy O'Beirne used to stay there when she was supposedly thrown out of the house.

Mrs Buggy's daughter, Pauline said that O'Beirne's statements about this are untrue.

At the book launch party in the Booth Road, Clondalkin, West Dublin, a friend of Kathy, Margaret Power, told this journalist that she heard Pauline Buggy say to Kathy: "You have that wrong. I have no recollection of your Mam ever staying in our house, or you for that matter. Maybe one night you did, but that was it." Asked by this author had Mrs O'Beirne and Kathy O'Beirne stayed in her house as portrayed in Kathy's Story, Pauline Buggy said, "That is all wrong."

Pauline Buggy said, "Mrs Nancy O'Beirne never stayed in my house. Kathy never stayed here, not that I remember."

6 In a Convent School:
a former pupil contradicts her story

Conned into entering a reformatory convent school by her cruel father, Kathy O'Beirne draws a harrowing picture of her life from the tender age of eight in the second chapter of her book, headed 'School from Hell.' In her emotionally touching account, both the nuns and her father are portrayed as one dimensional automatons of heartless brutality. This sharp division between 'goodies' and 'baddies' is something which is quite persistent throughout her work. She describes her lot as: "a child in the cruel grip of an unending nightmare."

And the nightmare that Kathy O'Beirne dreams is in the stark monochrome of black and white. (She even says so in p47 – "There was no colour in the room, everything was black and white.") But what set alarm bells off about Kathy's book initially in this writer's head was that the vast majority of characters in her book lacked texture and complexity, they are cardboard cut-outs of either good or evil.

Her father is portrayed as having cunningly misled her as to the reason why she was going on a car trip before dumping her there without remorse.

It goes without saying that the Reverend Mother in the chapter was "fat and ugly and did not look very kind." (p42) This was the same woman who allegedly grabbed a storybook out of the eight year-old's hand before proceeding to beat poor Kathy over the head with it.

Even darker than *Hansel and Gretel* for instance, in *Kathy's Story* the nuns supposedly block Kathy from going to the classroom for an education. Kathy said, "I was demoted from being a pupil to a slave." A life of drudgery and grubbing unfolded before her. She was being looked after in a "slave labour camp" (p52) by nuns, one of whom gave Kathy, as she alleged anyway, an invasive vaginal examination to ascertain whether she was "intact."

According to Kathy, lunch in the reformatory school was a meal of "bread and sludge," eaten in silence. After the evening meal, the resident girls were allowed to play for an hour in the recreation room but there was "no radio or television, no games or toys of any kind." Kathy alleges that the unnamed order of nuns, never allowed the girls any contact with the outside world. "We were only allowed out for a walk down the avenue once a day under strict supervision." (p 60).

The nuns accused by Kathy, the Sisters of Our Lady of Charity, on the other hand are adamant that Kathy only stayed with them in a reformatory convent boarding school, for a mere six weeks. One of the pupils who was there tells not only of her own tremendous experience at the school explains how it set her up for the rest of her life.

Maggie Lacey's experience of St Anne's School

Maggie Lacey is a vivacious and talkative 53 year-old lady who lives in the Liberties area of central Dublin, a stone's throw away from St Patrick's Cathedral. Disabled by the effects of severe arthritis, she is confined to a wheelchair when on the move, but this does not prevent her from currently studying for a degree in History and the History of Art at University College, Dublin (UCD). I heard of Maggie, when I mentioned to someone else I met, that I was writing a book on this subject. The woman turned out to be one of Maggie's best friends.

From the ages of 8 to 12, during the years 1962–1966, Maggie attended St Anne's school in Kilmacud, Dublin, the same convent boarding school that Kathy O'Beirne attended.

Maggie was placed in the convent boarding school by the local authorities because of her problems at home. She said that she was being physically abused by her stepfather, whom she characterised as a domineering and cruel man. Raised in the Arbour Hill army barracks in Dublin, she loves living in the Liberties area of Dublin, saying that it is: "full of great characters. It's very friendly and you can make great friends."

Maggie says that her stepfather physically abused her and was so mean that he used to lock up the food in a cupboard. It is a bit of a cliché, but he actually did hail from Co Cavan. Her mother was from a Traveller family, while her father was college-educated. According to Maggie, "My stepfather controlled the household, he used to lock up the food in a cupboard and we suffered a lot. Sometimes during the summer, I went to stay with my granny in Co Leitrim. She was aware there were problems but there was little she could do about it. I loved my granny, she was a tough old farmer's wife, but she was very helpful and in those days, life was tough for everybody.

"Anyway, as a result of what happened to me in childhood, I had great emotional problems and I was not the usual run of a child. I can tell you, I was very hard to handle and no relationship I have ever had with a man has ever worked. I always have to be the dominant one. The abuse has had long term effects on my life."

But for a woman who suffered so much harm as a child, she is thriving at present. She is even now, after all these years, very thankful to the Sisters of our Lady of Charity for the great help that they gave to her in her years of need. Maggie doesn't say that from a basis of religious allegiance or sympathy because she is not a practising Catholic. Indeed she has arguments about religion quite frequently with a devout Catholic neighbour who sees and helps her out a lot.

"The nuns were brilliant. I loved them," Maggie said. "To go from home to St Anne's, it was like going to paradise. I was taken out of my own home by the authorities and I had a lot of emotional problems with nightmares and tantrums. I was very bold and wilful, and challenged the nuns all the time. They never once hurt me nor did I have any problems with them." Indeed, Maggie is grateful to the nuns for encouraging her in her interests and talents, something she is carrying on even today.

"Our house mother was Sr Dominic, who looked after us just like a mother would look after her own children. There were many of us and she had to spread her love around, but she was very good to me. She saw that I was good at art, and she encouraged me at it. I didn't want to go to school and they didn't threaten or push me into it. She helped us in everything, even washing our face, cleaning our teeth, and brushing our hair.

"The nuns," Maggie said, "were very encouraging and they did their very best for us. We got elocution lessons for speech, and had posture lessons – walking about with books on our head. We had art lessons, drama and dancing lessons. To get that now, you would have to go to a private fee-paying school.

"We were also taken to the beach in Portmarnock or Greystones, but I didn't like that because I love the heat and I always found the beach too cold for me. I hate the cold."

The nuns, she said, also took the girls to the cinema, and there was a large projector in the school for films. On the odd occasion they were also taken shopping to help get material for the school – stuff like sheets and pillows.

In Maggie's experience: "The nuns were very encouraging, they looked after the girls' welfare and were good to us. I once had appendicitis and there was some problem and delay with the ambulance. I remember one of the nuns sat beside my bed all night holding my hand. My appendix eventually burst and I still have the sixteen stitch scar.

"We were all treated very well, and if I could think of one bad thing I would tell you. The food was basic but healthy. We had dessert every day, and the nuns had the same food as the girls. For breakfast we would have porridge or cereal with toast and tea. And for dinner we would often have grated cheese and onion along with brown bread and tea.

"Dinner was brilliant compared to what I had at home. I loved the treat of jelly and custard. At the school Mother Veronica was in charge of the whole operation and it was well run. The nuns had their own vegetable patch as well as cows for milking. Looking back, it was quite self-sufficient."

When asked about any beating or hardship that may have taken place, Maggie explained that none had ever happened to her, nor did she see or hear of any either. She saw violence only once in the school and that was one evening when they were watching TV. The girls were normally allowed to watch TV for an hour after dinner every night: "Well, on one occasion The Rolling Stones, then the height of rebellion, came on TV. An older girl went up and turned up the volume, but a nun then went to the TV and turned it down again. This happened again until the girl attacked the nun and tried to pull her veil off. We were all shocked, even then we knew it was wrong to pull a nun's veil off. Other nuns came and got hold of the girl and dragged her out. That girl was left the next day."

On one occasion, being ashamed that her parents never came to visit her, Maggie told one of her friends, who was a Traveller girl, that she (Maggie) had great parents who loved her. "We ran off from the school. I took her to my parents' home but they put us out of the house, and so we stayed at a traveller's camp for three days. Eventually the Gardai caught us and I was sent back. The nuns were very disappointed and asked me why I did it. I told them that I was boasting to a friend that I had nice parents. They asked me did I think I was better off at home? I said no. They understood there was no point in hitting or chastising me after all the abuse that I had received at home."

Listening to the experience of some of her friends at the convent boarding school, Maggie commented that she had heard some horrific stories of abuse and hardship. Maggie thinks, "I was one of the lucky ones. To go from the situation I was in at home to a place with the nuns, where I got three meals a day, clean clothes and a form of education where they taught me things. I was given opportunities that I never had at home."

There was a pretty set regime during the day. The girls got up early and had breakfast and there was Mass on some mornings. Then it was classes in the convent for a couple of hours followed by lunch in the dining hall. "After this," Maggie said, "we had arts and crafts until tea time, and after this we had an hour of TV. Some afternoons we had a run out in the recreation area, either running on the track or playing football. Then it was time for bed."

A model of help sharply reversed by media reports

In Maggie's opinion, the nuns had it all together. "They looked after us. A lot of the girls were abused or abandoned in some way and then went to the convent school where they were well looked after. This the opposite of the model you always hear and see on TV.

"I believe there are a lot of false allegations flying about. Now, don't get me wrong, I'm sure that there are also genuine cases of abuse, but I don't believe the amount of abuse being indicated to the public is true. I never saw anybody else getting abused by the nuns or heard of any stories like this – not once. I find it very hard to believe that all the stories of abuse by religious are true. I'm not a practising Catholic, so I have no axe to grind there, but I think it's wrong to make a false allegation. A friend of mine once asked me – 'Why don't you say you were abused by the nuns?' I could never do that because it would wreck my conscience.

"I can tell you one thing though, the nuns taught us right from wrong. I was such an angry person, I don't know how I would have ended up if the nuns had not brought me up. I'm afraid to think what would have happened if I had got into drink, drugs or crime."

Kathy O'Beirne claimed to be in St Anne's Reformatory School for Girls, for two years. The nuns themselves say they have records to show she stayed with them for six weeks only. This journalist asked them for the dates and the records but the Sisters of Our Lady of Charity refused to make these public, holding they were protecting privacy. Kathy's family have said she stayed with the nuns at St Anne's school for a short while in 1967. This was one year after Maggie was there, so Maggie has no recollection of a girl called Kathy O'Beirne. If Maggie left in 1966 and Kathy arrived in 1967, their paths would not have met.

One can see glimmers of the influence of her early life on Maggie today. She says herself that she has never had a long relationship with a man because she always had to be the dominant one. In addition, the layout and presentation of her house reveals it was arranged by someone with an appreciation of form and texture, contrast and colour. That love of art and an eye for colour is evident in the neat ground floor apartment where she lives her life. After speaking to Maggie for two hours, I said my goodbyes and took my leave of her well heated apartment, a place much warmer than breezy Portmarnock Beach.

7 Her Life in a Magdalene Laundry – NOT

In her book, crammed full with cruelty, suffering and vice, Kathy O'Beirne writes: 'The devil himself could not have dreamed up a better hell than the Magdalene laundry.' (p. 116) But there was no need for the devil to dream it up, because Kathy got in there before him.

Being in a Magdalene laundry and having a baby are two of the narrative maypoles around which the book revolves, and Kathy dances with a book contract in one hand and a dream of wealth in the other. However, both these narrative poles have been pulled down. Kathy was never in a Magdalene laundry, nor did she ever have a baby.

After many weeks of searching, I found a woman who had actually been in the industrial school in High Park (an orphanage for girls up to the age of 16, just off Collins Avenue in North Dublin) and then worked in the Magdalene laundry itself. Lorraine King was a former worker in High Park Magdalene laundry during the early Seventies when Kathy alleges to have been there. Lorraine said that she had consulted with former residents and they all agreed that this person, Kathy O'Beirne, had never been in High Park Laundry.

In addition, Lorraine commented that the descriptions of the daily life and even the physical layout of High Park in the book were very different from what they would have been like in the 1970's. The book, she said, "has not been written by someone who has been there." But what exactly is Lorraine King talking about?

Here are a few examples: In the second paragraph of the chapter on the Magdalene laundry Kathy O'Beirne writes: "The first thing I notice while driving up to the convent that day was a beautiful grotto to Our Lady on the left-hand side. Up from that was a church, a large red brick building with big bars on the windows." (p112)

Sadly for her case, when Kathy was supposed to have been in this laundry there was a large building in front of the grotto which blocked it from view. The description in the book is a view that Kathy or anybody who wished to visit High Park could have seen a few years ago, but not in the early 1970's when Kathy alleges to have been there.

Lorraine was born in December 1952 (and currently 55) was in the industrial school from 1958 to 1967 leaving at the age of 14. She then went back as a paid employee to work in the laundry reception room and stayed there until she was 17. She says she chose to work there in the early 1970s.

Lorraine told this journalist that, "I have just read the book's section about High Park, and I can tell you the woman Kathy O'Beirne is in 'airy fairy' land. The physical description does not even match up.

"If you are from Dublin, you would know where High Park was. It was on the Swords Road. It starts at Whitehall at the corner of Collins Avenue, where the Port Tunnel hole is now. From that corner there right across to Grace Park Road, down Grace Park Road to Griffith Avenue. It stops just short of Sion Hill Road. The place was absolutely enormous. There were four different institutions within that wall."

In the early Seventies, she suggested, that roughly 70 women worked in the laundry. "In the mid-1970's most teens, who I also knew, worked in 'An Grianan' training centre. This was set up by Sr Columba to help girls in trouble or who had behavioural problems, so they could avoid going into the Magdalene laundry. Sr Columba was progressive but was a tough woman in her own way. I had a friend who taught in 'An Grianan' for four or five years in the early Seventies, a primary school teacher who volunteered to work there. I also asked her and she never heard of a Kathy O'Beirne."

Lorraine said her teacher friend "never saw Kathy O'Beirne, she never knew of her or even heard her name before her book came out. We have obviously discussed it."

The grounds of High Park Convent were huge in the 1960s. Within its grounds, four separate institutions were contained, a convent, an industrial school, a Magdalene laundry and a private fee-paying home for old ladies who paid.

Describing High Park as it would have been in the Seventies, she said: "If you went into High Park at the time, you would approach it from Grace Park Road, there was a big big gate with an arch on it with Our Sisters of Our Lady of Charity of Refuge written over it.

"You would go in there and you would see Martanna House in front of you; to the right of that was the laundry. Martanna House was a hostel built in the mid-Seventies, for country girls working in Dublin, they would have to pay a rent there. They were free to come and go as they pleased within the restrictions, the same as similar hostels throughout Dublin at the time. That was just inside the gate.

"St Mary's was virtually round the back of that. That is what is now talked about as the Magdalene laundry. St Michael's was an old ladies' home for paying guests. St Joseph's, the industrial school took in children between the ages of a few weeks and sixteen years of age. St Mary's, now commonly called the laundry, was always referred to as St Mary's and housed the Penitents. We always called them the 'pentrins'; they were from 17 years upwards, and they were never known as Magdalenes or Maggies. Some of them were old women.

"The penitents lived in St Mary's; the children lived in St Joseph's; the old ladies lived in St Michael's, and the nuns lived in the convent. Every institution was independent of each other, and there was no communication between any of them. Yet you knew the nuns that were responsible for each section."

The Highlight of the Year

"The procession of the Blessed Sacrament for the feast of Corpus Christi was one of the highlights of the year when the children, the penitents and the nuns all came together. The first communicants were in front, throwing down rose petals. Then came the monstrance held by the priest, and surrounded by altar boys and whoever else, then the nuns in their pecking order, then the children in their pecking order, and then the penitents. The procession stayed within the complex, the High Park grounds."

Lorraine said: "High Park was horrendous. The place was bad enough as it was. It didn't need any embellishment. While there were some nuns there who were evil people, there were also nuns there who tried hard and were good to the girls. Within as far as they could be, because they were under their own restrictions as well. They were in an institution of their own kind, but, they chose to be there."

Adamant that Kathy O'Beirne was not in the laundry, gleaning from what she had written, Lorraine added: "There are things that a woman from the laundry would have known, but which are not included in the book. As for her descriptions of taking the laundry in, there is no way that any of the laundry girls would have had contact with the men who worked in the vans, as in Kathy's book.

"All the workers who had contact with customers were paid employees. And all the clothes that were brought in to be laundered, were brought in through what was called the 'Poly room' where every item of laundry was stamped. No Magdalene girls worked in there. The laundry then went into the back. I was a free person so to speak. I chose to work there and I was paid to do so. It was the customer-face end. There were about half a dozen girls worked with me there.

"When I worked there in the late Sixties, early Seventies, the nuns employed a manager, Mr Carpenter to run the laundry. The women did the work, the nuns supervised it, while Mr Carpenter was the manager."

A respectful burial was given to all

The Magdalene grave yard, Lorraine says, "was a little corner, half way between Grace Park Road and the Swords Road. If you look over from the hotel now on the Swords Road you would see where the Magdalene graveyard used to be."

One thing that really annoyed her about the book was Kathy's description of an alleged burial in High Park. "When a Maggie died," Kathy wrote, "she was brought down the long avenue in a handcart pulled by two men... The body was wrapped in a sheet and laid on the cart in the open. A black cross was placed on the body by one of the nuns. The black cross was the symbol of the devil and was used to ensure that the person who had died went straight to hell." (page 119)

O'Beirne asserts that the woman's body was basically dumped in a grave after a short prayer. And sometimes the nuns, with a few girls from the laundry and on occasion a few locals would attend. Hmm....

Lorraine was totally exasperated at this. "And as for throwing bodies into graves, I don't know what she was on. No way this would have happened. They would have been given a respectful burial. There is no way that a body would be wheeled up to a grave and thrown in like a carcass. They were always very respectful of the dead.

"There would always be a Mass, with the body of the woman kept in St Mary's. In fact, it is the first time I saw a dead body. I saw an old woman lying there with two old pennies on her eyes. I never thought that was true, until I saw it. She went into a coffin like any other normal person, and they had a Mass. There was no black crosses on a white shroud as in Kathy's book. That is a load of you know what."

Unlike in the book, Lorraine said that the dead were treated with great dignity. "There was no question of a carcass being dumped in a pit or grave."

There were no underage entrants in the laundry

While Kathy claims to have been in a Magdalene laundry at the age of 12, Lorraine said: "There is no way that a child of this age would ever have been in the laundry. The youngest ever would have been 16/17, and they would have been there only for a short time. It's very seldom you would see any that young.

"I would have known all the women in the laundry. Communication was not encouraged but you could not avoid it. We would have seen all the women file in and out of Mass every morning at half past seven. Very seldom there would be anybody that young. We were 16 years-old in the Industrial School, so why would they put a 12 year old in the Laundry?

"If she wrote the book as a fictional horror story, I would be happy to get on with it, but the fact is, she has maligned so many people. I have no time for that.

"I know she has taken Maggie Bullen's story. She had been in High Park and did get pregnant later on, and her children went for adoption. I don't imagine it was as bad as Kathy O'Beirne is telling. I know one of Maggie Bullen's girls. Kathy jazzed up even that story hugely. It is really quite simple. Kathy was not in High Park. She got the physical descrip-tion of the place completely wrong. She would have been too young and would not have been in the laundry at the age of 12 anyway, and there is no way that we would have missed any girl who was thirteen and pregnant."

Lorraine was aware of St Anne's school in Kilmacud and that a nun, Sr Perpetual Succour was in charge. This nun, she said, is currently called by her own name and lives in High Park today. It was this nun who sent out the invitations for the reunion of former High Park resi-dents in Mary 1999. Lorraine and the other ladies were invited was it was closing down, but Kathy O'Beirne was not not present for it; only former residents had been invited.

Another woman who was actually at the reunion is Valerie Murtagh. Now 63 years of age, Valerie, who lives near Liverpool, was in the indus-trial school from August 9th 1944 until she ran away in 1960. She had friends down in the laundry whom she used to visit regularly.

Valerie said she was ripping angry at Kathy for writing about High Park when it was obvious from her description of the place, that she had never been there. "I am so angry about this book. I want to stand in front of her and ask her to tell me where this place and that place was. She won't be able to tell me because she hasn't even got the basics right!

"Kathy O'Beirne has described High Park as she just had a walk around it a few years ago, but sadly for her, it was quite different three decades ago."

Valerie pointed out that the allegation in Kathy's book that the women were made to eat food with things moving in it (p118), usually caterpillars, was ludicrous. "I worked a good bit in the scullery peeling the potatoes etc. where there were three nuns as well and I can tell you, I never saw any maggots or caterpillars in the food whatsoever."

"As for her story that we were beaten with leather belts (p114), this is another detail which is false. The supervisors in the laundry used canes, which they hung on their belts, but they never used a leather belt."

Valerie went to a lot of trouble to dig out a lot of photographs both of the High Park grounds and the reunion that was held for nuns and past residents in 1999.

One interesting last detail that Valerie raised great doubts about is O'Beirne's assertion of frequent meetings and conversations with the Reverend Mother. "Meeting the Reverend Mother was such a rare occasion that you had a better chance of meeting the Pope! You might have seen her at a funeral or during the Corpus Christi Procession or on a big feast day, or when she wanted to address a large crowd, but rarely, if ever, did you meet her on a one to one basis. Yet in her book, as a young girl, Kathy O'Beirne is meeting and talking to the Reverend Mother all the time.

"Frankly, the woman was very busy and had more important things to be doing than talking to young girls all the time. You would talk to the nuns, yes, but not the Reverend Mother." Valerie hated her time in the High Park institution and so struck out on her own by running away. She has been a frequent visitor over the years and recently brought her own grandson over to visit Ireland and see where she grew up.

'Maeve' describes life in the whole complex

'Maeve', the radio name of a woman who spoke very strongly against the nuns concerning what she had heard about Maggie Bullen's burial a few years ago, came back on the Joe Duffy radio show in September 2006 to say that the nuns had a strong case on this occasion against Kathy O'Beirne.

'Maeve' later told this reporter that, "Kathy was not in High Park Laundry, was not pregnant and did not give birth there, along with a host of other things she said in her book about High Park Laundry. I bet she doesn't, even know what it was actually called and it wasn't High Park by the way."

'Maeve' who had attended the industrial school for 12 years, from 1958-1970 added that, "I also have photographs of the laundry as it used to be and bet your bottom dollar she would not be able to describe it how it was when she was supposed to have been there."

As one who had attended the industrial school in High Park for eleven years, 'Maeve' had the authority to say: "The entrance to High Park has changed drastically in the past 35 years. Kathy's description is one that has only been seen in recent years."

She also added that there was a very large list of obvious features of daily life, well-known characters and basic facts about the physical layout of the complex which anybody who had attended the Magdalene laundry would have known. However, none of these things are mentioned in Kathy's book. 'Maeve' is also adamant that no child was ever born in the Magdalene Laundry nor were any pregnant women admitted there.

Even the use of Kathy's language in her book marks her out as one who never attended the laundry in High Park. The women who worked there were never referred to, as 'Maggies', as the book maintains.

According to 'Maeve': "They were not called 'Maggies', we called them 'Pentrins' the nuns called them 'the women'. We in the industrial school were 'the children' and they in the laundry, were 'the women.'"

"Notice that it was 'women' who were in the Laundry, and not girls. Yet Kathy claims to have been in the laundry from the age of 12 years of age. Total bunkum of course, for which there is no evidence. As are the claims that babies were sold off to America after being driven up to Belfast to get the boat."

The central plots of Kathy's book revolve around her time in the laundry. She claims she was raped there by a lay visitor and had a baby a week before her 14th birthday. The nuns who ran the laundry have said from the start, first pointing out in private to Kathy, that they had an extensive trawl of their records as well as consulting with nuns who worked there, and were sure that she had not been there.

They then publicly stated that this was the case, also informing the ghost-writer and the publisher with a solicitor's letter that Kathy had never been in a Magdalene laundry. The publishers went ahead and published. And any publisher knows that a book about sex, money, religion and violence is a recipe for a best seller.

Making contact with 'Maeve', was one of the high points of writing this book because she was bright, witty and very good craic. She is currently studying at Harvard University in America and getting top results. Not bad for someone who left an Irish orphanage such as the High Park Industrial School. She left school at 12 and failed the Primary exam. In High Park she told me she was sent to the kitchens.

'Maeve' herself has a huge interest in Irish art and literature, and is a great fan of James Joyce, who frequently touched on the life of a Magdalene laundry. In his book *Ulysses*, the character Leopold Bloom was portrayed, in the Circe episode, as secretary of the Society of Friends of the Magdalene Asylum.

Asked about her memory of what the girls did in the Industrial school, 'Maeve' said they, "Scrubbed and scrubbed, cleanliness is next to Godliness. We actually did have a bit of craic though. From all accounts High Park was not as bad as the other Industrial Schools in Ireland really although life was hard in those days. I'm a 1958-1970 girl so I know."

Those who knew beforehand and kept silent

The 2006 publicity material from Mainstream Publishing states that, "Kathy O'Beirne has led the campaign for justice for Magdalen girls in Ireland for the past 11 years."

Amazingly, it came to light that the significant group campaigning for Laundry residents knew that allegations in Kathy's book were untrue but chose to say nothing until a certain controversy broke out, a year after it was published.

In July 2004, a press release from the 'Justice for Magdalenes' group stated that this new group was formed when former members of the Magdalene Memorial Committee joined with a group of Magdalene laundry survivors to form a new group to campaign for justice for women who were 'incarcerated' in Magdalene laundries.

The statement also informed people that, "One of the Magdalene survivors who is a member of Justice for Magdalenes has been involved in an ongoing garda investigation facilitated by Archbishop Diarmuid Martin. The survivor, who wishes to be known as Kathy, has campaigned alone for many years and has said that she is delighted to be working with a representative organisation."

Kathy strikes again, manning the barricades and ever ready to fight the good fight for justice and truth!

Claire McGettrick who is PRO of the 'Justice for Magdalenes' campaign group, based in Co Cavan said in a September 2006 statement that, "While the Justice for Magdalenes committee has been aware for some time that there were holes or flaws in Kathy's history, we have chosen not to engage in attacks or public rebuttals out of respect not only for what Kathy believes is the truth, but for the survivors and victims of both Magdalene laundries and other Irish institutions. Focusing," she said: "on Kathy O'Beirne and the ensuing media circus surrounding her book only serves to detract from this mission."

The Magdalene group campaigner said, that she knew even before the book was printed, from speaking to women actually in the Magdalene laundries at the time, that Kathy O'Beirne had never been a resident. McGettrick was also aware that Kathy had huge gaps of knowledge about the daily life within the laundry as well as the physical layout of the grounds. The group, she told this journalist had decided to say nothing but instead focus "on their mission to seek justice for Magdalenes."

Claire McGettrick added that former residents of High Park Laundry had contacted her group to say that 'Kathy does not speak or sound, in what she says, like a Magdalene.' "Concerning Magdalenes, it takes one to know one.

"We were also aware that information she spoke of about the High Park building was factually wrong. The physical layout of the grounds she gave, for example, was wrong."

Claire, who was not in a Magdalene Laundry herself, first became aware that Kathy had not been a resident after the making of a documentary on Magdalene laundries for a French television station. Kathy had actually spoken and acted as an authority on life as a Magdalene! It was then, after she had spoken that others had realised she hadn't been there, and people involved with the Justice for Magdalene group "had a quiet word in people's ear that Kathy was never a Magdalene."

Unbeknown to most Irish people, there is phenomenal interest in Irish Magdalene laundries on the European continent, particularly, Claire says, in France and Germany. It is quite amazing for many Irish people to think that Ireland's image abroad is more and more wrapped up with these laundries.

The most well-known film on the subject matter is the film, 'The Magdalene Sisters' directed by the Scottish actor, Peter Mullan. In his emotion-twisting polemic, the nuns are presented like Catholic

Frankensteins, or daleks out to exterminate all signs of life and love. Not shy about his own position as a fervent socialist committed to an anti-religious view of life, Mullan is not adverse to repeating tales of horror himself.

On February 7, 2003, Mullan repeated a story he heard to *The Guardian* film critic that many boys in an Irish orphanage were treated scandalously. But just how true does this sound?:

"A group of boys were driven into countryside outside Dublin in a school bus," he recalls. "They stopped alongside another bus wherein stood several young dental students who proceeded to remove all their teeth without any anaesthetic. I'm sorry, but that is Dr Mengele stuff."

Sounds a bit too barbaric to be true, I think, and where is the evidence? The episode is so far-fetched, when author James Frey put a scene of root canal treatment without anaesthetic in his book, it caused gasps of horror and then disbelief. But how about the Peter Mullan's film. Yep, it's a work of fiction with artistic license allowed, but how representative of life in a Magdalene Laundry was it? It will have to be for former residents of the laundries to tell their own account, yet, that can't be found in *Kathy's Story*.

'Kathy didn't even know how to get there'

Another episode which Kathy now probably wishes people could forget is the time that she asked a woman she knew to show her the way to High Park Laundry. A couple of years ago, before her book was published, Kathy contacted a friend of hers from Sherrard House, who will go under the name 'Angela'.

"Kathy asked me to pick her up at the Bishop's Palace in Drumcondra, Dublin. I went down in the car with my daughter and her little one and we met up with Kathy and another lady who was with her, who she described as her counsellor. This other lady was really lovely, a real lady, and awful nice.

"We went up there and met them on the step, she was seemingly coming out of a meeting, and Kathy said she was after having an audience with the bishop."

Kathy asked Angela, "Do you know where High Park is? I can't remember how to get to it, it was that long ago. Will you show us how to get there?"

Angela said no problem and led the way in her car while Kathy and the other lady followed in another car.

"We drove up," Angela said, "into High Park. We got out and Kathy started to point out certain places and say that was such and such a place, I looked at my daughter, lifted my brow and said, 'Yeah right!' As we left in my car, we drove past an old woman shuffling around the grounds who looked as if she didn't know where she was going or even where she was.

"Anyway, as we drove past, this old woman waved at us, with a big smile. Kathy waved back to her and said to me, 'Oh look, she recognises me from my time here.' The old woman could have thought it was Elvis. Once again, I thought of Kathy's story, 'Yeah right!'"

We now know that Kathy was never in a Magdalene Laundry, but as we are on the subject it is fair to ask what was life in the named Magdalene laundry actually like. Some people who were in High Park at the time have given us a frank and critical account of their time there. The nuns who ran High Park laundry got to say about it?

Two questions were submitted to them in October 2006 and then a further list of ten questions in 2007. I sent another e-mail to the spokesman for The Sisters of Our Lady of Charity on February 2, 2007:

"*Dear Sir,*

"*...I request once again, that the Sisters of Our Lady of Charity answer very simple and straightforward questions. I am doing a section of a book about life inside that Magdalene laundry and I would like the sisters to give us their side of the story.*

If answers are not forthcoming from the Sisters, many people will assume, that they refuse to answer because they have something to be ashamed of, or something to hide. Surely, it is in their interests that they answer the simple questions which I have put.

I kindly request that the Sisters of Our Lady of Charity answer the questions below as soon as possible.

yours sincerely,

Hermann Kelly, Journalist"

Finally after much encouragement I got a brief reply at the end of

March, 2007. The e-mail was entitled, 'Some comments from the Sisters of Our Lady of Charity.'

Question No. 1

What was the last year that High Park Laundry took in any new 'Maggies'?

'The women were never referred to as 'Maggies' within the laundry or home. This term was used by some local people.'

What was the youngest age that a new 'Maggie' would have been admitted into High Park during the early 1970s?

–Unanswered.–

Question No. 2

Can you give me the specific dates that Kathy O'Beirne was in St Anne's school?

'We cannot give specific information in regard to a person's time with us. Kathy has confirmed publicly her brief time spent with us in a home for young people.'

Question No. 3

For what reasons were the women in High Park Laundry actually there? Who put them there?

'In the 70's we took in women in need of accommodation. In the 1970s most women who came to us were in their thirties or forties There were many reasons women came or were sent to us. Some were rejected by families, some were regarded to have behavioural difficulties, some were intellectually challenged and some were single mothers.

'Not all were rejected by their families – in fact some families were very caring. A large proportion came to the door seeking a bed and many returned time and again. Admission was on the basis of need by the person and or family.'

Question No. 4

Why were the women kept in the laundry until after the age of majority, ie. 18 years of age?

'Question 4 is not understood. The vast majority of women in the laundry were adults.'

Question No. 5

Did the women receive any financial recompense for their work or was board and keep considered that in lieu?

'*The laundry was used to fund the upkeep of the women and their facilities. There was no other income*'

Question No. 6

What motivated the Sisters of Our Lady of Charity to close down the laundry? How had circumstances changed?

'*The laundries closed because of the age of the women and sisters. Many of the women are still with us.*'

Question No. 7

Do the nuns have any photographs of life inside the laundry and dormitory for the women?

'*It would not be appropriate to issue photographs for confidentiality reasons.*'

Question No. 8

In what year did High Park Laundry finally shut?

'*High Park closed in 1990 and Sean McDermott Street in 1996.*'

Question No 9 & No 10

Will one or a number of the nuns speak to me about their life and experience in the Magdalene Laundry?

Do the nuns know of any former residents who are willing to talk of their experience in the Magdalene Laundry?

'*We do not wish to speak at this time and neither are we aware of any women who would wish to speak publicly.*'

8 Bring out the Lie Detectors, it's time to get real

W ill the best-seller of 2006 become the literary fraud of 2007? Kathy's family certainly hoped so when they participated in a Channel 4 documentary, called *The Lie Lab*.

'You need to have your head examined' is a common phrase you might hear from an incredulous friend, but Channel 4 took this idiom one step further in the programme which was aired on June 16, 2007. In this documentary, produced by Bristol-based Quickfire Media, both Kathy and her family were asked to undergo a high tech lie-detection test.

In the November before the test, Kathy confidently told her local paper: "I knew the tests were happening and I was asked by the documentary people if I would do it. I said yes straight away. Nobody is forcing me to take this test, it's completely voluntary but I want to do it because I have told the truth all along."

She described the tests as a "once in a lifetime opportunity and it's exciting and interesting. I know in my heart that I'm telling the truth and this test will show that." *(The Clondalkin Gazette* 12/11/06).

Showing awareness of how the technology worked, Kathy said: "It will be very hard for me to tell a lie in this test because they can tell by the blood supply to your brain whether or not you're lying." Again demonstrating great personal confidence she added:

"I don't have to prove to them that I'm telling the truth because I know and God knows that I am. I'm doing this for the children that I look after so that they won't be hassled as they are growing up by people saying that I am a liar."

The more common polygraph test relies on the assumption that people become more anxious when they tell lies, but the problem arises that some liars don't become anxious at all, and can sail through the polygraph test with their lies undetected. The polygraph relies on external manifestations of certain emotional reactions, but these can at times be controlled.

This is the reason why polygraph tests are frequently unreliable and not used in court cases. But is there a more reliable method of lie detection? Professor Sean Spence from the University of Sheffield certainly thinks so, and has pioneered the use of functional magnetic resonance imaging (fMRI) to detect fibs. Contrasted with other detection methods, it relies on the finding that some regions of the brain (the prefrontal cortex) 'light up' with activity each time we tell a lie.

In a nutshell, the technology used in the Channel 4 programme scans the brain for activity to see which areas 'light up' and become active while the person answers contentious questions. It is practically impossible for a person to control their brain activity and so this test certainly appears to be more reliable that the polygraph test.

At this stage, the procedure is experimental, but researchers like Professor Spence say it is a promising tool in criminal investigation.

In the local paper Kathy scoffed at the commitment of the other side of the O'Beirne family to take the lie detector test. "I'd be the happiest girl in Ireland if they agree to do the test," she said.

So, it couldn't be simpler then. Kathy is so confident of her story that she freely underwent the lie detection test to prove it true. Wrong! She didn't do it at all. After initially agreeing to undergo the test, then signing a form with programme producers to that effect, when it actually came to doing the test – Kathy refused point blank.

The programme producers, Quickfire Media scrambled to offer her a range of dates on which she could come over, but when it came to the crunch, Kathy O'Beirne failed to take the lie detection test.

While writing a news feature on the subject before the programme was shown, I rang up Kathy both on her mobile and home phone number, got no reply and so left a message asking her to ring me back. Although she did reply to my call, she quickly rang up the executive editor of the *Irish Mail on Sunday* to threaten to get her legal team onto the matter. Paul Drury, the editor in question, called her bluff and suggested that she should go ahead and sue if that is what she wanted.

This was all before the article was even printed or she knew what was in it. Talk about getting your retaliation in first! Once again, nothing came of her threats of legal action.

Yet Kathy went on to claim that, "Channel 4 cancelled the lie-detector test on three occasions themselves. I didn't cancel it ... I took part in the film documentary and had no problem. I did it of my own free will. Nobody forced me to do it."

During the 60 minute programme, both Kathy and members of her family were interviewed and both sides gave their respective stories. As the programme was broadcast, Channel 4 put in the statement: "Just days before the scan, after months of negotiations, weeks of filming and the postponement of two previous scan dates, Kathy disappointingly [announced] that she will not be taking the scan."

Sean Spence, the psychiatrist from Sheffield University who was leading the tests said: "There may be reasons to do with not wishing to get into a scanner, of feeling claustrophobic about being in a scanner or feeling phobic about technology. There may be a number of good medical reasons why someone shouldn't have a scan, I don't want to downplay that. But if all those conditions are met and someone refuses to take part, then one inference may be that they don't want to test the veracity of their version."

On the other hand, her elder brother Oliver, took the test, answered the questions he was asked, and passed with ease.

On analysing the scan results during the programme, Professor Spence told Oliver that, "Both the brain scan and the response times follow your version of events. In so far as you could possibly know about the contents of Kathy's book, when you say that you are telling the truth in this study it looks like you are."

Parties on both sides of the story were interviewed for the programme as was the co-author Michael Sheridan. Kathy and her younger brother Joseph resolutely stood by their story throughout the programme and remained adamant that they had been abused at home. They also alleged that the rest of the family were only disputing the book at this time because they had lost a legal dispute about the possession of the family home.

Sitting at home in Dublin, watching the programme in Eamonn's home, the rest of the O'Beirne family felt a great sense both of relief and joy when they watched the final cut being aired. This was because they did not know until that moment what the programme makers had decided upon or how they would present the facts and arguments. Oliver told this writer that he was greatly relieved and felt that he had done his duty to clear his father's good name. He said the family were very happy and emotional when they saw the programme – but the drama wasn't over yet.

Follow up skirmish on national radio

There was also a follow-up skirmish on the national Irish airwaves the Monday after the Channel 4 documentary (18/6/07) when Michael Sheridan, two of Kathy's brothers and Professor Spence were asked on to the RTÉ 'Liveline' Show to talk about the Lie Lab test.

Explaining how the machine worked, Oliver O'Beirne described how the lie detection machine is basically a MRI scanner in which there is a 5 by 5 inch screen on which, "You had to read the questions and answer yes or no on the hand keyboard. It is reported to be 90 per cent accurate. I had no intention of coming out of the scanner until I had the job I intended to do done," he said.

Asked why he wanted to take such a test, Oliver ran through the whole affair of how and why he arrived at such a situation where he volunteered to take the test and show that the book by Kathy O'Beirne was, as Joe Duffy put it, "a pack of lies."

"It was the part about the family that we took offence to, that my father was abusive or violent. Then the part about the Magdalene laundries as well. I have stated where I went to visit Kathleen and what homes she was in. I never went to a Magdalene laundry, though many a Sunday I had to cycle to St Loman's [Psychiatric Hospital] over in Lucan."

Referring to the baby that Kathy talks about as her daughter in her book, Oliver said that if she ever had a daughter it would be his niece and he would like to pay his respects at her grave etc., but there was no daughter and no grave. "So where do you go?"

Mr Sean Spence, professor of adult psychiatry at the University of

Sheffield, said that he asked Oliver questions about what Kathy had said in her book, and "his answers were consistent with him telling the truth when he answered those questions. What I mean by that, is that he showed the right reaction times and also the right brain responses. So his responses are consistent with him telling the truth."

Prof Spence said what he knew about arrangements with Kathy was filtered through the production company and what he saw on the Channel 4 programme himself when it was aired. As far as he was made aware Kathy's failed to turn up because, "certain times were not convenient and towards the end of the process she appeared to change her mind.

"Four different dates were offered, over a time of six months. Dates were cancelled at relatively short notice. The last one was three or four days before the scan was to go ahead. I got the cancellation through the television company."

Michael Sheridan who is co-author of Kathy's book, claimed that he was at a disadvantage in that he had not seen the TV programme but was sure, (and he had the emails to show it), that it was the Quickfire Media team who cancelled the test on at least two occasions because one of the persons involved with recording the test was sick.

He claimed in documentation exchanged between Kathy and the TV production team, that she had made clear that she was willing to take the test. Mr Sheridan said: "She was asked to do it on a particular day. She suffers from a terminal illness, and her doctor told her before she travelled for the last particular test they offered her and he insisted that she go to Tallaght Hospital to check her level of blood platelets. She communicated this to the production team and they said, 'By the time you have that test done and come here, it will be too late.'"

Channel 4 vehemently denied this and said that Kathy had agreed four different dates with Professor Spence but pulled out of them. But Michael Sheridan was not finished yet because he then announced that Kathy was going to do a lie detector test with the Jeremy Vine programme on BBC radio:

"They have already recorded an hour's interview with her and they are coming over in the next week to do a lie detector test on her. They claim it is a highly sophisticated test with a 90 per cent plus success rate. She co-operated and gave Channel 4 a huge interview in London, they could easily have flown her up from London to the site of wherever the thing was when they got her over there. They didn't for some strange reason or another."

Oliver was then asked about his interaction with Channel 4. He had to cancel the test on two occasions because he was busy with work. Then asked by Joe Duffy, the '*Liveline*' presenter, would he have pulled out of the lie detector test if he had known that Kathy had pulled out or was going to pull out? Oliver answered: "No. Why would I do that? I said I would do something and committed to do it."

He added that when he had to cancel the arranged dates, Channel 4 were quick to facilitate other dates instead. Oliver was clear that the production team did everything to ensure that he could do the test. On the other hand, Michael Sheridan said that he participated in the show and received many communications from the production assistant.

Asked was he saying that Channel 4 were lying about Kathy's refusal to do the lie detector test, Michael Sheridan replied: "Perhaps they need to go to Professor Spence and get a lie detector test. Anyway, it is not Channel 4, it's the production company. I have the communications from them on my laptop of their whole approach."

Asked by the interviewer whether any of his team became sick and were therefore responsible for cancelling any of the tests, Professor Spence said, "Possibly at the beginning but not at the end."

"Subsequent to cancellations," Joe Duffy asked, "did you offer four different appointments, Kathy agreed to do them but she did not turn up?" Professor Spence replied: "What I can tell you is that we offered that number of appointments and can tell you that she didn't arrive. I certainly did not cancel the last two appointments. Maybe we were responsible for the first two, in collaboration. But we were not responsible for the last two, and of course, everything is negotiated through an intermediary, so I can't know why Kathy did or did not come along."

Not to be outphased, Michael Sheridan teased the O'Beirne family about why they had (as he claimed) taken two years to raise a protest about the book, to which Eamonn replied that he contacted the publishers but that Mainstream Publishers had failed to respond. Eamonn then accused Michael Sheridan of not having researched the material properly before writing the book, pointing out that he had only spoken to a few family members.

On a more serious issue, Sheridan then dropped in what he had been muttering in private to journalists for some time. He said that the gardai, on foot of complaints, were investigating allegations of sexual abuse within the family.

The programme host, Joe Duffy was quick to jump in and clarify that if he (Duffy) wished to, he could make allegations against his own family and the gardai would be bound to investigate those as well. Therefore to say there was an ongoing garda investigation into sexual abuse, meant just that. It did not necessarily make the complaint true. In this case, the complaint came from Kathy and her brother Joseph, one who has remained relatively quiet up to this point.

Co-author Michael Sheridan – notice the technique

Notice the replication of technique used during the 'Liveline' programme. When Kathy O'Beirne was questioned on the same radio show in September 2006 on whether she had ever had a child as she alleged, the family who knew her said no. But just as things moved towards a conclusion about not having one baby, she suddenly stated that she had not just had one baby but two babies. It certainly distracted attention from the first query.

The same is also true for Michael Sheridan when he talked about Kathy's failure to do the lie detection test for the Channel 4 programme. While the question starts off; 'why did Kathy not go through with the lie detection test for Channel 4, has she something to hide'? etc, Michael Sheridan distracted matters by throwing a novelty into the conversation – actually she's doing a different lie detection test with the Jeremy Vine show for BBC radio. We wait with bated breath for its conclusions!

The same goes for both Kathy's and Michael Sheridan's reactions to criticism of the contents of their book. When confronted with Kathy's family members who say that the allegations in her book are not true, both Kathy and her co-author, instead of simply defending the veracity of their book, start to bring in additional issues with nothing to do with the book.

Issues such as the legal ownership of their parent's house and Kathy's new allegation of sexual impropriety within the house. If the book is true, then surely it can be defended as such without bringing up issues which distract from focussing on it?

Before he wrote *Kathy's Story*, Michael Sheridan was the editor of Ireland's first ever dedicated crime magazine – *Irish Crime*. When interviewed by the *Sunday Business Post* newspaper in November 2003 to publicise the launch of the new magazine, Sheridan expressed admiration for international exponents of the crime genre such as *True Detective*, *Master Detective* and *True Crime* which he said *Irish Crime* magazine would be modelled on:

"You can't ignore a formula that has worked so well. Interest in crime runs across all age groups, with women especially likely to buy," he said. "This year there have been a dozen true crime books, all set in Ireland ... true crime gets into the best-seller list. I felt if there was this appetite, why wouldn't there be room for a crime magazine?"

Well before Michael Sheridan and *Kathy's Story* appeared on the publishing scene there was a very popular strand of miserable literature. Mix this with public revulsion and media scrutiny about the sexual sins of religious and you had a certain winner on your hands, no? Surely, you can't ignore a formula that works so well?

A story was printed in *The Evening Herald* newspaper (where Michael Sheridan used to work) on August 20, 2007. It stated that Kathy O'Beirne had exclusively revealed to the paper that she had done a polygraph (lie-detection) test done with a professional examiner, Carol London-Williams. Kathy claimed that she had passed this test with six questions which included (in the only example given), whether her father beat her or not. The examiner in question, who carries out private lie detection tests in Scotland, told this journalist she could neither confirm nor deny that she had carried out a test on Kathy O'Beirne, as this was a matter of client confidentiality. *The Evening Herald* said it was the first independent group to see the lie-detection report.

Kathy's brother Joseph stands by her – until now

The newspaper headlines have it that the O'Beirne family opposes Kathy's book, but Kathy also has a brother Joseph who has come out in her support.

Joseph (43) is the youngest boy of the O'Beirne family and his siblings say he was very much his mammy's boy. A separated father of five children, Joseph blamed his difficult childhood for his lack of achievement in later life.

After the family press conference in September 2006, Joseph gave an interview to the local paper, *The Clondalkin Gazette* in which he claimed that he and his brothers were physically, (though not sexually) abused by their father.

"My father was a hard man. I remember all the brothers when they were told to get out of their bedroom and they were told to put a blanket round them and my father told them to get out and they all marched down the field with a blanket around them."

On reading this the other brothers laughed hilariously. Eamonn said: "This is just hilarious. It is so ridiculous I don't know what he is on. Does he think we are all going to get up in the morning and run around a field in Clondalkin with a blanket. Utterly ridiculous, totally untrue." The other brother's agreed with Eamonn. But this was not all Joseph had to say.

He also recalled, he claimed, his brother John, being beaten stupid: "[One of my brothers] said on radio that my father never hit him. That my father never hit him? I was there at the time, out in the hall, that my father lifted up the steel pan and burst him over the head with it and put him flat out on the ground. He did hit him."

His brother John, counterclaimed that he would remember anything that happened like that. But Joseph's story is not finished yet.

He further claims that he had been sexually abused during his own childhood by two older boys in the area. He says that he has given the gardai statements of his claims about the abuse. He is swift to emphatically add in though, that he was never sexually abused by his father:

"I was abused when I was a kid, when I was younger, and it was going on, for a long time. I am very happy now about coming forward because he took my childhood away from me and I want to come forward now and speak about it. I am actually happy now, I am delighted."

So delighted in fact, that for some reason, he has decided to write a book about his whole experience.

When I spoke to him by phone in June 2007, Joseph said he was two thirds of the way through this book. If that is true, it would make his family a veritable publishing empire. There will be few fir trees left around Clondalkin after this affair is put to rest.

His brothers and sisters counter-claim that he has been influenced by his eldest sister Kathy, and is being blinded by the lure of a potential book deal. They said in August that they had heard Kathy and Joseph had a falling out or a cooling in their relationship.

I rang Joseph on Wednesday August 8, 2007 to ask him for his final stance on *Kathy's Story* before this book went to print.

Joseph's answer: "Some parts of Kathy's book I stand behind yes, but some no. I am standing on my own and staying away from Kathy and from the family. Let Kathy stand on her own, that is her business."

9 Were Threats and Intimidation ever used by Kathy O'Beirne?

Brian's Story – handed a will that showed the way

The Saturday before the September 2006 family press conference, Kathy went into the butcher shop in which Brian O'Beirne works and handed him a copy of her last will and testament. Brian read it to find that he was named as the sole beneficiary. [This journalist has a copy of the will stamped by Kathy's solicitor].

Five minutes after he was handed this will, Brian described how, Michael Sheridan rang him up and asked would he come up to Kathy's house – there are a number of journalists present and he should support his sister. [Michael Sheridan has confirmed to this journalist that he indeed had rung up that particular day, and spoke to Brian. Sheridan said he asked Brian to repeat what he had said earlier.]

This train of events, however it came about, and who knows, maybe it was just a cosmic coincidence; was a big mistake and misjudgement by Kathy. For up until this point, Brian had tried to stay out of the dispute for his own reasons, but now he said, he had principles, and would not be bought.

In Kathy's book, Brian is mentioned a number of times; thanking him for his support (p. 7) and remembering his kindness (p. 45). As he said himself: "I have always stuck by her. I am soft like that. I wanted to sit on the fence and say nothing, because I work in a public job and thousands of people in Clondalkin come into the shop where I work every week. I wasn't looking for a profile, but just to keep my head down."

Asked what caused him to come out against Kathy's book. What was the turning point? Brian said: "I bought a mobile home down in Wexford and I wasn't up talking to Kathleen as much as before. I was talking to Margaret, and reading what was in the papers and listening to what was on the radio. I thought, 'Jesus, I'm after letting her get away with saying so much about my father that isn't true. It's unbelievable. I have to make a stand here somewhere.'"

"The real turning point," Brian said, "was when she came into the shop, the Saturday before the press conference and handed me a copy of her will, and I was the sole beneficiary. She asked me was I standing by her?"

When Kathy first handed Brian her will in the butcher shop, he was very upset: "For a while I thought she was going to kill herself. I was literally in bits, and was shaking, I could hardly talk, I was so upset. I had to go home from work very soon after she left.

"Five minutes later, Michael Sheridan rang me up and said, 'The paper journalists are up in Kathy's house. Will you go up and support her in her claims?'"

"I said 'I will not go up. For Kathleen to call my father an ogre, for having done something that never happened. I said no.' After that I had to go one way or the other. There could no longer be any sitting on the fence. I will not be bought. I will not lie for her. I'm very soft, but I have principles. I will not be bought and that is it.

"But there are now so many facts coming out. For instance, there are a number of people around Clondalkin who were in these places, in the Magdalene laundries and have told me that Kathleen was never there. They have said to Kathleen's face, 'You are a liar. I was in a Magdalene laundry. And you never were.'"

Making direct threats to Journalists

A journalist from *The Sunday Mirror*, Niall Donald interviewed Kathy O'Beirne on the second Friday in August 2006. In it, he tells her he spoke to four of her brothers and sisters who said her father was not an abuser and that they have no memory of a Magdalene laundry ever being mentioned in the house.

When Niall Donald rang up Kathy to tell her he had just spoken to her brothers and sisters, he asked what she had to say in response. This includes what appears, and perhaps I am wrong in this interpretation:

Kathy saying that if he prints what her family has said, she may commit suicide, intimations that if her brother were to commit suicide, that Niall would be responsible.

More ominously again, Kathy threatens that the journalist would be "dealt with." In addition she said she was not a blood relation of Oliver, Eamonn, Mary and Margaret O'Beirne and she didn't grow up in the same house. She also added in that she had documentation from the nuns showing she was in a Magdalene laundry under their care.

Below is a truncated version of the conversation. You may judge for yourself:

Niall Donald: [After outlining that he spoke to Eamonn, Oliver, Mary and Margaret O'Beirne and what they said.] "Well, that is what they said."

Kathy O'Beirne: "Well, they are not my family and so they can't say anything about me. If they do say anything about me I will just take them to court."

Donald: "What? They are not your family?"

O'Beirne: "I'm not going into it. I'm not going into it. [laughs] We are related, but I am not their sister."

Donald: "You are not their sister?"

O'Beirne: "No, I am not their sister."

Donald: "But you grew up in the same house or whatever?"

O'Beirne: "I didn't grow up in the same house, because I was taken out of the house... [makes allegations of abuse – then says she doesn't want stuff about not being related in the paper] I don't want them mentioned in the paper at all or anything about me if that is going to happen because the shit is going to hit the fan here and between you and me, everybody is going to be in trouble."

Donald: "What goes in the paper is the business of the editor..... It is not unfair to talk to someone else."

O'Beirne: "It is unfair if you are going to print shit in *The Sunday Mirror* just for to get readers for your paper. What do you want me to do? Go out and commit suicide? Because that is what I nearly did before over those." [end of tape side 1]

O'Beirne: "Look you. If anything happens to the rest of my family, you will be responsible....And if this stuff starts coming out, my brother has tried to commit suicide three times over this and over the rest of those people. So if anything happens to them, who is going to be responsible? If you print that, who is going to be responsible?"

Donald: "Well, I can tell you Kathy, it's not going to be me, but there you go. I'll be honest with you Kathy, I wouldn't feel responsible for that either." [Assures Kathy that what is written will be 100 per cent accurate and only material that is on tape].

O'Beirne: [After threatening to get her solicitor to speak to the paper's editor – and telling him that she has recorded everything] "Well I can guarantee you that I have a letter stating from the nuns that I was in the Magdalene laundries and their care, which I received on Thursday. I received it on Thursday with my legal team."

Donald: "From the Sisters of Our Lady of Charity?"

O'Beirne: "Yeah, so you can print whatever you like. I don't really mind. I'll let my legal team handle it...."

Donald: "That is not a threat to me. I get paid a wage."

O'Beirne: "Niall, I have to be honest with you and you can print this in your paper. If anything happens to anyone connected to me I will have you dealt with. And I mean that. And you ask anyone that."

Donald: "You will 'have me dealt with'?"

O'Beirne: "Yeah. I will have you dealt with. Yeah."

Donald: "What does that mean?"

O'Beirne: "I will have you dealt with and so will the 300 of my followers, and I mean that. There are enough people already committed suicide...."

Donald: "I don't find that fair to be threatened like that."

O'Beirne: "I say that openly for the paper."

Donald: "So I can print that can I?"

O'Beirne: "I will get onto to RTÉ in the morning and I will say what *The Sunday Mirror* is trying to do to me and to other people....You are stirring shit now and getting in touch with people...."

Donald: "If you can send me this document about the laundries then it is all over...."

O'Beirne: ...."If you print that about those people. I am not even related to them. I am distant related to them. But that is about all. We are not blood. We are not blood related at all. And feel free to ring my solicitor to confirm what I have just told you. And you can write that as well."

Donald: "I will have to talk to the editor now, but Kathy, if you can send me this document that you were in the Magdalene laundries, honestly that will be the end of the article."

O'Beirne: "Who were you talking to?"

Donald: "To your brothers Oliver, and to Eamonn, one of your sisters Margaret and your other sister Mary."

O'Beirne: [Makes other allegations of child abuse about those outside the family].... "I am going to give that all to the papers and there is going to be murder...."

Donald: "All you are doing at the minute Kathy is threatening me.... If you can produce documents for me which contradict what they [Kathy's brothers and sisters] say that will be great."

O'Beirne: "I can tell you what you are putting in the paper is lies and I can tell you now that I will sue the paper...... I will get onto the editor and tell him that."

Donald: "That's OK, people sue papers all the time. That is your right." [asks for her solicitor's number]

O'Beirne: .... [gives her solicitor's phone number and repeats allegations of child abuse] "I have court orders about my brothers. I am telling you now I have all my proof up and above board."

Donald: "Can you show me that proof? I'll come out now and you can show it to me."

O'Beirne: "I can't do it now, I am speaking at a Christian concert. I can't go now."

Donald: "Tomorrow maybe? Tomorrow afternoon? Anytime up until it goes to print. You show me the stuff and it won't go in. Of course. If it's not true no one wants that going into the paper....If you can show me this stuff is bullshit it will die, and will never be printed....If you can show me it's not true then, bang, it's all over. I'll be fair. I would hate to put in something that is not true. It would upset me....I do care about getting it right for its own sake Kathy. Especially on something as horrific as this...."

O'Beirne: "It doesn't really bother me. I have my facts, my proof and everything else... I have just received a psychiatrist's file that handed me over to the Magdalene laundries. Isn't that strange?"

Donald: "I'll come out and you show it to me and read it and that will be it. I don't even want to take a copy of it.... I'm not trying to screw you over. I don't want to get stuff wrong...."

The Sunday Mirror printed the news article by Niall Donald on August 20, 2006.

Hermann Kelly gets some special attention

In comparison with threats to "have you dealt with" or being asked who is going to be responsible if a certain person commits suicide, my interaction with Kathy O'Beirne was less dramatic, but still very telling. After I wrote an article for a newspaper even on occasion, before it was published, Kathy O'Beirne would ring up the editor of the newspaper and threaten to sue.

It happened with *The Irish Catholic*, twice with *The Sunday Times*, twice with *The Irish Mail on Sunday*. With *The Irish Independent*, even before the article had been printed she sent in a solicitor's letter threatening legal action, wildly claiming that because I spoke to her brother Joseph and asked him for an interview that I was harassing members of her family.

Such a clear pattern was emerging that I was able to e-mail Paul Drury, executive editor of *The Irish Mail on Sunday* on October 15th 2006 to advise him what would happen after the article was printed: "Hello Paul, just to let you know in advance what is likely to happen in reaction to article. Either Kathy O'Beirne and /or Michael Sheridan shall ring up early on Monday morning. Kathy shall make wild unsubstantiated allegations against me. She shall then make hefty threats of legal action towards you. Luckily none of the allegations are true and none of the threats will be carried out. It has happened a few times already. Not only to me but to other journalists as well. It isn't personal."

Two days later I got an email in reply: "You were quite right, Hermann .... that's exactly what happened."

Campaigner against false allegation is threatened with home picket.

Florence Horsman-Hogan, the founder of L.O.V.E., (Let Our Voices Emerge – a group set up to help people who have suffered false allegations) relates how Kathy O'Beirne phoned her up and threatened to have a picket protest of hundreds of people placed outside her home. if she continued her group's campaign to have Kathy's book pulled from the shelves. "I suppose," she said, "it's only inevitable that I would get a call from Kathy herself.

"However, the call on the third week of August 2006 only strengthened my concern that Ms O'Beirne is not a very well woman to say the least. She made some fairly outrageous remarks, one to the effect that she's had 300 support calls since the evening before the phone call – that's at least 15 calls an hour for 20 hours (she called at 17:50 pm).

"Kathy O'Beirne also invited me to her case in the High Courts the week after the call, but wouldn't tell me what it's about, in which case I declined the kind invitation. There were a number of other fairly bizarre remarks, but one I took exception to – she's threatened to bring out gangs to picket our home. She threatened to bring hundreds of Magdalene women to protest outside.

"Now, that's not nice! For a start, this is a family home with children (and a rabbit, and dog), but also I don't like threats, particularly from bullies."

The L.O.V.E. group quickly issued a statement that the gardai in Clontarf, and Shankill, Dublin were notified of Ms O'Beirne's call and threats. "This campaign is a matter of truth and record and does not require any action which could alarm or upset the Horsman-Hogan children.

"Evidently Ms O'Beirne is unhappy at her family coming forward last Sunday to deny her allegations in the book," states Ms Horsman-Hogan, "but she can't bully any of us by threats. This remarkable and courageous development by the O'Beirne family has at last, delivered a well deserved hammer blow to the credibility of this 'horrific fairy tale.'"

"We will not be bullied by Ms O'Beirne, and if she thinks threatening me with a picket on my family home is going to make us back down, she can think again. Kathy can produce the evidence now required at anytime and I will put it on the L.O.V.E. website – in the interests of justice and fairness for all involved."

A vulnerable young woman took up Kathy's offer to help but ....

Just up the road from the original family house in Clondalkin where Kathy still resides, there is a petrol station and shop, right beside the large Bewley's Hotel in Clondalkin. A young woman of 26 years of age, Lisa Howlett works in the petrol station shop and knows the area very well, having grown up in Clondalkin all her life. She was born and reared there; or as they say in Derry, it was in Clondalkin that she was 'bred and buttered.'

Kathy O'Beirne, from what her family and friends say, and from what she has said herself, has always had a huge interest in young children; this became evident again in the last year. In the Autumn of 2006, a picture of Kathy O'Beirne and a baby girl appeared in the local newspaper, *The Clondalkin Gazette* with the caption, 'Mamma Kathy.' Unusual? The child in question was Lisa's new baby girl.

Lisa told this reporter that when she became pregnant and visibly so, Kathleen who frequently visits the petrol station shop, began to show great interest in her and in her plight.

The father of Lisa's child had gone off the scene and she had a falling out with some members of her family who had moved to Galway and with whom she had little contact at the time. In this situation, when she was relatively vulnerable, Kathy, she said, showed her attention, appeared friendly and offered her help.

"She became a bit too close when I was pregnant, because I was on my own really. I thought she was being friendly with me. She was being very helpful and offered me great support. She was buying the baby clothes, and I thought she was being really nice. A lot of people had warned me to stay away from her, including my family, because they did not like her at all.

"The people at work did not like her either, because she was always giving off to them. But I thought I would give her the benefit of the doubt. And to be honest with you, I now feel like a fool."

Kathy at the baby's birth

"I had a few friends," Lisa said, "who wanted to be there when the baby was born, but at the last minute they couldn't do it, and Kathy offered to be there for me. I appreciated it and said 'that was fine.'"

"On the day, my friend could not make it and I asked Kathy if she would come in, I was friendly with her at this point. She came straight in. Well, as soon as the baby came out, she grabbed the baby. The nurse went ballistic at this. From that day on the control really started to kick in.

"Even the day that Olivia was born in October 2006, Kathy was going around the Coombe Maternity Hospital saying I was her foster daughter and Olivia was her foster granddaughter."

During this time of friendship, Lisa went frequently to Kathy's home in Clondalkin. There she became aware that Kathy claimed she had had a number of children herself.

"Once the baby was born, certain things weren't adding up. Kathy had pictures of babies in her house. She claims she had three daughters. She told me she was raped, the second one Daisy and a miscarriage four years ago. She has pictures of babies on her wall, but they are not even hers.

"She showed me a photograph of a dead baby in a coffin and said it was her baby. I was very upset when I saw the photograph. I believed it was hers. Then she claims she had a baby called Daisy and there was a photograph of Daisy on her mantelpiece, but the picture looked very up to date, if you know what I mean. Alarm bells were ringing in my head and then she started to trip herself up.

"One day, for instance, she couldn't remember her baby's name. She forgot Daisy's name. I asked her 'Are you going to the cemetery to see Daisy's grave?' She said 'Daisy, who's Daisy?' I said, 'Your daughter, Daisy.' – Just how could you forget the name of your child if it died, how could you forget? – Kathy said, 'Oh yeah.' - If you had a daughter that died you would know their name, for sure. You don't forget that.

"Looking back now," Lisa said, "I can see that she latched on to me, but at the time I thought she was being really nice. I was on my own, my family were in Galway. She was buying the baby clothes and said she would mind the child when I went back to work full-time, and I agreed to that, and went out to buy stuff for the baby, bouncers etc."

However, as things became more intense, Lisa became increasingly uncomfortable:

"I became uneasy after she started to ask to look after the baby quite a lot. I didn't feel comfortable, I wanted to be left alone with my baby. I felt she took control quite a lot. A week after the baby was born, Kathy took the baby overnight to her house and I felt so uneasy. Then, when I began to say 'no' to her requests to look after the baby I felt uneasy."

There was then an incident in October 2006 when without telling Lisa where she was going, Kathy took her baby Olivia to a funeral. From this funeral of an old neighbour, Lisa heard back that "Kathy was passing the baby around 'like pass the parcel' and that made me really annoyed."

Lisa later heard that Kathy was telling workers in Tesco (people she didn't know were friends of Lisa) that the baby was hers. She as a fifty year old woman was telling people she was dealing OK with the night feeds, 'It was difficult at first' etc. This made Lisa very angry when she heard what was happening.

And then heard later again that Kathy was saying Lisa was putting the baby up for adoption because she couldn't cope. That was just about Christmas and Lisa confronted her on it. "I was getting really paranoid about the whole thing, about what was happening," said Lisa.

Kathy asked for a release letter to take the baby abroad

But the last straw was when Kathy asked Lisa for a letter of release, so Kathy would be permitted to take the child Olivia abroad. Lisa told how Kathy enquired what was going to happen when she went back to work and who would look after her baby Olivia when Kathy went away, as Kathy hoped to travel a bit. Now, a child in Ireland at present can have its own passport and is no longer recorded on their parent's passport.

"Kathy said she was going to either Edinburgh or Sheffield, over in Britain and I asked her what was going to happen. She suggested that I get a passport for Olivia. She kept on about me getting the baby a passport, so I went out and got the passport done. I was stupid enough to go along with it."

"She then asked me to give her a letter stating that she could take the baby out of the country. Stupid enough, I was going along with this, I wasn't even thinking."

Asked what Kathy was going to do with the baby, Lisa said Kathy was going to Britain to see a "Sarah, [a Sarah Veevers was involved in the production of the Quickfire media production of the *Lie Lab* programme] and she wanted to take Olivia over for this, and me sometimes. I wasn't up for this." Lisa then told Kathy that this wasn't going to happen, and things began to cool between them dramatically.

Looking at the events that unfolded, Lisa said: "The way I feel now, I feel really angry towards this woman. She ruined the whole experience of the baby for me.... I just feel very angry. Kathy started to really frustrate me, and she would get annoyed when I said you can't take Olivia now. This was growing all the time."

"Kathy would say then, 'if I can't take her now, I won't take her next weekend.'"

Lisa finally went to look for a crèche because she no longer wanted Kathy looking after Olivia. "The day I paid the fee for the crèche, she came up to me and asked did I not want her to look after 'that effing child' and I said 'No.' That evening she came up to my house with a pram full of Olivia's stuff and threw them at the door. I had the baby in my arms, and she shouted, 'Thanks for using me.' That was the day I said, 'No more.'"

"Kathy was also claiming to be fostering two Nigerian girls who live on my road. One of the girls is three and the other girl is five years of age. She said she was 'sponsor fostering' these two girls through the church, as she now goes to a Presbyterian church in Lucan where the girl's mother goes as well. I believed her until all the stories came out."

"The girls live with their mother, their father is not there. This day that I received a text message I went down to the mother and told her that Kathy had been going round saying that she was 'sponsor fostering' her kids. The woman was very upset. She said there was no such thing. 'They are my babies' were her exact words to me. She was very upset. I then got this text message the next day":

'Hi Miss Lisa, this is Kathy's brother Do not go 2 the children's house and be Telling them that u dont let Kathy mind U baby. Keep away from them or u will get a letter from my solicitors.'

"This text which I received claims to be from Kathy's brother, but if you ring the number it is actually Kathy's voice."

[Sent at 8.54am on Jan 23, 2007. This author rang up the number and it clicked into Kathy O'Beirne voicemail.] Olivia made a report to the Gardai about what had happened.

Mary O'Beirne's Story – received vicious texts and malicious posters. But who sent them?

Mary believes that it was her sister Kathy who put posters at her husband's work place and posters on the doors of her children's school in October 2006.

"It is getting dangerous," Mary said, "my husband went to work this morning and stuck between the shutters at his place of work was this poster in handwriting. I then went to bring my seven year-old to school and on the two school doors were two more posters. I believe it is her handwriting, I knew it the minute I seen it."

One of a number of posters, hand written in bold case and put outside the school of Mary O'Beirne's children, read as follows:

"The friends of Kathleen O'Beirne who went to school with her are sick and tired of the lies her family are spreading around about her. What about Mary O'Beirne who gave her address as St John's Road to get her children into a Clondalkin School. What about Eamon the Flasher when he was seventeen. They have more to hide than Kathleen. We stand behind her 100%."

Kathy wrote a Christmas card for Lisa Howlett's baby Olivia in 2006 on which she writes (in mostly capital letters):

"Baby Olivia Hugs and Kisses Love You Lots (2006) From Mamma Kathy XXXOO"

One does not have to be a handwriting expert to spot that the handwriting appears similar. Perhaps that is just chance? Also at this time, the two sisters, Mary and Margaret, began to receive, from an unknown mobile, a large number of increasingly offensive and threatening text messages.

The O'Beirne family have no proof of who sent these text messages, but handed the phones and messages over to the Gardai and asked them to carry out an investigation. The Garda Inspector of Clondalkin, Peter Duff, wrote to Eamonn O'Beirne in early 2007 concerning the complaints that the family had made and wrote: 'I expect a file to be sent to the Director of Public Prosecutions in the near future.'

A source close to the Gardai has confirmed that a file was sent to the DPP in June 2007 over allegations of harrassment against a number of the O'Beirne siblings. Time will tell what the outcome of the Garda investigations will be.

10 Bribed to Commit Perjury: Kathy's best Friend

Kathy asked a childhood friend to lie and act as a false witness by saying that she had seen Kathy being raped by a priest of Dublin Diocese in the late Sixties. Though offered hefty financial inducement to go along with Kathy, her friend refused to do so.

A tall woman of 48 years, Margaret Power lives with her husband in London, where she has worked as a hairdresser for the last 21 years. Margaret was best friends with Kathy for a very long time, indeed all her life, up until the time that Kathy published the contents of her book. She has quite an astounding story to tell herself. Like Kathy, Margaret grew up on the Booth Road and they attended Scoil Mhuire, Clondalkin together, though Margaret was two years behind Kathy. Margaret's older sister, on the other hand, was in the same year as Kathy.

The two girls always called each other by their surnames. Kathy always called her Power, and Margaret always called her O'Beirne. They never went by their first names to each other ever. Margaret speaks here in her own words.

Best Friends, growing up together

"Kathy and I were really good friends from when we were kids. Really good friends. No one else would play with her or anything like that; she was always bullying. In fact, even bullying girls that were older than her. They were scared witless by her, she used to come out with scissors and cut their hair, beat them up and all. I mean, Kathy was a problem since she was very very young. She was always aggressive and quite violent. But some people felt sorry for her because she was such a loner.

"From an early age, as well, she loved to steal. Really she was a kleptomaniac. Not only did I see her in action, but I joined in and did it with her.

"If anything was stolen, when we were together, you would always get something out of it. If she stole a packet of biscuits, you got a biscuit, if she stole 10 bob, you got one. That's the way it went. You always got a cut if you stayed along with her. You got paid for doing a job so to speak."

And about her age: "Kathy now tries to say she is three years younger than me, but in fact she is two years older. I am 48, Kathy is 50 now.

"I was the only one who would hang around with her, and who had any time for her. All the other girls hated her. She was a bit afraid of me though, and if she went after one of the girls they would threaten, 'We'll get Margaret Power after you !....'

"One Christmas day, my sister got a new pair of roller skates and Kathy pulled her down and pulled them off her. I went out, found her and bit her. She's fairly biting back now though!"

I saw her go off to St Anne's School

Asked about whether Kathy had ever been in a Magdalene laundry? Margaret said, "I am 100 per cent sure that is not the case.

"I remember the day she went off in the car to St Anne's [Reformatory boarding] school. Her father told me she has gone to boarding school. He didn't let on it was for 'nutters.' She about eight or nine maybe, in and around that age. She was only away for a few weeks and then she was back, as bad as ever, both of us running around Booth Road, running riot.

"My mother and father were always trying to keep me away from her, but she was my mate at the time like. She was an awful young one.

Kathy was also in St Loman's [Psychiatric Hospital]. But she was also there for a short space of time too. I visited her in there."

Kathy's Parents – painting a proper picture

"Oliver O'Beirne, he's dead now, God rest his soul. He was a strict man, but he was not the man that she made him out to be in the book.

He was tough, but he had to be tough with her number one anyway.

"He gave her a slap or two, but that was only to calm her down. She would be out causing trouble and she was very violent herself.

"But the allegations in the book that he dipped her hand in hot oil are untrue, I would remember. She was never bandaged up or hospitalised for anything like that. And anyway, doing something like that would leave a permanent scar or a claw hand, and O'Beirne doesn't have a claw hand.

"She never ever said to me that her father was doing anything like what she says in the book. The allegations are complete tripe.

"Mrs O'Beirne was the same as the father. She was quite strict as well. She was a tough woman, and not the doting angel Kathy makes her out to be.

"The O'Beirne's were from the country and quite religious. The children were always called into the house in the evening to say a decade of the Rosary.

"I can tell you this for certain. Kathy never once said to me that she had been physically abused by her father or sexually abused by any of her brothers in all our years of friendship and confidence.

"Kathy never said she was ever abused by a priest or a nun. Her allegations in the book that she was raped before her Holy Communion, that's all lies. She never once mentioned it in all those years to me. She told me most things and confided in me all the time.

"Kathy did say she had been abused by a certain individual when she was younger, [Margaret named this man, a working man now living in Tallaght, Dublin] as far as O'Beirne told me, that is coming up for court. But then again, O'Beirne says she is taking cases against many people but nothing ever happens."

Running around with Kathy after we finished school

Asked what Kathy O'Beirne was up to after she left school, Margaret remembers that Kathy O'Beirne, 'was always hanging around. She was always around.

"She spend her youth hanging round the house. She was in a hostel for some time. She went into Sherrard House Hostel for a while, but that was it. She chose to go in there herself because she had greater freedom to do whatever she wanted, and I remember going in there with her one day.

"In her later teen years Kathy used to bring some older woman out to Clondalkin whom she had met in around town. As she spent more time in the hostel in Dublin and I got a job training as a hairdresser I saw less of her. She was also a great one for going round the hospitals visiting kids. She got very close to a child down in Our Ladies [Our Ladies Hospital for Sick Children, Crumlin].

"Kathy has a bowel problem since she was young. She mentioned this in her book [page 142]. And this seems to be one of the few things that was true in it ; the problem was something like Crohn's Disease. I was horrified when I read in her book that the supposed baby was to have died of a bowel complaint. I thought that was awful.

"She also did time in the 'Joy [Mountjoy Prison in central Dublin which is mentioned in Kathy's book]. She's an awful robber, and definitely a kleptomaniac if there ever was one. I remember she was in the 'Joy and her appendix burst. I think she mentions that in the book and that did happen. I know someone who was not far away on the prison wing and they said they heard her screaming and that.

She may have worked a few weeks in Urney's chocolate factory but that was it. A few weeks max. We used to cut grass in people's gardens. That was the only job Kathy O'Beirne ever did but rob."

Talking about old times as her mother was growing weaker

"A few years ago, before I went back on a visit to Ireland, I was asking after O'Beirne because she had been keeping very low. She was impossible to contact and made no effort to contact me.

"A couple of weeks before her mother died, [in the month of December 2001] I was with Kathy and we went outside for a smoke. We were talking and I just knew she had something she really wanted to say to me. Now, she looked a wreck, and was giving off about her family and saying that no-one else could look after their mother like her. That she couldn't leave her mother, even for a few days.

"I was saying, 'Jaysus, that's awful.' – I was swallowing the story to be quite honest. She was busting to say something and I said, 'there is more wrong with you than looking after your mother and all that. Come on, what's up? I know you've got to say something.' She broke down to cry, and said, 'do you remember what happened to us all those years ago?' I said, 'I do.' She was talking about childhood abuse that I had experienced.

"I said, 'Why don't you come over and visit me?'

"I went over to England and tried a number of times to contact her by letter and by phone but there was no reply. I never heard from her again until last June [2005]."

I couldn't wait when Kathy asked me to her book launch party

"I can tell you one thing. The sickening thing she did to me last year. If it had happened 40 years ago, I probably would have forgotten, but this only happened last year. The horrible bitch, what she's done, she's unbelievable.

"I was on the phone to my mother in Ireland and asked about O'Beirne, to which she said O'Beirne was writing a book. I said, 'Go out of that, sure that one can hardly write her name.'

"O'Beirne contacted me just before I went to Ireland and said, 'Are you coming to our party? There's a book coming out'. Anyway, I went over, went to see her and went to the party for the launch of her book. I could not believe it when I read it. The book is just incredible.

"We were talking the day before the party, and she asked would I go and see the local priest. You would not believe it but O'Beirne arranged for me to go and see Fr Lumsden in Clondalkin Parish, which I did. [This was over abuse that Margaret had experienced.] Kathy was present when I spoke and I later learnt that this was a big mistake. Her brother Brian also came to give Kathy emotional support. But next thing, she had arranged for me to meet the Gardai. They said they wanted to talk to me for about six hours. I said, 'I'm not having any of this. This is ridiculous.' – I was in an awful state. This was all about stuff that Kathy had told them. She had told them that I was going to be her witness!

"O'Beirne also wanted me to go to her solicitors and sign a document for her. I said, 'I am here to sort out myself, not to go to your solicitor.' I said, 'I am not going to go. If I want a solicitor I'll get one for myself.'"

[When asked about this incident, Fr Lumsden in Clondalkin Parish said that the name mentioned by Kathy O'Beirne was not one that he had heard of in the diocese before and that people long-involved in Clondalkin parish life had not heard his name either. He had made enquiries about the matter. Kathy, however, quickly came back to say that she was going to handle the matter through a different agency]

"But there, O'Beirne asked me to lie and act as a false witness that I had seen her being raped by a priest of Dublin Diocese. I refused to do so.

"On the night of her book launch, she had asked me to lie. To lie about one of the priests in the parish. She asked me to say that I had seen a priest rape her. – I said to her , 'I most certainly will not. That is just lies.'

"Her allegation was complete bullshit. Basically I told her to get lost. I said, 'There is no way I'm going to lie about the clergy.'

"She did say there would be a few bob in it for me. She is money mad that one.

"She said that if I went along with her on her story that she was going to buy a bungalow for the two of us. She thinks I want to get back to Ireland to live with her. [laughs]

"I must say, she caught me unawares. If I had've been ready for it, I would have decked her. She said she would get us a bungalow in Ireland if I lied for her. There is no way.

"The priests name was Fr 'Gamma' (not named due to libel laws and the person's right to his good name) and I do know that she named this priest to the Gardai and to the archdiocese of Dublin."

O'Beirne has a claim in against a priest in Dublin diocese. That one particular priest, who is still alive, was alleged by O'Beirne to have raped her and that Margaret had witnessed the incident. The allegation is that a priest in Clondalkin parish took Kathy and Margaret for a ride in his car and raped Kathy. It was alleged the incident happened in 1969, when Margaret was still at school.

On foot of queries made by Dublin Diocese at the behest of Kathy

O'Beirne, Phil Garland, head of Dublin Diocese Child Protection Service went over to London to interview Margaret in April 2006. They spoke for over two hours. The outcome was recorded, and a statement was drawn up: "He drafted up this conversation and statement. It was perfect. And said he was going to forward it on to the Gardai," said Margaret.

A source close to the Gardai in Dublin also confirmed to this journalist that the Gardai started to investigate Kathy's complaint against Fr 'Gamma' in November 2006 after Kathy had made a formal complaint. The man in question, is about seventy, has left the ministry and is married.

Margaret was appalled at the allegations that Kathy made: "I am definite, there is no way did that priest abuse her. No way. And I will not stand in a court in Dublin and lie for her.

"She says in her book she was abused by priests through the homes and now she is saying it was a local priest from the parish.

"She also said that 'Monsignor Alpha abused me.' [allegations against a second priest, who is now dead] He was a lovely priest, and the Parish Priest in Clondalkin during the 1960's. I'm not sure if she put this complaint into the Gardai or Dublin Diocese. I can tell you one thing, no such abuse took place."

[A source close to the Gardai confirmed to this author they had spoken to O'Beirne about this allegation].

"O'Beirne told me that she has named three local priests. One of the allegations was against a local monsignor.

"One of the complaints, she said, was against, Fr 'Three', a priest who is resident in England at the moment. 'The Gardai,' O'Beirne said, 'are looking into getting him extradited back to Ireland.'"

Kathy told Margaret about the complaints that she made against the three priests, alleging that she had been either abused or raped by them.

According to Margaret, "The allegations against the three priests are bullshit, absolute lies.

"I am disgusted with what she had done. I valued her as a friend. I always went home to see her and we would chat. I am gutted to think she has done something like this. She is one horrible bitch. She has to be stopped for she will keep on going and going. She has hurt a lot of people.

"I thought we were good ol' buddies.... but she turned out pretty septic in the end. Horrible. She is horrible and dangerous.

"I have been reading *The Irish Post* for years and have seen the advertisements looking for people to make claims off the Church, and Dublin Diocese from their school days and that. I said, 'I don't want anything to do with that.'"

Margaret revealed that O'Beirne has also made an allegation of abuse against a named Garda Sergeant, formerly attached to Clondalkin Station and who is now dead. Margaret named the man Sergeant 'Huggy', and I have confirmed with a source close to the Gardai, that they have spoken to Kathy O'Beirne about this person.

Kathy alleged that she had a baby in her book.

"In August 2005 I went back to Ireland to talk with her. She said she was writing a second book and that I was in it a lot. I thought, 'You bastard. You've had eleven years of counselling and eleven years of thinking and spent three years writing this book.'

"I said, 'I want to read it before you sign off on it. If it's true, you can then go ahead and write more of it, if that's what you want.'

"Once again, when she was going over to Edinburgh with the script of her second book, she rang me up. I said I was feeling a bit down. She said how beautiful it was up there in Scotland, that I needed a break and that I should come up and she would pay for everything.

"I knew what she was playing at, so I played it up and said, 'But how would I pay for that?' O'Beirne said, 'But I'll pay for everything.'

"There and then, I told her to get lost, and that was the end of that. I was disgusted. Did she think she was going to buy me?"

'You just don't know what she is going to come up with in her second book, after the first one. She said she was going to mention a second baby. Seemingly, I was the only one who knew this. But she didn't even have one baby, never mind a second."

Kathy O'Beirne told Margaret that in her second book, she was going to talk about her second daughter. "I said 'What?' She was never pregnant. She never had one baby, never mind a second. She was a great one for having kids around her. We all were out pushing prams and stuff. But she never had a baby and she never told me that she ever had one either. I would remember if she was pregnant.

"When I was over in Ireland she took me to Glasnevin Cemetery [in North Dublin] to supposedly show me the grave of her child.

"We were standing at this monument thing and I asked her to show me the baby's name and she said she didn't bother getting the engraving done. I said , 'You better get your act together, and you just telling the world about a baby.' I asked her to show me the first name, she said, 'its not there.' I asked her to show me the second name, she said, 'it's not there.' I said, 'you're an awful liar.'

"There was no first baby, there was no second baby. These stories are all absolute lies..... I got so upset at the graveyard that I had a sore stomach."

Margaret Power concluded: "There is very little that is true in that book, but there are a lot of lies in it. Is there nothing that can be done about this rubbish being published?"

Well, there is. On Friday February 10, [2007] two Garda detectives from Ireland, a man and a woman came to London to interview Margaret. Speaking to Margaret the day after they had interviewed her, she told me that the Gardai were both very nice and interviewed her for three hours. They had an escort with a detective from Scotland Yard being as it was in a different jurisdiction. "They have plenty of information now. They seemed content going back now. Both the Gardai seemed familiar with Kathy O'Beirne. I told them I was going to talk about what has happened from 2003 until the present day. They were very surprised with what I told them. I would say completely flabbergasted. And I told them the whole truth. The complete story. I feel it's a great load off my shoulders. A huge relief ..... The woman garda told me that Kathy was ringing her up every week, asking how things were moving in the case, about prosecuting the priest. I can tell you, things should be moving on now, but not in the way she [O'Beirne] expected. It's now time for the Gardai to use what I told them. I can tell you. What

I feel like doing now, is going over there, putting my arms round Kathy O'Beirne and choking her. That is how angry I am with her. She has destroyed her own immediate family. They can't get on with their lives. My own family got very upset by the whole thing. My brothers were very upset, and it has caused terrible problems. It is just starting to mellow out a bit now, but it will never be the same again. A few things will never be put to right. Never.

"I can't believe how sneakily she came upon me. I thought she was a loyal friend. I was gutted to think that I knew someone for so long, and she tried to screw up people's lives the way she did. Absolute bitch."

A source close to the Gardai in West Dublin was able to confirm in late July 2007 that a file about this matter was sent to the DPP.

The Gardai were waiting to hear back if a prosecution would be taken by the Public Prosecutor.

Margaret Power was told that Kathy O'Beirne has made allegations of abuse or rape against three different priests and one garda sergeant. These are complaints, Margaret believes that have been made in the last three years and of which we are aware. It is possible that there could be more.

Margaret had never heard of a Fr Fergal O'Connor, a priest against whom O'Beirne has made a totally seperate claim.

11 The Second Burial of Fr Fergal O'Connor

Fr Fergal O'Connor OP, the next victim of Kathy O'Beirne's false allegations, established a residential hostel, Sherrard House in the early Seventies to help homeless girls.

Although never mentioned or explicitly alluded to in Kathy's book, three former residents of this refuge have spoken up to confirm that Kathy spent over three years along with them. One of those, Mary Lavin tells how disgusted she was that Kathy made false allegations against the founder of the hostel just before he died.

Mary Lavin was a resident of Sherrard House and former friend of Kathy O'Beirne. She told me: "Kathy is not telling the truth. I was in St Anne's [Reformatory School] as she was, and nobody was treated badly. There were punishments yes, but no-one was treated badly.

"Sherrard House itself was a breeze. It was a very easy regime with a relaxed atmosphere. The staff were all young people. There were rules of course, as in every home. If you broke them, you were put out for a few days, and went to stay elsewhere. The man who started the hostel," she said, "the Dominican Fr Fergal O'Connor OP was a lecturer at UCD. He was fantastic and a real gentleman. The good that that man did, yet he went to his grave with a broken heart. It was terrible.

"He was barred from the hostel, a hostel that he had started to help these girls, at the end of his life because of things that Kathy said. It is absolutely terrible."

She thought too, that "the book is made up of other people's stories greatly embellished. Definitely, without a doubt, these things did not happen to Kathy."

Yet Mary, still feels sympathy for Kathy: "I feel sorry for her. She is sick. She's disturbed. She is as clever as they come, and always was. But

122 KATHY'S REAL STORY

it doesn't justify what she is doing."

A Dominican priest, Fr Fergal O'Connor was a well-known and widely respected lecturer in Political Science at University College Dublin (UCD) from the Sixties onwards. In his time he taught the recent Minister for Justice, Michael McDowell and former Taoiseach, (Irish Prime minister) John Bruton.

While at UCD he was instrumental in setting up the hostel for homeless girls as well as a group of volunteers, ALLY, to take pregnant, single girls into their own homes while they were having their babies. He was universally regarded as a talented lecturer and priest of outstanding kindness and compassion. To Kathy O'Beirne, this was a matter of no consequence.

Fr O'Connor died on 29th September 2005 at the age of 78. But just over a year before he died, while suffering terrible pain from the grip of advanced arthritis, those who knew him say that Miss O'Beirne claimed that he had raped her in Sherrard House Hostel in the early Seventies, and also drove seminary students from a religious order in his car up to the girls hostel where she was, so they could gang rape her. They also say that Miss O'Beirne claimed that Fr O'Connor physically beat her up.

Those who knew him, for the first time now publicly tell how these false accusations caused him incredible pain and heartache. A short time before he died, he was given the all clear regarding the accusation.

Fr Cyprian OP, is a fellow Dominican priest and close friend of Fr O'Connor. They were both roughly the same age as well as resident together in St Saviour's Priory in north central Dublin. Regarding Fr O'Connor's physical condition, Fr Cyprian commented:

"He developed arthritis in his early twenties, and at the time was told he had a very short time to live. All the time I knew Fergal he had serious arthritis, and as time went on, he became increasingly crippled by it. I have met a lot of people, but I have never known anybody who was so totally and utterly, every day of his life, in total pain. He could not find a place in the bed where he would lie in comfort. He was a quivering mass of pain, from head to foot towards the end of his life, day in day out, without ceasing. And no one ever heard him complain of his condition.

"He had to take medicines at various times, but no matter what he took, it had an adverse effect upon him. Usually the drugs upset his stomach so much he could not keep them down. At the end, the drugs were insufficient to ease the pain. On top of that, at the very end of his life, his legs broke out in severe ulcers. To look at them was painful. But there was nothing that could be done for him."

Asked how Fr O'Connor could have raped Kathy O'Beirne if he was so crippled, Fr Cyprian said: "That was the joke. As long as I have known him he had arthritis, but it grew progressively worse as he got older. As it ended up, he couldn't open a door, or cut a slice of bread or anything. The sheer impossibility of him, inflicting physical pain on anybody was ridiculous. Anybody who knew the man, could only wonder how she could make such an accusation. Fergal O'Connor was so crippled with arthritis, he was incapable of lifting his arms above his head."

His work at Sherrard House and with Ally volunteer group

"There is no doubt," Fr Cyprian said, "that the groups he set up have done great work. Sherrard House in Dublin which helps homeless girls continues this work. And it was extraordinarily difficult work. Not all the girls were fully appreciative of the help, because of lack of home formation and parental help, and in some circumstances, they could be quite difficult.

"For a man so intelligent, he was never a purely academic person. Every weekend of his life, he spent up in Sherrard House itself, helping to do practical work to save money, such as supervising the plumbing and carpentry. In later years, he spent hours on the phone trying to help these women. The women there in Sherrard House worshipped him. Even the most difficult woman there would be up with bunches of flowers to him."

The talented lecturer

"Fr O'Connor was a very popular and influential lecturer. Although the last thing in the world that Fergal would court is popularity; he always told it as he saw it. He was a tremendous follower of Plato and he challenged people to think through their ideas and relate it to contemporary society.

"Indeed, I could hardly have my dinner in comfort when he was around. He liked to challenge thinking so much. Fr O'Connor was one of the first priests to go on the Gay Byrne's [RTÉ TV] *Late Late Show*. Because of his method of speaking and challenging ideas, he caused a mighty stir at times. He was a joy to the media because he was controversial."

The allegations by Kathy O'Beirne

"Fr O'Connor was accused of aiding and abetting sexual abuse. He was accused of driving young people over to her. A group of seminary students from a religious order, who at the time helped out at the hostel, so they could have their way with her. He was accused of driving clerical students to the hostel to have sex with Kathy O'Beirne. *She made these accusations before she turned on Fr O'Connor.*

"Kathy O'Beirne then accused Fr O'Connor of sexually abusing her, of raping her while she was in Sherrard House, some time in the early Seventies. She also accused him of physically abusing her, or beating her up. It was so unbelievable but it was already believed at this stage, in early 2004, that she had accused someone else of raping her and this was found out to be false."

The effect on Fr O'Connor

"At the very end of his life, as the investigation was going on, Fr O'Connor was barred from entering Sherrard House, the hostel he had set up to help girls in need, or from entering into any contact with people involved with Sherrard House, even by phone.

"There is no doubt that the allegations made against him by Kathy O'Beirne weighed very heavily on him. As a very close friend, he did not have to say how he felt about this accusations and the effect it had on him. I knew, from meeting with him and talking to him about it, that it preyed on his mind terribly.

"At Fr O'Connor's funeral, the preacher, Fr Larry Collins said obliquely, that for all the physical pain that he suffered, the greatest trial of his life came at the very end. It was a great spiritual suffering. In reaction to the allegation made by Kathy O'Beirne, Fr O'Connor was profoundly dismayed by it. Not so much for himself but for the organisation; for fear of its effect on Sherrard House hostel and the people who worked there.

"I think deep down, he knew in his bones, that the allegation was so utterly and grossly false, that it could not be sustained. But that it should have been accepted and acted upon by those in authority, when it should have been immediately and patently obvious that the girl was an unreliable person. That is why he wrote the refutation."

The actions of those in authority

"To him, it was as clear as daylight, that anyone with a shred of common sense should not have entertained the allegations. But, at the moment, because of the type of society Ireland is at present, if the slightest whiff of anything like that arises, you are almost defenceless. It is almost assumed automatically that you are guilty until proven innocent.

"No-one who even remotely knew Fergal, as we knew him, could even imagine, this to be true. But bishops are in a very difficult position at present; if an allegation is made, they are almost required to report it automatically. If the bishops do not report allegations they can be held to blame afterwards.

"As far as I know, the allegations were made to Dublin Diocese and passed on subsequently to the gardai. Bishop Diarmuid Martin of Dublin was simply following the guidelines that the bishops set for themselves. It was then investigated by the Health Board, although the Gardai were involved. As far as I know he was interviewed once by the gardai, and he was very vigourous in his defence.

"I also know that he wrote a document, a complete defence of his position. He spent many hours dictating out a formal refutation of the allegations to a helper, who typed it out on computer as he spoke. The typist was a volunteer from his days at the hostel. He himself was physically incapable of typing himself. But he spend weeks at that.

"In another sense, he believed that the allegations could not touch him, simply because they were false. He held to the old Latin maxim 'Magnus est veritas et prevalebit – The truth is great and it shall prevail.'"

The final outcome

"Through all this sorry saga, Fr Fergal continued to have the complete trust and confidence of his Dominican brothers and was never at any stage asked to cease his priestly ministry. He was very highly respected in the order and at university for the work that he did.

"As far as the order is concerned there was never any substance to the allegations made against him.

"At the conclusion of the investigation, Fr Fergal O'Connor was notified, that the Health Board were satisfied that he could continue as before, and go back to work. This conclusion came just a month before he died. He died having this satisfaction at least."

Asked was Fr O'Connor a good man? Fr Cyprian replied: "I do not know what the word saint means if Fergal was not one. He was not a craw thumper, anyone who heard him on the *Late Late Show* could tell you that. But he was a saint. And what Kathy O'Beirne did was terrible."

The talented lecturer who was touched many lives

Brian Patrick Hillery is a 29 year old Management Consultant for Deloitte & Touche in London. The nephew of former Irish President Dr Patrick Hillery, Brian studied under Fr O'Connor, and had this to say about him:

"My final year at University College Dublin in 1998 was a memorable one, not simply because I spent much of it locked away in the college library frenetically preparing for my final exams, but because I had the privilege of forging a lasting and memorable friendship with Fr Fergal O'Connor.

"I chose to study political philosophy in my final year under the tuition of Fergal; the focus of our course was *The Republic*, Plato's monumental work of moral and political philosophy. For me, like many others fortunate enough to have studied under Fergal, his brilliance as a teacher was unquestionable, the impact of his lectures etched on the mind long after the lecture theatre had emptied.

"I recall my first encounter with Fr Fergal vividly. He ambled into the theatre, slightly stooped, a crutch propped under one arm, and after a brief introduction he initiated a thought-provoking and heated debate on how free we, the student body of UCD, were. Just as nonchalantly as he had arrived he left, leaving us, his students, bewildered. Fergal delighted in argument and was fearless in provoking it; he was in his element in the lecture theatres and hallways of UCD, engaging his students in unscripted face-to-face philosophical debate.

"Fergal wanted his students to find the answers to important questions, questions about what it means to be good, and how human virtues should be translated into a just society. He made us realise, perhaps for the first time in our lives, that what we thought really mattered, that what we believe and how we live have a direct bearing on one another. He instilled an understanding in us that to study philosophy can also be to practise it. Fergal helped us realise that our beliefs about justice, wisdom, courage and temperance are central to our whole life, to who we are.

"Fergal believed his role as a teacher was to help people – his friends, his students, just about anyone who would join in his conversations – to develop and nurture something he believed was already alive in all of us: a susceptibility to the good. Fergal once commented on an essay I submitted that 'our chief concern in life must be the pursuit of the good, and this demands that in every action, every situation, we must endeavour to find the good. Surely this is the most important theory for everyone.' Philosophy, Fergal would often tell us, is a love striving for the truth; it is a process or a journey, rather than a piece of information that can be acquired or learned.

"Though bound to the constraints of a religious order, he had the freest of minds. It was testimony to his Socratic credentials that on at least one occasion a member of the Oireachtas damned him as a corrupting influence on Ireland's youth! While Fergal was fearless in his pursuit of social justice, he was also extraordinarily kind. He helped numerous people in his own discreet way. His generosity and love knew no boundaries.

"That is why he endeared himself to so many and the reason why he had an almost tribal-like following in the lecture theatres and hallways of UCD. However, this following was not confined to his university life. In fact, there were a very large number of people who sought Fergal's constant advice and help throughout his lifetime. Many of these individuals were in daily or weekly contact with him. To these people, he showed unreserved love and gave of his time selflessly.

"I travelled from London to attend Fergal's funeral out of respect to someone who had a profound and lasting impact on my life. Fergal never mentioned the allegations that were made against him and it was only when I attended his funeral that I realised how much hurt and pain they had caused. It was as though Fergal did not want burden others with his pain and yet was always there to offer advice to those who needed him. I am privileged to have had the opportunity to develop a friendship with someone who embodied what it means to be great in many ways.

"At Fergal's funeral, it was no surprise that Fr Larry Collins, vicar provincial of the Dominicans, commented on how many people had described Fergal as 'great' or 'one of the greatest'. He had a profound and lasting impact on those around him."

Mrs Finola Bruton's experience of Fr Fergal O'Connor OP

As a student studying Politics and Political Philosophy at university, Finola Bruton, the wife of former Fine Gael leader and Taoiseach John Bruton, met Fr Fergal O'Connor OP for the first time in 1974, when he was her professor.

Even at this stage, she was immediately aware that he was severely crippled by arthritis. "He was very bad with arthritis, even the first time I met him. It was obvious. Although he was not on crutches, he had to walk slowly and to keep himself moving, he would force himself to walk up stairs. He never complained although he had been hospitalised many many times in his life," Mrs Bruton recalled.

"He could not lift his arms above his head, nor shake hands because of the pain that squeezing his hand would cause. Instead, he just put out one finger to hold. I subsequently learned that he suffered from severe rheumatoid arthritis from his early twenties. I can assure you, not only was it a physical and mental impossibility that Fr Fergal would beat someone up – but if you knew Fergal O'Connor, it was also an emotional impossibility.

"As a human being, Fergal O'Connor was an exception. I have not met his like before him or after him. I do not think that I will meet the like of him ever again."

Mrs Bruton now recounts that Fr O'Connor was extremely intelligent, had great clarity of thought and was always searching for the truth. He believed that a culture should always be challenged.

"He was my professor while I studied at university, and when I lived in Sherrard House in two different occasions, he was up there every evening. He then trained me in as a counsellor for ALLY, which was a separate organisation, run from the Dominican Priory which looked after pregnant girls.

"The ALLY group would interview and liaise with families and get counselling for the young women. The Irish host families who participated in the scheme took in young women and minded them in the latter part of their pregnancy."

"Fr O'Connor organised flag days for ALLY and the hostel for homeless girls. He used all his charm and skills to get volunteers and families to help." Finola spent a lot of time working with ALLY and the hostel at Sherrard House:

"Fr Fergal then married John and I, and I left for the wedding church from Sherrard House. I would say that I spent more of my time speaking to him for a large part of my life that any other human being."

Finola says that Fergal O'Connor, "set up this hostel and did this work with young pregnant girls as Christian service. He interpreted his role as a priest, as a servant of Christ, helping people in need."

Sherrard House Hostel, when Finola was there at least, "ran by the philosophy, that if girls did not like it there, they could leave. Their stay there was totally voluntary. There was no enforced placements. It was on that basis that the hostel worked. It provided a certain security for many girls. As a fully engaged university lecturer, Fr O'Connor went out of himself to help others in need, motivated by Christian charity."

The culture of the time

"To those who knew Kathy O'Beirne in the hostel," Finola said, "her story had absolutely no credibility. She got away with it at a time when people were willing to run with these stories. It is a normal temptation when some stories of abuse have turned out to be true to believe all stories. It is important that these should be fought when they are untrue."

Mrs Bruton discussed the matter with Fergal O'Connor after the allegations were made by Kathy O'Beirne and she remembers that "first of all he fought them and refused to apologise. He had great moral courage. The people involved in Sherrard House also found the allegations against Fergal O'Connor outrageous as well. He had touched the lives of too many people before this and had well established credentials, so to speak. Everybody whom I met, knew that he was totally innocent."

It was asserted by Kathy O'Beirne in one of her statements that Finola Bruton was staying in Sherrard House while Kathy was resident there. Finola Bruton, however, has no memory of Kathy ever being there at all, while she (Finola) was there. "I was never in the hostel at the time, she says, she was there. Perhaps she thought that this would aid her case.... but it was simply untrue."

Finola agreed that once the allegation was made by Kathy O'Beirne that Fr Fergal was neither allowed to enter the hostel or have contact, even by phone with those who worked in it. She said: "That was horrendous. He often spoke to me about this and it hurt him deeply. He had spent his entire life, since coming to Dublin, looking after the homeless, building up and designing that hostel. Of course, it hurt him being excluded from the place he founded. However, he always spoke about the matter in a gentle and dignified manner. He was not the type of man to be bitter, and had Christian acceptance of this cross. He had resilience and hope. But it did hurt him."

At the age of 11, by which time Kathy claims to have been beaten and raped, a beaming Kathy poses beside Jean, the young bride of her brother, Tommy.

In a photo from the late 1970's. Kathy smiles as she lifts her little niece Rachael. Soon after she claims, her father would not let her stay in the house.

At the wedding of her younger sister in 1991, smiling bridesmaid Kathy stands along with her proud father Oliver, the 'cruel and evil' man who she accused of horrific abuse.

CLÁR NA nDALTAÍ I SCOIL NÁISIÚNTA

1.7.'65	2706	Ní Beirn Caitlín	18.10.'56	C.R.	Oibreoir nuacht Oidhrí	Scoil Mhuire Gil Cruise I		

1966	175	II	1.7.'65	II	1	1	2	2	1	·	·	·	·	4	4	6	3	4		
1967	60	III	1.7.'66	III	1	2	3	3	1	·	·	·	·	6	5	5	3	3	8.7.'67	Smithfm. So. scoil
1968	141	V	18.10.'68	V															18.10.68	

Kathy O'Beirne school records in Irish showing her attendance at the local national school until age 12 and a half years of age. It also shows she went to another school for a short time.

A portrait of the O'Beirne family at brother Eamonn's wedding in 1978. Kathy is at the extreme right hand side.

Style Council 1980. All the O'Beirne boys. Just before John's wedding are (from left) Joseph, Oliver, Tommy, Eamonn, and Brian.

Kathy O'Beirne in July 2005. Pic courtesy Tony Gavin/ *Sunday Independent*

Oliver O'Beirne, the father.

Michael Sheridan, co-author of *Kathy's Story*.
Pic Collins/G White.

Howzat! Oliver and Eamonn O'Beirne hold up their sister Kathy's birth certificate showing she is not 45 but 50 years of age and more importantly, their sister.

Five of the O'Beirne siblings at their press conference in September 2006 showing the gathered media what it was all about – their parent's memory and good name.

Above left:

Tom Hayes, the secretary of Victim Alliance Support group.

Above right:
Lisa Howlett and her child Olivia, who Kathy befriended for a while.

Left: False allegations campaigner and founder of L.O.V.E. charity, Florence Horsman-Hogan.

below: Maggie Lacey who stayed in St Anne's Reformatory Boarding School, Kilmacud and had a great experience. Kathy stayed in the same school for 6 weeks.

The Dominican priest, Fr Fergal O'Connor OP, who lectured at University College, Dublin and founded a hostel for homeless girls. Kathy stayed at Sherrard Street Hostel and 25 years later accused him of crimes against her. He was a charismatic and hugely respected lecturer.

Fr Fergal O'Connor around the time the allegations were first made by Kathy O'Beirne.

Margaret Power, Kathy O'Beirne's best friend who was asked to lie and give a false witness statement.

Kathy asked a friend to drive her here. The High Park complex in Dublin, run by the Sisters of Our Lady of Charity. The building immediately to the left by the car is the Industrial School, then the Chapel, further down the four buildings are St Mary's Magdalen Asylum. (Commonly known as High Park) This view if you came from the Swords Road Entrance or through the farmyard via Collins Avenue.

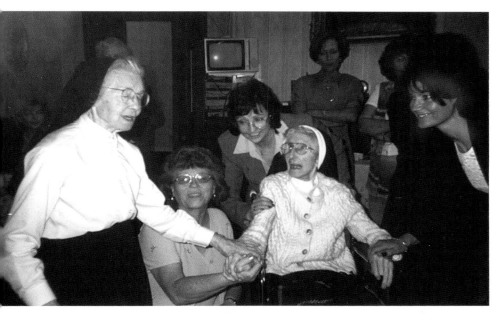

At the May 1999 get-together for woman who had been in High Park industrial school and laundry. Take my hand and I'll give you a song. Valerie Murtagh is kneeling on left.

Above: Paul Anderson (34), from Crumlin, West Dublin who was found guilty of making false allegations of abuse against a priest and jailed in June 2007 for 4 years. Pic Collins/G White

Left: Former nun, sister Nora Wall after being sentenced to life and five years imprisonment for rape in Dublin Central Criminal Court (23/7/99). Her conviction was later quashed and declared a miscarriage of justice.
Pic Collins / M O'Sullivan.

Journalist Bruce Arnold has written extensively on abuse by, and allegations of abuse against, Catholic religious. He also defends a report on Artane Industrial School by a Fr Moore. His wife, Mavis has published a book about a tragedy that happened in a Poor Clare orphanage in Cavan during 1943. Pic: Collins

John Prior who made multiple allegations against the Christian Brothers. Pic: Collins.

John Kelly (left) of the Survivors of Child Abuse (SOCA Ireland) shakes hands with the Chairman of the Investigation Committee of the Commission to Inquire into Child Abuse, Mr Justice Sean Ryan. Date 07/05/04 at the Shelbourne Hotel. Pic Collins / C Keegan.

Can anything be learnt from the tragedy?

Concerning the whole area of false allegations in general, Finola said: "I have a problem with a situation in which someone is guilty until proven innocent. I have a problem that anybody can make any wild accusations, a person can be stripped of their ministry, and punished in the most humiliating of manners. I don't think the Church in searching to help victims, which it ought to do, and searching for the truth, which it ought to do, and in seeking to investigate all these matters, which it should; I do not believe in any of these searches, that the end justifies the means.

"The morale of some priests around the country is hurt because of a prevalent culture in which, if a priest is sick and does not turn up for Mass, people ask did he not turn up because he has been withdrawn from ministry following an allegation of child abuse.

"These things must be investigated but they must be done properly. No-one, including people like Colm O'Gorman, [director of abuse survivor and advocacy/campaign group, *One in Four*] have a monopoly of feeling when it comes to the matter of child sexual abuse. We have to be very careful how we conduct our investigations.

"That is something on which I would be critical of the Church and critical of the manner in which the investigation into allegations against Fergal were conducted. Bishops have an obligation to protect their priests from scurrilous allegations. Who else, with all authority, can protect them? If, in your search for truth, you use the principle that the end justifies the means, you are creating even more injustice.

"In this regard, I do not believe that Fergal was served well. His own order were tremendous. From the beginning they believed him and stood by him. His family were also wonderful while they suffered as well. The people involved in Sherrard House Hostel were also wonderful and stood by him. Everyone who had any dealings at all with Fergal gave him their support. That was comforting to him.

"I believe that God sends good people to help others along in life, and in my life, Fergal was that good person who helped me. He was that person for many, many people."

Head of Irish Human Rights Commission speaks up.

"This is an extraordinary case of character assassination," says Dr Maurice Manning about the allegations heaped on his friend and teaching colleague, Fr Fergal O'Connor.

Dr Maurice Manning, president of the Irish Human Rights Commission, is a highly respected academic who went on to become a member of the Oireachtas for twenty-one years, serving in both the Dáil (Parliament) and the Seanad (Senate). He was a member of the New Ireland Forum and the British Inter Parliamentary Body. He also served as both Leader of the Seanad and Leader of the Opposition in that House. Dr Manning first met Fr Fergal O'Connor when he was a student at UCD, and was supported by him when he (Dr Manning) was appointed lecturer at UCD at the young age of 23. He had heard of the allegations levelled at the Dominican by Kathy O'Beirne only after he died, but speaking of what he knew of Fr O'Connor when he first met him in the mid-Sixties, Dr Manning said, "What struck me when I first heard of these allegations was that Fergal was physically incapable of any of it. You could blow him over, he was physically so vulnerable. The man was virtually a cripple from the moment I first met him. He could not walk properly his feet were so sore, his hands were all crumpled up. He had no strength in his limbs and he smoked steadily, no doubt, to take away the pain he endured."

Speaking of his character, Dr Manning said, "Fergal was a saint. He lived for other people and radiated something special which people found overwhelmingly attractive and made them want to be near him. He was a first class lecturer, without doubt one of the very best if not the best teacher I have ever witnessed during a long time in academia. His lectures were something to behold, and attracted students from all over the student body, philosophy and engineering students came, quite often his lecture hall was standing room only. He really could teach and engage the students, and I would say enrage them also because he would cause them to question their near universal middle-class assumptions.....He had a great way with women for he had a very idealistic view of them, and he would always be surrounded by people. He was never afraid to speak his mind and also had his enemies. He was attacked in the Seanad by the House's Fianna Fail leader, and was seen as too liberal by both the Church and the State at the time, and slightly dangerous in that he questioned the status quo. He had his enemies also in the university but the head of the department was very supportive. He lectured at a time," Dr Manning said, "when Dublin's Archbishop John Charles McQuaid tried to keep a tight hand and controlling influence, especially on the philosophy department." Dr Manning lectured in Politics at UCD alongside Fr Fergal O'Connor and knew him well. When asked by this writer, whether Fr O'Connor's suffering of false allegations of abuse was a human rights issue, Dr Manning suggested that it was a vital matter for law reform in Ireland.

Senior female barrister speaks of his pain

I met Ms Patricia Moran SC at the meeting point in the bustling law library within the Four Courts, Dublin. Patricia is a senior counsel, and one of the pioneering women at the Irish Bar when, unlike today, there were very few woman barristers. She had two uncles who were Dominicans and she knew Fr Fergal well from when she was about 15 years of age. As she went on to study at UCD, she also became involved in an enthusiastic group of students who went to debate and intellectually joust with him and each other on a regular basis. Patricia told this writer, Fr O'Connor was "an incredible lecturer, who could hold hundreds of students spellbound and above all get them to think for themselves."

This deep friendship continued on into later life and up until the time that he died, Patricia would go to visit him every week or fortnight. "To spend a hour with Fergal was an experience, a privilege, something which you wanted more of. It was hard not to meet him and not to be changed, and not want more time with him. He was absolutely unique as in individual. I have never known anybody so alive in all my life. His body was crippled, he could not even dress himself, or do things we all take for granted, but his spirit and his mind were always overflowing. A great light was always on. Every time I visited Fr Fergal I always felt that I had been honoured to have been privy to such a fine mind."

Patricia was one of the people in whom Fr Fergal confided his great pain at the allegations made by Kathy O'Beirne. Fr Fergal told her, she said, that O'Beirne not only accused him of rape and driving other men up to rape her but also of physical violence towards her. Something of which he was absolutely incapable: "This was not only physically so, but to rape or cause violence to another person, he would be totally incapable of it, it would be totally against his very nature. Fergal loved women and had a deep understanding of them. He could not have given any more of himself in the way, he laboured to look after the young woman who came to him for them and did everything possible to look out for them."

Commenting on the effect which Kathy's allegations had on Fr O'Connor, Patricia said, "the anguish he experienced was nearly inde-scribable. It was so painful, so damaging. On the surface, he would try to rationalise why she was trying to do it, and put it down to her mental state etc., but he was also deeply deeply hurt, to the core of his being. Can you sense for one moment, what it must have been like to be legal-ly barred from setting foot in the hostel that you started? Can you imag-ine what it would be like not to be allowed even to speak to people you have worked with for decades to help other people? The effect of the allegations was devastating. I still get upset when I think of it. The pain of these allegations was compounded by the fact that they dragged on for so long without release." Patricia said that the matter dragged on for much longer that just one year. "It went on for a few years. That was inexcusable and what he was hurt by, was the long delay caused by the failure of the Health Board, not so much the Gardai, but the social workers of the Health Board to finally investigate and put the matter to a close. It dragged on for years and by the end he was totally drained. He tried to keep positive and not let it effect him, but I know it hurt him deeply."

What the documents say
The board of Sherrard House Hostel declined to make a statement about the allegations made by Kathy O'Beirne against Fr O'Connor as outlined by some of his close acquaintances. However, one person aware of this whole matter, who we may call "Patrick", passed on some documents, and gave me a number of comments.

Among these documents was a letter signed by Phil Garland, director of the Child Protection Service of the Archdiocese of Dublin, and sent to the Dominican provincial leader on 17th May 2004. It said that Kathy O'Beirne had a meeting with the diocesan Child Protection Service director on 14th of May 2004 and made a number of allegations. This letter stated –

"The Child Protection Service in the Archdiocese of Dublin has become aware of child protection concerns in relation to a number of matters that have been expressed by Ms Kathy O'Beirne. These concerns include the following:

"Numerous allegations in relation to the physical, sexual and emotional abuse perpetrated on residents of Sherrrard House, 19 Upper Sherrard Street, Dublin 1.

These allegations included:

1 The sexual abuse of children perpetrated by members of ... [a religious order in Place A]. The abuse is alleged to have taken place in Sherrard Street and in [Place A].

2 The facilitation by neglect of the gang rape of a fourteen year old girl called "Mary." The rape was conducted by five unknown men after "Mary" was excluded from Sherrard House.

3 The maintenance of a regime which was emotionally abusive to all residents concerned during the time period of the late 1970's. In addition there was a substantial amount of physical violence.

"This information has been related to me by Ms Kathy O'Beirne. She has requested to be contacted via this office. She has indicated a willingness to talk further with the Health Board and the Garda Síochána."

According to the source from Sherrard House, the person who accompanied Kathy O'Beirne to the meeting with Child Protection Service of Dublin Archdiocese was a woman counsellor from the *One in Four* group, who is named on the extract of the meeting which this journalist now has in possession. Kathy had also instructed solicitors to write to Fr O'Connor three and a half years previous to this meeting, seeking her files from Sherrard House.

In the meeting extract it is recorded that: "Kathy recalls that she was fifteen and a half when she went to Sherrard House."

She also alleges that Fr O'Connor drove the girls from Sherrard House over to [Place A] in his car and that three of those that came across from [Place A] were priests and clerical students who abused girls while they were in Sherrard House. "Kathy said there were a few children born out of those relationships between the priest/students and the girls."

Kathy also alleged that after a girl "mousy Mary" was excluded from Sherrard House by a house mother, and that this woman and Fr O'Connor knew the fourteen year old girl was in danger: "Mary was banging on the door to get into the hostel. The five men took her off and gang raped her." According to Kathy, "the girls never seen 'mousy Mary' again."

The meeting extract states, "Kathy recalls that the older girls were charged £30.00 a week rent by Fr O'Connor and the girls had no way of paying that. Many of them went down to Baggot Street area and turned to prostitution to earn the money to pay to Fr O'Connor every week. Kathy said that Fr O'Connor never sexually abused her but he mentally tortured her and abused her in every other way. He locked her out from 9.00pm to 9.00am as well."

The meeting extract prepared by Child Protection Service director, Phil Garland ends by saying that Kathy wanted a public apology from Fr Fergal O'Connor "because he put her through a lot of suffering."

Outside these documents, "Patrick" said, that the Health Board insisted that Fr O'Connor withdraw from contact with Sherrard House while the investigations were being carried out. Both the Health Board and the Gardai made separate investigations into the allegations of Kathy O'Beirne against Fr O'Connor.

Separate from this, those close to Fr O'Connor engaged a senior lawyer, Mr Garret Sheehan, who in turn instructed a former senior garda officer to take statements from all the house mothers and many of the girls who had been in the house. "Patrick" added that, "The report was very comprehensive. Not one of the girls agreed with anything that Kathy O'Beirne said."

The Health Board wrote to the Homeless Girls' Society [the board of

Sherrard House] on 21st August 2005, "I write to advise you that having investigated this matter we have come to the conclusion that abuse alleged by Ms O'Beirne in Sherrard House is unfounded on the basis of the information available to us at this time."

On Tuesday 27th of September 2005, An Garda Síochána wrote to Sherrard House, "I wish to inform you, following a comprehensive investigation by An Garda Síochána into various allegations made by Kathy O'Beirne, a file was submitted to the DPP for his consideration. I am in receipt of correspondence dated 10th of August 2005 from the DPP which states that a prosecution cannot be considered in this matter."

Fr O'Connor died on September 29th 2005 at the ag of 78.

"Patrick" said that what happened was appalling. Fr O'Connor rang "Patrick" up just before he died to say that he had been vindicated. "You could hear," this person said, "the emotion in his voice."

The person said, "the emotion here still runs very very deep about this, about what happened. All the girls too were both angry and devastated."

The hostel for homeless girls which Fr O'Connor helped found, while maintaining a low profile, continues its tremendous work of helping vulnerable young women. Fr O'Connor's name continues to be held in the highest regard and affection by those who knew him.

12 An Area Study in False Allegations – Is Clondalkin a microcosm of Ireland?

*K*athy's Story is probably the best known of the allegations of sexual abuse against Catholic religious to have originated in Clondalkin, but it is certainly not the only one; not by a long stretch. A number of other prominent cases have been flagged there in recent years.

The small area of Clondalkin in west Dublin has its fair share of false allegations. If every area in Ireland was the same, it would add up to very a high number of fraudulent allegations indeed.

In May 2003, someone we shall call Fr 'Beta' (to protect his anonymity), a priest in the wider Clondalkin area, was accused by a man of sexual abuse. Even though the priest resolutely refuted the allegations from the start, he was still told by the Archbishop of Dublin to withdraw immediately from parish duties while the matter was investigated by the gardai.

This created quite a bit of anger amongst his fellow priests in the diocese, and caused the National Conference of Priests of Ireland to complain that the priest, by virtue of being asked to step down without proof of wrongdoing, had been stripped of his right to his good name.

According to Church's guidelines for dealing with allegations of child abuse, which have been in place since 1996, bishops and religious superiors are allowed to exercise their discretion when deciding whether an accused cleric should step down from his ministry. In practice though, however flimsy or outrageous the allegation, the accused priest is nearly always asked to step down from his public ministry.

In this case however, by Christmas of 2003, after a full garda investigation into the claims, Fr 'Beta' was informed that his case had been definitively stopped as they had no evidence to support the allegations made by his accuser. He was reinstated in his active position during Midnight Mass with parishioners giving him a standing ovation as he was reintroduced.

A letter of commendation was read out from Cardinal Connell, the then-archbishop of Dublin saying that Fr 'Beta's good name had been vindicated. However, that his name had been vindicated shows that the priest in question already had his good name stripped away in public. By being asked to step down without having previously gone through due process, his good name and reputation had already been greatly harmed – quite unjustly.

Reacting to news that Fr 'Beta' had been cleared of the allegation, Fr Dermod McCarthy, the head of religious broadcasting at RTÉ, told *The Irish Independent* at the time: "I am delighted for my colleague Fr Beta, who, after seven months of torture, could have received no better Christmas present than this acknowledgement that he was wrongly accused."

However, Fr McCarthy went on then to criticise the way in which the case had been dealt with by the Dublin Archdiocese. "It seems that in the case of a priest his right to his good name and reputation as a citizen of this country can be set aside at the first hint of an allegation, however baseless," he said.

The Paul Anderson Case

In June 2007, a thirty four year-old man from Crumlin in west Dublin was convicted of making false allegations of abuse against a priest of the Dublin Diocese. Paul Anderson was found guilty of falsely accusing a priest of attempting to bugger him while been given tuition for his First Holy Communion more that 25 years ago.

In court, Anderson denied making a false statement to detective garda Brian Kavanagh on June 18, 2003 in Kevin Street garda station. This man alleged that the named priest had committed acts of indecent assault and buggery on him in the Spring of 1981. Anderson, who was €9,000 in debt at the time he made the allegations, denied telling investigating Gardai: "I thought of the story first and then the priest's name."

He also denied saying: "Yes, he didn't rape me but he was a cruel man and I just said it," and that the priest "used to frown down on us because he thought everyone who lived in the flats were scum."

Anderson, who is a fairly stout man, with a small goatee and glasses, still claimed in court that he had been sexually abused. However, the court heard evidence showing that neither Anderson nor any other pupil from his school had ever been sent to the priest for Holy Communion prayer tuition.

In addition to this evidence, the jury was also shown a video recording of an interview in which Anderson told gardai his allegations were not true and that he apologised for making them. This videoed interview he did with gardai, half an hour before he was released was shown to the court contradicting what he said under cross-examination.

Standing by his story, Anderson told the Dublin Criminal Court that 26 years ago, his mother sat outside the room while he was being assaulted by the priest and that all others were just "lying to protect the Church." The jury however, weren't to be swayed by his appeal. After deliberating for six hours and staying overnight in a hotel, the jury found Anderson guilty by a 10–2 majority verdict.

Between the time of the court verdict and sentencing, Fr 'Beta' told this writer that he "wasn't ecstatic, why should I be? Something was stolen from me, my good name and now I am having it returned. It is not that I am receiving anything else extra, to tell you the truth," Fr 'Beta' said. "I am highly relieved it's over. I am also angry and disappointed that the whole affair has dragged on for four years for this to come to court. Nor am I happy the way I was initially treated by the Church."

The matter had been down for court appearance on a number of occasions but Anderson made specious threats of suicide to ward off the trial. The priest chose not to be named, because he did not wish his name even remotely associated with such matters. An order was made to that effect.

The priest told the legal counsel prosecuting Mr Anderson that he nearly "died of fright" when Cardinal Desmond Connell first informed him of the sexual abuse allegations made against him. He said he found the allegations "repulsive" and the whole situation "very difficult." In his victim impact statement Fr Beta wrote that Anderson's false accusation "was more like a case of armed robbery," in which his name and reputation were being used in an attempt to extract money from the Church.

"I would have honestly preferred had the perpetrator shot me through the head rather than have put me and my family through the pangs of anxiety and the profound sufferings we endured over the past four years."

As a direct result of Anderson going with the *One in Four* group to Dublin Archbishop's House armed with the false accusation, "he hair triggered the Church guidelines with immediate and devastating effect on me and on the practice of my priesthood." Fr Beta was "instantly and publicly suspended from ministry," and was forced to leave his home and live with relatives.

"Without any due process, my diocese – in this Guantanamo Bay reaction – had me stand aside from my work as a priest," he said.

Expressing his gratitude to the gardai for their professionalism he thanked those who he said "gave me back my life." He expressed his appreciation to two gardai in particular "who approached this case with meticulous attention to detail that uncovered the truth and led to justice being done."

Although he found the whole episode very hurtful and traumatic he added that the ordeal had given him "a deeper insight into the mind of Christ," who had also been falsely accused. "And since his standard of forgiveness was 'seventy times seven times' then surely I must be able to find it in me to forgive Paul Anderson – which I now do – and I do so wholeheartedly.

"So may I sincerely ask that this be taken into merciful consideration by the Court when sentence is being passed," he said.

He dedicated "the considerable trauma and suffering to genuine victims of the atrocity of abuse. I hope that what transpired in this case will not stop any genuine victim from coming forward to seek justice and redress for such a crime. The safety of children has always been for me and must always be of paramount importance."

The parish priest at University Church on Dublin's Stephen's Green, (who is a colleague of the accused) told the court that Anderson first wrote to him asking for "financial assistance to cover the cost of counselling for depression," while the secretary to the Monsignor who handled abuse complaints for the Archdiocese said Anderson made repeated phone requests "for help to pay a bill for more than €2,000 from his counsellor."

After the 17 day trial concluded, at the sentencing, Judge Patricia Ryan said that the court had to signify the seriousness of this offence by imposing a prison sentence of four years. After the case, the innocent priest in question said that he had prayed for mercy for his accuser while friends admitted that he was left "totally devastated" by the allegation, and criticised the four-year wait before his name was cleared.

Is Clondalkin a microcosm of Ireland? It is hard to know, for one would have to study the extent of abuse allegations in other parts of the country and compare. But what is certain, is that a high number of false claims against innocent religious have originated in Clondalkin, and as a consequence many priests have been treated very unjustly.

[More examples from Clondalkin were cut for legal reasons]

A bad week for the One in Four group.

One in Four is a counselling and advocacy group for people who have suffered abuse. It is headed by former Progressive Democrat party candidate from Wexford, Colm O'Gorman. The group which he leads is heavily subsidised by the Irish Government.

Writing an opinion piece in *The Irish Times* on 29/3/2006, Colm O'Gorman, the director of *One in Four* stated: "In the past few months a number of commentators have suggested that grave injustice is being done to priests falsely accused of child sexual abuse. Such suggestions rightly concern fair minded people, but remarkably, no evidence of any kind has been presented to suggest that false allegations are being made or that the rights of those accused are being abused."

He also suggested that, "In seeking to protect our children we may be forced to act in ways that seem contrary to the rights of those adults accused of child abuse."

These expressed sentiments may be a cause of unease or alarm for those anxious to ensure the rights of all are upheld without fear or favour. It was the *One in Four* group which accompanied Kathy O'Beirne as she went to make allegations against Fr O'Connor. The *One in Four* group also took Paul Anderson under its wing and accompanied him to see the Archbishop of Dublin with the accusation that he was abused by Fr Beta.

After this came out in court, the group rushed to defend its actions saying it would be failing in "the most basic level in our collective responsibility to protect children" by not reporting a credible child abuse allegation. It was the group's standard practice, a spokesman said, to pass on credible allegations to the appropriate authorities.

"Any time a credible allegation is made, it must and should be reported, ... Credible means capable to be true.

"How any diocese responds to a concern like that is obviously a matter for the diocese, but best practice would dictate that if the allegation is credible, then, as is required by the church's own guidelines, the person involved would be asked to step aside when the allegation is investigated, and I understand that is what happened in this case," the *One in Four* spokesman said. That was at the end of July 2007.

The Case of Fr John Kinsella

Barely a week earlier the same advocacy and campaign group was left in an embarrassing position when a group of three men from Wexford which *One in Four* was advising, were forced to drop their case alleging abuse against a Fr John Kinsella which was being heard at the Dublin High Court.

The civil action ran for several weeks and involved over 20 witnesses. In it, the three male plaintiffs alleged that during the late '70s and '80s this priest sexually abused them while he was working in St Aidan's Cathedral, Enniscorthy, Co Wexford.

Fr John Kinsella refuted and completely denied the allegations since the first day they were made. He was asked and agreed to step down from ministry in 2002. At the same time the priest completely refuted all allegations, and the diocese claimed that the action was statute-barred because of the long delay in bringing the proceedings.

When the claims were first made in 2002, the DPP declined to proceed with a criminal prosecution. So in this case, the three men were taking a civil action seeking financial compensation. A civil action succeeds on the balance of probabilities and does not have to be proved beyond a reasonable doubt, so it is easier to succeed and has a lower burden of proof.

However, during the trial a number of inconsistencies between some of the statements and known facts appeared. To top this off, Fr John Kinsella also counterclaimed for damages for making false accusations.

After weeks of witnesses and cross-examination, the legal counsel for the three plaintiffs, Mr Jack Fitzgerald SC asked the judge to strike out the action, and also to strike out counterclaims by the defendants. Fr Kinsella, who was both insistent and vocal about his innocence from the time the allegations arose, was visibly relieved when he left the High Court.

The court action was dramatically struck out mid-hearing with no order. The papers claimed that this joint action by the three men was the first civil diocesan abuse case to go to full trial at the High Court. It failed.

13 Ireland's abuse Problem – first the Betrayal, then the Portrayal

There is no doubt whatsoever that abuse of children, of the most horrendous kind, was carried out by Catholic religious, not only in Ireland but in other countries as well. It is a source of great pain to the minors who were abused, and a huge scandal that someone representing Christ and the Catholic Church would abuse children. The abuse that took place was compounded again by the inadequate response of those in authority to immediately stop it taking place, and in failing to both present the abuser for justice and failing also to prevent that person from continuing in the priesthood. Protection of the vulnerable should always be their first priority.

It is difficult to cite exact figures for the number of convictions for child abuse by Catholic religious because the Irish courts do not keep records of various crimes according to occupation or state in life. Even one occurrence of abuse is too much, but there have been a good number of clergy/religious convicted over the last 15 years in Ireland. But certain things we do know. Dublin archdiocese reported in May 2007 that from 1940 until the present, that 8 priests have been convicted on criminal charges related to sexual abuse, with 3 others currently facing trial. This includes both diocesan and religious clergy.

During that time, the report notes, more than 2,800 priests (1,350 diocesan and 1,450 religious) served in the churches of Dublin. Up until this point, there have been 112 lawsuits against priests who worked in the Dublin archdiocese. Of these, 72 have been resolved so far, with the Church paying out 7.8 million in legal costs and damages.

A few well-known cases.

Sexual predator Fr Sean Fortune, 45, died in disgrace after overdosing on a lethal cocktail of drugs and whiskey at his home in New Ross, Co Wexford during March 1999.

This cleric abused many young men but chose not to face dozens of charges before a court and jury. He was facing 66 charges of buggery, sexual assault and gross indecency against 29 young men under his care in the 1980s.

Fortune sexually abused post-pubescent males of the same sex. At times, Fr Fortune and those like him, have been incorrectly termed paedophiles. However, according to the clinical definition of paedophile used by the American Psychiatric Association (APA), a paedophile is an adult with a preferential or exclusive sexual attraction to prepubescent youths.

The APA's *Diagnostic and Statistical Manual of Mental Disorders* 4th edition, gives the following as its diagnostic criteria for Paedophilia: A. "Over a period of at least 6 months, recurrent, intense sexually arousing fantasies, sexual urges, or behaviors involving sexual activity with a prepubescent child or children (generally age 13 years or younger);...."

According to book, '*Message from Heaven – the Life and Crimes of Fr Sean Fortune*' by *Irish Times* journalist Alison O'Connor (2000), Fr Fortune carried out a range of crimes, not just abuse. He was also being investigated for the misappropriation of money linked to Government FÁS training courses and a media training course he ran in the parish.

His horrific crimes came to light in 1995 when Wexford man Colm O'Gorman complained to Gardai about what had happened, thus kicking off a Garda investigation that resulted in Fortune's prosecution. For this action alone we should be grateful to O'Gorman. It was clear that Fr Fortune was allowed to run riot over a long period of time, and the Government sanctioned report into events in Ferns Diocese, called the 'Ferns Report' showed that the response of the diocese at the time was totally inadequate.

The report identified over 100 allegations of child sexual abuse made between 1962 and 2002 against twenty-one priests involved with the diocese.

It is understood that one of the priests identified in the report as Fr Alpha had a civil action against him struck out with no order.

Two Ferns's priests, Fr Donal Collins and Fr James Doyle were both convicted of sex abuse of teenage boys by the courts in 1998, and both have also been laicised by the Church.

Dubbed 'Ivan the Terrible' by his victims, Fr Ivan Payne, a priest of Dublin diocese preyed on boys (aged 11-14) for years dating back to the late 1960s. He was sentenced to six years in prison at the Circuit Criminal Court in 1998 after he admitted to 13 sample charges of indecent assault on nine boys on dates from 1968 to 1987.

They included attacks on altar boys around parishes in Dublin (Cabra and Sutton) and also attacks on youngsters in the city's Crumlin Children's Hospital, where he was chaplain. He was let out of the Curragh prison in Co Kildare in October 2002 after spending four and a half years in confinement. It appears that Fr Payne sought out shy and introverted adolescents to abuse. One of those boys who Payne molested, Andrew Madden wrote a book entitled, 'Altar Boy' about his experiences. The archdiocese later apologised both for the trauma suffered by the victims of Fr Payne and the failures of those in positions of Church authority to deal with the matter properly.

After an RTÉ programme about this issue in 2002, Cardinal Connell of Dublin admitted that, "Incalculable harm has been done to those who were abused. Further scandal has undoubtedly been caused by the fact that, having approached the Church in expectation of the best possible care and the most sympathetic response, some people suffered further hurt. We have been slow to understand the depth of their trauma and the nature of their needs." He apologised for "the terrible betrayal they have suffered. I do so," he said, "in my own name, with a keen sense of our failures to deal more adequately with the problem, as well as in the name of all of us who in any way represent the Church."

Fr Brendan Smyth (1927–1997) was a notorious paedophile who over a period of 40 years, systematically raped and sexually assaulted a huge number of boys and girls in parishes in Belfast, Dublin and the US.

Smyth joined the Norbertine religious order in 1945. It appears that leaders of this order were aware of Smyth's crimes as early as the late 1940s, yet they failed to report him to the police forces either in the

North or the Republic of Ireland.

Instead, whenever allegations were made against him, Fr Smyth was moved from parish to parish and between dioceses. In some cases, the order failed to inform the diocesan bishop that Smyth had a history of sexual abuse and should be kept away from children. Arrested in 1994, and convicted soon after, Fr Brendan Smyth died in 1997. During October 2005 one of his victims succeeded in having the title 'Reverend' removed from his gravestone.

Christian Brother Maurice Toibin has been convicted in relation to Letterfrack (see later, p172) and a Christian Brother Jack Kelly of the Southern Province was also convicted and given an eight-year prison sentence for sexually abusing 11 boys. According to a source in the Christian Brothers, to the best of their information in August 2007, four Brothers were convicted in regard to sexual abuse of whom only one related to residential institutions. Six former Brothers were also convicted though not all went to jail – two were suspended sentences. None of these six were convicted in respect of residential institutions. In 1965, there was a total number of just under 1,300 Christian Brothers in Ireland.

Media reaction to abuse revelations

A few outlets of the Irish media have chosen to forge a special vocabulary in striving to build a public image about the occurrence of child abuse.

Sociologist Harry Ferguson noted as early as 1995 the frequent media use of the term "paedophile priest," given to amplify the deviancy of a select group of individuals. Indeed, it helped to give the very misleading impression that abuse of minors is a practice exclusive to or virtually exclusive to Catholic clergy. The inordinate concentration of the media on the sexual sins of the clergy, to the virtual exclusion of other groups is most clearly glimpsed in the use of this term, "paedophile priest."

According to Michael J Breen (*Studies* Autumn 2000) this phrase was used 332 times in *The Irish Times* between August 1993 – August 2000.

The "paedophile priest" term comes up 265 times in *The Irish Times* archive between January 1996-August 2007, yet the terms "paedophile farmer", "paedophile lawyer", or "paedophile teacher" or "paedophile journalist" never occurs. In the same 1993–2000 time period, the term "paedophile farmer" appears five times but only in the context of the debate generated by Harry Ferguson, on why this phrase is not used.

In a 1995 edition of *Studies* Journal, Harry Ferguson pointed out that most of the contemporaneous high-profile cases of abuse (including Kelly Fitzgerald, the Kilkenny and McColgan cases), in fact involved farmers who were "good family men", yet the media hadn't created a "paedophile farmer" label. He was publicly criticised by the Irish Farmers' Association for bringing the good name of farmers into disrepute. This criticism only managed to prove his point. No one would dare coin or use the term "paedophile lawyer" etc. because there would be consequences; and it was of no great utility for social change.

Compounding this selectivity, the frequent use of photographs and TV images of rampant abuser, Fr Brendan Smyth also pointed towards an undue media fascination with, not just the word, but the image of the "paedophile priest."

This was exemplified in 1998, when an *Irish Independent* photo of Father Brendan Smyth, reacting to taunts as he was being taken into court won the Irish media's Photograph of the Year Award.

The judges described it as "a powerful photograph of a loathsome individual," while the *Irish Independent* reran the photograph along with the headline "Captured, the face of an evil monster."

The Irish Times (February 12, 1996) again noted that the award for the overall Journalist of the Year in the 1996 Northern Ireland media awards was won by Mr Chris Moore of Ulster Television's *Counterpoint* programme "for his ground breaking documentaries on the *paedophile priest*, Brendan Smyth."

Fr Smyth became the poster boy for some church-bashers in Ireland, but concentration on the sins of the clergy deflected attention greatly from the occurrence of abuse in general society.

A number of journalists have used the selective reporting of sexual abuse as a weapon in an ideologically-driven attempt to attack and undermine the teaching authority of the Catholic Church.

The report entitled 'The Sexual Abuse and Violence in Ireland' (SAVI) commissioned by the Dublin Rape Crisis Centre and published in 2002, shows a high level of abuse in Ireland. Its executive summary stated that one in five women (20.4 per cent) reported experiencing contact sexual abuse in childhood and a further one in ten (10 per cent) reporting non-contact sexual abuse.

To paint in broad brush strokes, a strong majority of abusers are adults – roughly one third are relatives, one third neighbours or people in authority and one third are strangers.

The SAVI report also found that 3.2 per cent of sexual abuse was carried out by religious or clergy. As an author of the report, Prof Hannah McGee made clear in an interview in *The Irish Catholic* of September 2003, that it does not follow by strict extrapolation that 3.2 per cent of abusers in Ireland are clergy. This is because clergy, like swimming coaches or teachers have easy and frequent contact with minors. In theory at least, this figure of 3.2 per cent , she said, could be accounted for by, as she said, "small number of very active abusers." We know at least some of the clergy who carried out horrendous acts of abuse, did it on a very high number of innocent victims.

But reflecting on the surprisingly high level of abuse in society, is it not amazing how relatively little time is spent on examining the abuse carried out on the other 96.8 per cent of the population?

Guilty until proven innocent. Analysis of the Church's reaction to child abuse allegations

The Church has heard and dealt with allegations of child sexual abuse before. In the 16th century in Italy for instance, if a priest was accused with firm evidence, he was immediately brought to canonical trial, the evidence heard from all sides and if found to be guilty the wayward cleric was immediately excommunicated.

The phrase in English, thrown out 'bell, book and candle,' comes from the traditional act of excommunication when the person was officially expelled from membership of the Church. In the process, a ringing bell was stopped, the book of the Gospels was slammed shut, a lighted candle was extinguished.

Immediately after excommunication, the guilty priest was literally defrocked, handed over to the the civil authorities of the day to be, well, burned at the stake.

While I'm not advocating a return to this practice of making criminals /sinners into fire lighters, it does demonstrate that the Church was aware of the harm done to the child, and to the Church, by the heinous actions of a wayward priest. The Church reacted swiftly but with due process and if the defendant was found guilty the punishment was severe. In this era, the Church first brings allegations to the notice of civil authorities.

In the last few decades, not only in Ireland but in other countries as well, the reaction of the Church leaders to allegations and evidence of abuse was found to be in many cases, woefully inadequate and to be honest, frequently both scandalous (in the full theological sense of the word) and criminally negligent.

It has been frequently recorded that on hearing of child abuse allegations during the Seventies and Eighties for example, instead of holding a thorough examination and bringing in the local police; the erring priest was frequently moved to another parish where he would then re-offend.

Even though Christ's teaching is very clear about the gravity of 'preventing one of these children from coming to Me' on many such occasions, the abusing person was sent away for counselling. The bishop listened to his lawyer and his secular-trained psychologists who at the time wrongfully believed that these perverted tendencies would disappear with a few years of counselling.

When it fully came out in the open what was happening, it became clear that some bishops were guilty of the ultimate betrayal, both to the innocent children as well as the teaching of the Church itself about protecting the innocent. On too many occasions a crime was covered up rather that investigated and dealt with properly.

In the Nineties when the extent of what was happening was exposed for all to see, many bishops who, up to this point, had been negligent regarding the rights of children and the harm that was being done, who failed to curb and prevent the wrongdoing to some clergy; turned instead to the other extreme. The bishops are now reacting to the stigma of failing to act properly in the past by acting in a way which can often lead to another injustice – the public humiliation of an innocent person.

As it now stands, the practice of the Church has moved from one extreme to another. Whereas before, it was the children who suffered, now it is the priests who are made the whipping boys in virtually all cases. Today, if there is an accusation of child abuse against a priest, no matter how unfounded, no matter how long ago, no matter how flimsy and uncorroborated with the testimony of others or of evidence, the priest is almost always publicly humiliated and his good name destroyed.

The document, 'Our Children, Our Church' subtitled, 'Child Protection Policies and Procedures for the Catholic Church in Ireland' was published by the Irish bishops in 2005. That document states on page 47 that "Where it is established that there are reasonable grounds for concern that child abuse has occurred, the Director of Child Protection shall, on behalf of the bishop or religious superior, or chairperson of the Church organisation, report the allegation to the civil authorities immediately."

The document does go into some detail on what is to be considered "reasonable grounds for concern." However, as the head of the National Conference of Priests of Ireland has pointed out, in practice, no matter how unconvincing or outrageous the allegation, the accused priest is nearly always asked to step down from his public ministry.

In an RTÉ Television interview on October 1, 2006 Archbishop Diarmuid Martin of Dublin said that he realised that he has angered some priests who say measures introduced are "over-strict" and often result in clergy being stood aside from ministry when they are innocent.

After describing how he felt "violently angry" on hearing stories of priests abusing children, Archbishop Martin added that, "The credibility of the Church has suffered. If I talk to parents about child sex abuse, they are horrified to imagine their own child at risk."

He said: "It is now a question of regaining confidence – and you have to earn it. I try to do that by having norms in place to deal with any future allegations. There have been priests taken out of ministry who are innocent. They can be very angry with me and have a right to be angry with me.

"I do believe that anyone in any caring profession against whom a reasonable accusation emerges should stand aside until that is fully investigated. That is because of the need to protect the most vulnerable, who are children, in this very painful process."

But he admitted: "Sometimes those who are innocent go through horrendous suffering and the assessments are extremely invasive."

On the *Liveline* show after the Paul Anderson case was heard (28/6/07), Phil Garland of the Child Protection Office for Dublin Archdiocese said that, according to the guidelines brought in within the last four years, a priest is not now asked to step down "automatically." He said he first has a meeting with the Gardai and Health Service officials. Priests and relations of priests who had been falsely accused and asked to step down strongly differed with this assessment on air.

From one extreme to another

Whereas before the children suffered while some bishops remained secure, and sometimes allowed the abusing priest to be chaperoned another parish or session of counselling, now things have moved to another extreme. While once again, the bishops remain safe and secure, the weakest allegation is currently accepted while priests are hung out to dry. Could you imagine the hurt and humiliation of an innocent man who has tried to do his best for others all his life, when he is asked to stop his public ministry as a priest?

If you were a priest, how would you feel as an innocent person when it is announced by your bishop that you have been asked to take leave until further notice?

It is the accepted principle of law that a person is innocent until proven guilty, but in this instance, that principle is suspended, almost reversed to become "guilty until proven innocent." Why does the principle of "innocent until proven guilty" apply to others, but not priests who are accused of wrong-doing? On this matter at least, could it now be a case of innocent until proven religious? It is a sad fact that by virtue of being asked to step down, without any proof of wrongdoing, a man has already been stripped of his right to his good name.

What is lost sight of is the principle that a person is regarded as innocent until proven guilty and secondly that in all instances, there must be due process.

Kicking a man out on the street on the first hearing of an allegation is not due process. It is a grave injustice. There should be public action taken against a person only when an investigation has shown there are grounds to believe the allegation against him/her is true.

But as it stands, a priest is asked to stand down almost automatically once an allegation is received. And it does not seem to matter how old the alleged incident, nor how flimsy the evidence to back it up. It is time that the pendulum of reaction came back to the middle once again; it has already spent too long at both extremes. Fr John Littleton, leader of the National Conference of Priest of Ireland in September 2005 said that he was aware of cases where a priest had been cleared by both civil and religious authorities following receipt of a child abuse allegation against him, but the bishop had decided not to restore him to his ministry.

Fr Littleton suggested that after a priest was found to be innocent after both Church and State investigations and the bishop still refused to allow him return to his ministry, "then in justice the priest would have every right to take an action against his bishop and sue him," he told *The Irish Independent*. He continued: "The basis for this is that every citizen has a right to his good name and to have that vindicated in a court of law."

According to a well documented article in the British Catholic journal, *The Tablet* of July 14, 2007, Vincent Nichols, Archbishop of Birmingham and man in charge of Copca (Catholic Office for the Protection of Children and Vulnerable Adults) acknowledged last year that an accused priest is unlikely ever to be reinstated. Of the 40 clergy accused of abuse in England and Wales by 2005, four had been dismissed, yet only two were restored to ministry. That is a lot of men left in limbo with their reputations destroyed.

Fr Beta in west Dublin insisted that his case go the whole way to court and his good name be vindicated. Perhaps that is the way to go, at least it shows those who make false allegations that there are consequences for the pain they cause to others.

14 Abuse Claims fall Flat

John F Kennedy's cousin is blackmailed

A climate has currently been created in Ireland where virtually any claim of abuse against a Catholic priest or religious is accepted at first hearing. This has left a number of individual priests open to blackmail attempts. A high profile example victim of this clerical blackmail is a relation of the famed Kennedy Clan in America.

Fr Michael Kennedy in Dunhill, Co Wexford was subjected to a malicious blackmail attempt by two brothers who were local gravediggers. He had on occasion helped them out financially when they said they were hard up; indeed, Fr Kennedy gave one of them, James Donovan money and a job.

Some years previously he had also given one of the brothers €200 when he claimed his mother had died, only to find out later that the lady in question was alive.

It emerged in court that James Donovan threatened to accuse Fr Kennedy of sexual assault unless he gave him €800. James Donovan claimed he needed the money to pay off a drug baron in Limerick. Nasty threats were made against Fr Kennedy by James Donovan who called the priest a pervert and a child abuser. The allegation was reported to his Bishop.

Judge Michael O'Shea and a jury heard in the court how Fr Kennedy had refused to pay over money to the two men and how he immediately contacted the gardai to set up a sting operation. When the two men arrived to pick up the money from Fr Kennedy, the gardai were on hand and this led to a frantic car chase through the local town and countryside. Yet, one of the brothers, Rossa Donovan still phoned Fr Kennedy on his mobile and told him he was "dead."

The two men were charged for the offence of demanding money with menaces from Fr Kennedy outside Dunhill Church on May 7, 2003. James Donovan (32), of Dungarvan with 38 previous convictions, pleaded guilty and received a two-year term, while his brother, Rossa Donovan (29), having 93 previous convictions, pleaded not guilty to the blackmail charge and was sentenced to three-and-a-half years imprisonment.

After the court case, Detective Garda Seamus Kavanagh read a statement explaining that Father Kennedy's absence in court was because he has "suffered torture for three years." The statement also said that Fr Kennedy felt priests to be easy prey: at the current time in Ireland, all a person had to do was make an allegation against a priest and he "was gone" and the Church had to pay out millions of euro. It was his opinion that what the Donovan brothers did to him was disgusting and that priests have no protection. Being honest, he said he found it difficult to forgive his blackmailers.

Nora Wall and her quest for justice

Late on a dark February evening, just three years ago in 2004, a thin middle-aged woman heard for the first time, that the DPP would not contest her application to the Irish High Court for a certificate of miscarriage of justice. Nora Wall, a former Mercy nun had, for a while, become the most despised and hated person in Ireland, the crime for which she was convicted repulsed the nation, as they read about it in the newspaper and heard it discussed on the radio. Her crime: the gang rape of a ten year-old girl was not, however, to pass into legal infamy. No, rather the monumental miscarriage of justice which she herself suffered was to be read in the headlines of many newspapers.

"Nailed to the Cross – not on the Hill of Calvary but on every TV screen and newspaper," was how she described her lot. "Instead of the inscription INRI [Jesus of Nazareth, King of the Jews], the replacements read 'beast,' 'sadist' 'evil' 'Mercy devil.' Yes, openly scourged and stripped of all humanity and dignity."

Nora Wall, formerly known as Sr Dominic, was sentenced by Judge
Paul Carney in June 1999 to life in prison after she was wrongly convicted of raping a ten year-old girl. She became for many the "face of
evil," in some respects, the new Myra Hindley.

"Hanging and dying on the cross – a jury verdict guilty of 11-1
brought a-free-for-all in the media. People 'planted' here and there from
the Four Courts shouting all kinds of abuse or obscenities to help the
cameramen snap a reactionary shot for more graphic headlines," she
wrote.

She had been accused in court of holding down the girl to be raped
by a man, Pablo McCabe, an alcoholic with severe mental problems,
"on an unknown date in 1987 or 1988."

The newspaper headlines that followed the charges were graphic
and sustained over many months. On the day of her sentencing (June
23, 1999) The *Star* had the headline, "I hope evil nun gets a long jail
term." *The Sunday World* trumpeted: "Rape Nun's Abuse Pact With [Fr
Brendan] Smyth."

Journalist Paul Williams in the July 11, 1999 edition of *The Sunday
World* wrote:

"EVIL NUN Nora Wall, convicted for helping to rape a ten-year-old
child, also secretly provided children for sick paedophile priest Father
Brendan Smyth.

"*The Sunday World* has learned that the depraved cleric regularly visited St Michael's Childcare Centre in County Waterford where Wall –
then known as Sister Dominic – was working. Last month Wall was the
first woman to be convicted of rape in Ireland.

"She was found guilty of helping to hold down a 10-year-old child
who was in her care while her drunken accomplice Pablo McCabe
raped her. Victims claim Evil Wall provided kids to the paedo priest.
Victims of evil nun Nora Wall have claimed that she provided children
to paedophile priest Father Brendan Smyth."

These allegations were completely untrue. She took *The Sunday
World* to court for libel and won libel damages of €175,000. The printed
apology took up a short single column on page three of the paper's
October 27, 2002 edition.

Concerning the original court case, Judge Paul Carney who sentenced both the accused, Wall and McCabe, went even further, describing the alleged action: "This was a gang rape" he thundered. "The leader of the gang was the only person in the world who was charged with the protection of Regina Walsh. I don't think I need to say more than that."

Nora Wall (51 at the time) was given a life term of 20 years, while her co-accused, Pablo McCabe was given a 12-year sentence. Sensationally, Wall became the first woman in the history of the Irish State to be found guilty of rape, and also the first person, male or female to receive a life sentence for that offence. Why was the sentence so harsh?

Taking a look at the cultural climate of the time may give a few pointers in the right direction. The TV documentary by Mary Raftery entitled *States of Fear* which claimed to reveal systematic child abuse in religious-run residential institutions had been broadcast shortly before and may have contributed to a climate where Catholic religious especially could, with impunity, be regarded as the source of evil crimes.

The editorial of *The Irish Times* (17/12/2005), in which Mary Raftery writes an opinion column commented that: "The charges were laid at a time when allegations of the abuse of children in institutions had entered the public domain. The case was heard within a month of the broadcast by RTÉ of the *States of Fear* programmes. The jury could not but have been affected, it seems, by the horrific abuse exposed in that series and by the complaints of the child victims that no-one listened to them."

One of Nora Wall's legal defence team privately suggested that she had been convicted in a climate of near hysteria created by the media. The three *States of Fear* programmes produced by Mary Raftery were broadcast on RTÉ, the national broadcaster in the Irish Republic, in April/May 1999. Nora Wall and Pablo McCabe were convicted in June and sentenced on 23 July 1999.

Nora Wall was to become the embodiment of all these despicable crimes, and the person who was to feel the backdraft of the hysterical climate of the day. When she was charged only a very small number of journalists held out the possibility that, just perhaps, she was innocent of the charges.

Born into a respectable and well-to-do farming family in 1948 she decided to join the Mercy Order in 1967. With them she worked in St Michael's Cappoquin, Co Waterford from 1975 to 1990, leaving her order in 1994. When she left St Michael's in 1992, an official from the then South East Health Board gave her a glowing reference: "Applicant is an extremely warm and caring personality with a natural flair for challenges. She is exceptionally kind and considerate with an outstanding character. Ms Nora Wall is a professional childcare worker whose abilities I have always found to be of the highest calibre."

It was during her time looking after children in this care facility that her problems originated. Regina Walsh, the girl who alleged she was raped had made previous allegations of rape against other people as did the prosecution witness, Patricia Phelan, who had also made unsubstantiated allegations of sexual assault against others, including her own father, her brother and an uncle.

Prompted by knowledge of her previous history, the DPP had declared that Phelan could not be called as a witness in similar cases ever again. This meant, that she should never have testified in the Wall/McCabe case. But she did.

The accuser originally claimed that she had been raped by both the accused on her 12th birthday. A date when Pablo McCabe was actually recorded as resident in a Dublin Hostel, awaiting entry to Mountjoy Jail. When this became apparent, another charge for another date was quickly brought before the court.

"My Way of the Cross couldn't have been more painful, extreme or despising," said Nora Wall. "Everything was there aplenty – cross, condemnations, nails, thorns, spears, sponge, towels, helpers, rejections, disowning, consolers, and public stripping and lashings by the media."

Between being convicted and being sentenced, journalist Mary Wilson of RTÉ ran a series of interviews with young people who had been cared for by Nora Wall. These young people were effusive in their praise. How could Wall, a woman who inspired so much love and respect in those who knew her, be guilty of rape? For the first time, questions were raised in the public mind. Well-known columnist,

Kevin Myers was one of the few to come to Wall's defence. This did not however, prevent the trial judge from calling her a "gang rapist" nor the national newspapers screaming obscenities at her such as 'Vile Nun,' 'Pervert Nun,' 'I was Raped by Anti-Christ,' etc.

Regina Walsh was interviewed in *The Star* newspaper on June 17, alleging that she had been raped by a coloured man up a side street from Leicester Square in London. By pure chance this was read by a Kilkenny man, Michael Fitzpatrick who recognised Phelan standing beside Walsh in the newspaper photograph. He had been a victim of a false allegation of sexual assault from Patricia Phelan, and so he approached Nora Wall's brother. When the defence brought Phelan's previous actions to the attention of the court, the case collapsed overnight.

After the two were in jail for four days their sentences were quashed. This dramatic turnabout took place after it emerged that the key prosecution witness had given damming evidence despite an instruction from the Director for Public Prosecution that, as an unfit witness, she should not have been permitted to do so.

The judge completely changed his judgement in light of the new revelation about the witnesses. Both accused were released from Mountjoy Prison immediately. The nation drew its breath. People did not know what to think. There was confusion at first. Nora Wall went back to her family home, where her brother Jim said he "never believed for a moment that Nora was guilty." But when his sister was found guilty earlier by the court he was "numb for half an hour."

Four days after being convicted and sentenced to life imprisonment, the DPP then conceded that Phelan should not have been called as a witness in the original trial to corroborate Walsh's account of the alleged rape. Nora Wall's brother-in-law, manager of the Waterford Ladies Football team, Michael Ryan, spoke of the devastation the guilty verdict and the life sentence had brought on the Wall family. "The hurt and the pain are indescribable," he said. "An innocent woman has been put through the mill and dragged through the courts and the mire."

The judgement of the Court of Criminal Appeal delivered on December 16, 2005 by Justice Kearns made very rough reading for the

Irish justice system. The court concluded that it did not, "find it necessary to distinguish in terms of gravity between the various newly-discovered facts which the court is satisfied show that there has been a
miscarriage of justice in this case. The prosecution which did take place
inasmuch as it involved the tendering of corroborative evidence by a
witness known to be unreliable was thus, in that format, a prosecution
that should not have been brought.

"There was further, a most unfortunate breakdown in communications or systems failure between the respondent's office, that of the
Chief State Solicitor, the Garda Síochana and prosecuting counsel
which the court is satisfied constituted a serious defect in the administration of justice brought about however unintentionally in this
instance by agents of the State."

It became clear that as part of the prosecution evidence "Regina
Walsh recalled the alleged episodes of rape by reference to 'flashbacks
and/or retrieved memory.'" Both young women had made multiple
allegations of rape against other people before this case.

After the trial, conviction and sentencing of Nora Wall, Patricia
Phelan "voluntarily made contact with Sr Mona Killeen, who had been
a lifelong friend and supporter, and admitted to her and subsequently
to members of An Garda Síochána also, that she had lied in her statement and in her evidence upon the trial of the applicant, in saying that
she had witnessed the involvement of the applicant in the alleged rape
and sexual assault of the complainant, Regina Walsh, when she had
not."

By November 1999 the DPP accepted "fully and ungrudgingly" that
both accused were to be presumed innocent of all the charges reined
against them. Patricia Phelan subsequently made a statement to gardai
in April 2001 admitting her previous statement and accusations were
false, and that her eyewitness account under oath in 1999 of seeing
Nora Wall rape a 10-year-old girl were lies.

In December 2005 at the Court of Criminal Appeal, Nora Wall was
successfully applied for a certificate declaring a miscarriage of justice.
Mr Justice Nicholas Kearns stated the court was satisfied that newly discovered facts showed that there had been a miscarriage in her case.

[The full discoveries of the criminal appeal can be found in Appendix 1 at the back of this book.]

Before Nora Wall received her certificate of a miscarriage of justice she wrote the following lines to those who supported her: "'Nothing is as strong as gentleness, and nothing as gentle as strength.' In time the reality of this 'trumped up case' brought its own truth. What a price to pay when you have been deemed guilty before you even get a chance of defence.

"From the first day of my arrest in October 1996 my journey to prove my innocence or bring any sense of sanity to such an allegation was a constant cul-de-sac. Imagine some family members reading in a national newspaper of an 'ex-nun from West Waterford difficult and uncooperative under investigation.' I wonder how that reporter got such information before I could travel to tell my family of my plight....

"My Thanks and Admiration will be forever with all who trudged and journeyed with me on my Way of the Cross. Grá agus buíochas anois agus i gcónaí (Love and thanks, for now and always)," wrote Nora Wall.

The Nora Wall case, as it was called in the media, garnered some amount of sympathy for the woman. However, while mentioned in passing, even more tragic is what happened in the life of Pablo McCabe. What befell both people was equally horrible, but it can also be noted that while Nora was a well educated woman from a strong, stable, and loving family; Pablo McCabe was a petty thief, an alcoholic, a homeless man who suffered from mental illness. He had got a rough deal all his life.

50-year-old Pablo had been diagnosed a schizophrenic. In court he was described by his own legal team as a "vagabond and hobo." He spent his early years in the care of the Sisters of Mercy in St Michael's, Co Waterford, and he regarded it as his home. That is why he repeatedly came back to it, a place of refuge and help. In evidence, he said that he was a regular visitor to St Michaels during the 1980s, and it was then that he first met Nora Wall as he was trying to trace his mother. He was totally innocent of any wrongdoing in this instance. But in the anti-Catholic hysteria that was whipped up at the time, he was counted as collateral damage. He was innocent of a crime he did not commit, yet it was never established how his signed confession came about.

Some high profile cases of false allegation around the globe

The woeful and totally inadequate handling of child abuse allegations in the past, in Ireland and America has led to a total reversal of the situation today where now absolutely any allegation tends to be believed and no matter how frivolous, given wide and lavish media coverage. A lie is half way around the world while truth is getting its boots is a humorous metaphor for what can happen in the current circumstances. Many high profile Catholic churchmen have been on the receiving end of false allegations, all of which received world-wide media coverage until they were found to be untrue.

Cardinal Edward Egan of New York in August 2002 was accused by a man of having sexually abused him when a boy in 1969. Egan publicly acknowledged the accusations but said they were "totally false and beneath contempt."

His accuser was found to have made similar accusations against 20 high profile figures in America including politicians of national stature. A police investigation publicly concluded in December 27, 2002 that they had, "found no credible evidence on which to proceed."

Archbishop George Pell of Sydney (before he was made cardinal) in a highly publicised case, stood aside in 2002 while a church inquiry investigated claims that he had sexually abused a 12-year-old boy in 1961. Pell denied his accusers allegation, saying they were lies. On August 20 of that year, a former Victorian Supreme Court judge investigated the claims and concluded there was insufficient evidence to back up the accusation that had been made.

Cardinal Joseph Bernadin of Chicago, before he died of cancer, was accused in late 1993 by a former Elder High School student of buggery during a pre-seminary programme. One year later, Steven Cook , the accuser, an AIDS sufferer, recanted the allegations and admitted publicly that he had invented them. That is a small sample of internationally high profile cases, but I return to some cases closer to home.

Declared innocent by a jury of his peers – Fr Edward Kilpatrick

Fr Edward Kilpatrick is a priest of Derry Diocese, and currently parish priest of Murlog, near Lifford in Co Donegal. At the age of 53, Fr Kilpatrick, an intelligent, quiet spoken yet straight-talking man, was accused by two former altar boys of sexually assaulting them during the period 1975-1982.

In 1995, the accusers, one a 30 year-old civil servant and the other a 32 year-old teacher went to the police to make these accusations. Both accusers, one of whom was quite publicly a homosexual, made an accusation which quickly led to 19 charges of gross indecency and indecent assault. Fr Kilpatrick remained resolute throughout the ordeal.

When the accusation were first made, he made a public announcement of the accusation from the pulpit at the highly attended Vigil Mass, assured his parishioners he was totally innocent and called for their support. He also invited the press to be present and told them he would fight the accusations all the way. The parishioners knew him and although shocked, the local people gave him their support. There was no hiding publicity on his part or avoiding hard questions. Indeed, he was very forthright throughout the whole episode, even voluntarily presenting himself to the RUC prior to the court hearing.

Virtually turfed out on the street by the local bishop after the accusations were first made, Fr Kilpatrick was formally asked by his bishop to stand down pending the outcome of police inquiries. There were many inconsistencies both within and between the stories of the two accusers. As it went to court, things were looking quite shaky for the priest.

However by pure chance, his defence lawyer met another solicitor in Co Antrim who advised the lawyer to hire a private detective and do a bit of research. This turned up the phone records of the two men and showed that the claimants, who were not supposed to know each other, had been in contact with each other and the prosecuting RUC – Northern Ireland police officer. Both accusers had also made preparations to take civil actions to claim compensation even before a verdict had been reached.

Amongst other evidence this all came out in court, and Fr Kilpatrick was cleared by a jury in Armagh Crown Court in May 1997. After 18 torturous court appearances over two years, there was finally a unanimous declaration of innocence. The judge commented that the case could have been thrown out on a number of technicalities but because the priest was a public figure, he let it go to full trial in order that he could be cleared by a jury of his peers and his reputation salvaged.

Paul Farrell: The effects of false abuse claims on my life

Former Christian Brother, Paul Farrell, received widespread sympathy after his conviction for child sexual abuse was overturned after six years in legal limbo. The 58 year old now-married man, had been found guilty of indecently assaulting a then 15-year-old boy in a Galway institution more than 20 years ago, and in July 2001 was sentenced to a year in jail by Dublin's Central Criminal Court.

A tall burly man who lives in Dublin, Mr Farrell had been convicted on two counts of indecent assault on dates between November 7th 1980, and March 31st, 1982, when he had worked as deputy director of St Josephs residential school, Salthill, Galway. However, allowed to appeal, he had been out on bail following this conviction.

Paul Farrell was suspended from his job as a teacher, at which he had worked for 32 years when he was first charged in August 1998. The allegations arose for the first time in January of that year. When he was convicted in July 2001 he immediately lost his job, was suspended without pay, and was forced to work in operative-type jobs.

He first met his wife, Marion when he worked in the Salthill residential institution, when she came to voluntarily take children out for visits. A relationship grew over time and he soon left the Christian Brothers to marry 21 years ago. They had a very difficult time in the early years of their marriage when their own child died at eight months of age.

The former Christian Brother appealed his conviction to the Court of Criminal Appeal which overturned his conviction on November 25, 2003. Following his acquittal in the Court of Appeal he was reinstated into his position as school principal, but because of the effects of his experiences he felt he could not continue in the position and opted for early retirement.

A number of grounds of appeal were advanced by the lawyers on behalf of Mr Farrell, during the hearing at the appeal court. The barrister claiming that the original trial judge had erred both in law and in fact.

Giving the judgement, the three judges, Mr Justice Geoghegan, presiding, with Mr Justice ONeill and Mr Justice Murphy, said the court would quash the conviction and there would be no retrial. The Court of Criminal Appeal found that the judge in the original trial had:

1. failed to warn the jury of the dangers where there was no corroborative evidence;

2. failed to raise with the jury, credibility issues that followed such a lapse of time between alleged events and allegations being made, and;

3. had presented speculation and conjecture as fair comment.

The initial reaction of Paul Farrell to this event was first one of relief. From the day the allegation first arose, he said his life had changed dramatically. After the allegations and the publicity it generated, he found it, he said, "impossible to interact socially." He became afraid of being near other people's children. If he went to see a film at the cinema with his wife, and a 10 year-old boy sat down beside them, he felt he had to move, all for fear of allegations being made.

He felt, due to his experience, that he had lost the ability to interact with children, such was the damage that had been inflicted on him by the allegation. As he could no longer function as a teacher, his career was brought to a sudden end.

For a couple that loved children, who used to take groups of children off to the Marian shrine of Lourdes, and take in an autistic boy from a nearby foster home at weekends for five years; it all had to stop. They loved children, and it was it was extremely painful.

For Marian and Paul Farrell's lives will never be the same again. Despite the overturning of convictions against Paul in the Court of Criminal Appeal, their relief at the judgement could not mask the damage that had been done and their anger at the injustice of it all. Here are Paul's own words, as he offers help to those being dragged through a similar situation:

Being Falsely Accused – It Was A Living Death

"I am sure, like me, you will never forget what you were doing when you got that phone call from gardai or your solicitor. I was cooking a chicken stir fry at a quarter to seven on the evening of the Monday after the Omagh bombing. I was never to feel the normal peace or tranquillity that goes with the satisfaction of doing a days work in my school ever again. A terrible beast had been born.

"An interview with gardai propels you into a world where you have shameful things thrown at you in spite of the fact that you always prided yourself on being a relatively successful and dedicated teacher, parent and ordinary decent citizen of a State you had pride in. Now that State had become a beast that was going to squeeze the life out of you. It drags you into more interviews, has you arrested and brands you a criminal no matter how innocent you are. It forces you to make journeys across the country and sit in alien courts only to tell you after hours of waiting, the date of the next hearing.

"At home the beast has moved into your house. Having been suspended from your school you have all day to live in his shadow. Going out, you wonder who is looking at you and what are they thinking. In town you try to distract yourself in book shops, libraries, cinemas but it does not work because the beast keeps following you. Seeing a garda car, you are sure it is about to stop for you, they want another interview, they have more allegations. You walk about looking at the ground in front of you because that allows people that you know avoid you, while protecting yourself from the embarrassment of knowing they are there at all.

"Your personal life at home has died. You don't laugh with your wife anymore. If you have school-going children you shudder to think what they are going through but you are helpless to change the situation for them. The beast is in charge.

In my case the situation descends into hell when I am appearing in the Circuit Court in front of a judge who may pander to a jury recently educated by *States of Fear*. The result is a foregone conclusion, conviction. The original trial judge remains the 'honourable' and I become the convicted and the whole country knows about it through newspapers and television.

"Fortunately there are some honourable men in the Four Courts and they grant me an appeal. Two and a half years later I win the appeal on multiple grounds where the honourable judge had misdirected the jury. I was now free and what a relief. But it's a short lived relief. Long delays follow in waiting to be restored to my position only to find I am too traumatised to ever stand in a school again. Effectively my career is at an end and I am left with the only option open to me; seek early retirement and see my career prematurely ended.

"The state of shock and fear that my wife and I have lived under for six years has now turned to anger. The social workers who dealt with my accuser who made the allegation, still have their careers. The detective guards who I believe [maybe] failed to conduct a proper investigation failed also in guarding me against a false allegation. The DPP who went with the media flow after *States of Fear* still earns his salary. Having being dealt with so unfairly by the institutions of the State I once had faith in and respected, the experience leaves me with a very cynical attitude to Health Boards, Gardai, DPP and the court systems.

"This is only a short resume of the last six years. We are trying hard to replace the anger and cynicism and I think we will succeed through the help of friends who have stood by us all through our encounter with the beast. Just in the last two weeks a new kind of peace has begun to dawn after a holiday in the Far East. Perhaps it taught us that the world is not all bad and that while there might be 'something rotten in the state of ...' Ireland. It is just some things, and not all things. There are good people living in this state also whose voices are beginning to be heard above the rot and with the assurance of the truth behind them their voices will become louder and prevail.

"Coming as we do from a Christian tradition perhaps it's at times like this that we get the strength of faith. Being falsely accused is like a Good Friday; hopeless, helpless and tempted to end it all. But we have been promised an Easter Sunday. While for many of us, the time between the Friday and Sunday is a weekend that goes on for years we have lived in the faith and hope that it would finally come and just now I feel there is a dawning happening."

You would think once the trial is over, and any conviction is quashed that Paul Farrell's trauma would be over. Shortly after the Court of Criminal Appeal threw out the criminal conviction, Mr Farrell received a letter from the Redress Board that the same person making the same allegation had made a claim to the Board seeking redress/compensation.

This author has seen the document. Believe it or not, this is all totally legal and above board in Ireland. A person is prevented from taking a civil action and then seeking money from the Redress Board as well, but an accuser is entitled to take part in a criminal action and then seek money from the Redress Board. The same allegation can be thrown out in a Criminal Court in Ireland, but unchanged, be pulled out of a hat again before the Redress Board. Is that justice? I think not.

Paul's wife Marian told this author when we met in Swords, north County Dublin in February 2007 that they were so upset and traumatised by their experience that both had seriously contemplated suicide. She recalled that she came home from work one day, and said: "Sometimes I feel I should take the car and drive it into the River Liffey, so the water will give us peace." To which her husband, Paul, replied: "I never thought I would hear you say that, but I have thought so many times of taking an overdose of tablets and putting an end to it."

That two people would think like this, even momentarily, shows the trauma they have suffered.

State owes falsely accused an apology said Senator

Farrell's treatment did not go unnoticed however. After the wrongful conviction for juvenile abuse was overturned, a senator from the Progressive Democrat Party, Tom Morrissey, called on the State to apologise unreservedly to the former Christian Brother. The senator said that the overturning of Mr Farrell's conviction raised some serious questions about the manner in which this case was conducted.

"Paul Farrell and his wife," he said, "have been robbed of six years of their life together and their careers have been destroyed. Mr Farrell has no redress against his former accuser. His life has effectively been destroyed and the State must help him try and put the pieces back together."

Speaking on Wednesday 26th November 2003, Senator Morrissey said, "The State owes Paul Farrell an apology or at the very least an acknowledgement of the serious deficiencies that occurred in the investigation of this case. Members of the gardaí and a number of State officials also have, I believe, serious questions to answer. Justice demands that in a civilised democracy, when the State makes a mistake it should own up and pay the price. Paul Farrell, who gave 30 years service caring for the unwanted in our society, deserves no less."

Senator Morrissey also tried to raise the matter in the Senate the day after this statement, but the Speaker of the House (*An Cathaoirleach*) refused to allow the issue even to be debated. It is an interesting issue that he raises:

Mr Morrissey: "I wish to raise the issue of the overturning of the conviction of a former Christian Brother, Paul Farrell, two days ago by the Court of Criminal Appeals."

An Cathaoirleach: "We do not have any control over the courts."

Mr Morrissey: "I have a question for the Leader on this. Paul Farrell gave 30 years of his life to teaching in an institution and was principal of an inner city school in Dublin. He was convicted on the flimsiest of evidence and the judge was found to have erred in three matters of fact ..."

An Cathaoirleach: "I do not think we can discuss rulings of the courts. The judiciary is independent and we cannot discuss its rulings."

Mr Morrissey: "That is not the point I am making. Some years ago, the Taoiseach rightly made a full apology to victims of institutional abuse in this country. This case is an example of similar institutional abuse of a former Christian Brother. I ask the Leader to consider asking the Taoiseach if he will make an apology to people who have been similarly abused by the institutions of this State."

A few did abuse, but not all are therefore guilty

On the same day that Paul Farrells conviction was quashed, Christian Brother Maurice Tobin (71) was jailed for 12 years when he pleaded guilty to sexually abusing 25 boys at Letterfrack Industrial School between 1959 and 1974.

Judge Kenny, in his judgement commented that Tobin had been involved in violently sexually assaulting the boys and young men and he wondered why this sex abuse was allowed to go unchecked.

Galway Circuit Court heard Br Maurice Tobin plead guilty to what was described as 'a shocking litany of sexual abuse' – 23 cases of indecent assault and two of buggery. He was obviously quite prolific, and 16 of Tobins victims were in the court. Seven of the young men gave evidence that their lives had been destroyed.

The Christian Brothers in a statement, said they deeply regretted the hurt and pain caused to those who were abused by Brother Tobin. They were greatly saddened and the Order offered its sincere apologies to those who had been abused and to their families. Superintendent Tony Dowd of Clifden, outlined the type of abuse each of the 25 victims suffered at the hands of the accused – now found guilty and convicted.

Murder most horrid – damning accusations without foundation

Letterfrack was a reformatory industrial school run by the Christian Brothers in Connemara, in the west of Ireland. Due to the constant media onslaught of many years, it is in the eyes of many, a name synonymous with beatings, brutality and according to a number of prominent commentators, murder.

A large number of allegations were made about Christian Brothers in Letterfrack. Some of the accusations being quite horrendous, and very public. Kathy OBeirne, as mentioned earlier in the book, said on national radio that "hundreds and hundreds and hundreds of bodies buried on the lands of the Magdalene laundries all around Dublin and around the country, and in Letterfrack. And they did not die from being undernourished. A lot of these children were murdered."

In an interview in *The Sunday Independent* on December 22, 2002, playwright and actor Mannix Flynn spoke of his time in Letterfrack. He was promoting his new play, 'James X' that was about to begin in Dublin's Project Arts Centre. A well-known actor and activist, with a very troubled early life, Flynn had been previously classed as "criminally insane."

Flynn told journalist Bridgid McLaughlin that, "The State has failed me and my fellow travellers. We need Mary Robinson to look into it. When you're in a place like Letterfrack, all past life disappears. Your soul and spirit are murdered in a matter of minutes. When you sleep at night you think of the young boys murdered in the grass below you. And their graves are everywhere. Kids murdered for no reason, and buried like dogs all over the 5,000 acres of Letterfrack wilderness.

"We now know that the 125 headstones, with names and ages from 10 to 17, are only a fraction of those killed. Does anyone care in a State we call civilised? Will there be a tribunal? It is doubtful. One wonders who cares about unwanted children anyway? A priest who abuses and brutalises kids for up to 40 years is released after serving a year. Why? On humanitarian grounds! Where is the humanity for the special needs kids murdered in Connemara? We all know their death has been dreadful."

In the picture caption, Flynn was quoted as saying: "It's a holocaust we're dealing with. In every bit of land around Letterfrack there is a child buried."

Holocaust, murder, secret burials, boys buried like dogs all over Letterfrack – surely that is an understatement! But he isn't finished yet:

"I was 11 when I was sent to Letterfrack industrial school. Letterfrack in beautiful Connemara was this State's idea of a Special School for Special Needs. The only thing special about it was its exalted position as the monster terror hole of subhuman abuse of children. For me, it was a completely traumatic experience. The warrant for me to go to Letterfrack wasn't even signed. The whole apparatus for sending children to Letterfrack was illegal.

"A lot of lies and death certificates just disappeared. It was an inhospitable and shockingly degrading place, 250 miles from Dublin. I was scared shitless, coming across hundreds of young fellas who never saw you before. There were 170 boys, five brothers and about seven or eight others employed there. They had their own sort of regime. It was like being pulled out of the Rotunda [area in Dublin] and put into a major war zone. That was the kind of life it was.

"Every night, we all cried out for our mammies and daddies. *I can still hear the bloodcurdling screams.* I was in Letterfrack for two years, they don't let you out for Christmas until after the first year."

In May 1999, Mannix Flynn took part in Mary Raftery's documentary for RTÉ called *States of Fear*. In this hugely influential campaigning programme, Flynn talked about how there was usually blood in the yard from children being beaten around it. But in this *Sunday Independent* interview he was to go much further:

"On the very day I arrived in Letterfrack one of the brothers orally raped me. It was savage. Horrible," he says. A few weeks later, another brother beat him with a leather strap for smoking. Later that night, the same brother brought him to his dormitory, stripped his pyjamas and lashed Mannix for an hour. "By sending me there, the State facilitated this rape, this torture," he says. "One night, one of the employees came to my bed and took me into the toilets.

"I was half asleep and didn't know what to do. He threatened me and held me by the hair, he held his hand over my mouth and he anally raped me. The threat and fear of violence emanated from the whole building. On a daily basis you'd see some child savagely beaten to a pulp by a grown up, flogged on the windpipe with a truncheon. It was like something out of *Schlinder's List*. You weren't just clipped on the ear, you were beaten until you were turned into whimpering simpletons," he says, "and to think that this was all enabled by the Gardai. And this is only the tip of the iceberg.

"The whole point for people to realise now is that hundreds of children were locked away in Letterfrack, *hundreds of children were raped and murdered. It's a holocaust we're dealing with. In every bit of land around Letterfrack there is a child buried.* My only solace in Letterfrack was when I could wander into a field. We farmed for all the brothers and the locals. I'm a good man with a pitchfork," he says drily, "I know more about balers, barley and cows than you could imagine. The brothers had the cheapest labour in Ireland.

"*The gardai in Clifden, fair play to them, uncovered a massive paedophile ring* and it ran from the low minions right up to the top. These gardai who investigated this took it upon themselves to work very seriously on it. It's unfortunate that their efforts have yielded such little return. I saw the incident room in Clifden garda station myself. There were thousands of old files with corroborative statements. The public haven't got a clue what's really going on."

It is hardly possible to make up greater accusations than these. And it was not the only time he did it. Over a number of years, Mannix Flynn has made the same blood libels on the national airwaves. Vociferously shouting down any opposition he met on the way. But don't think for a second, that he is regarded as some loose canon by the State. Indeed, as a reward for his artistic ability, a few weeks after this interview Mannix Flynn was elected a member of Aosdana, the select national association of creative artists; and later again, in January 2004, was made a Director of the Irish Museum of Modern Art. He has had a high profile in a number of State-funded art projects.

Bruce Arnold's claim of boys buried in the woods

Nor is he alone in making these allegations. He was one of a very active unit of movers and shakers. English-born and Dublin-based newspaper columnist, Bruce Arnold has made sweeping criticisms of the Christian Brothers, hurling horrendous accusations at them in print over a number of years.

For Bruce Arnold, "There were not just 'bad times', or 'bad people'; the savage, unrelenting cruelty was systematic, constant and comprehensive....[Peter Tyrell, a former resident of Letterfrack] was caught up in a system where his incarceration was really not much different from the Stalinist gulags." (*The Sunday Independent* November 19th 2006).

Three years previously on June 16, 2003, Arnold claimed that in Letterfrack, "We know now that the total [number who died in Letterfrack] is much higher and boys are buried in the woods as well." Hefty charges indeed, but Flynn and Arnold are joined by a vocal and influential crowd of assorted activists, journalists and campaigners.

In response to allegations made earlier, the Gardai had set up a special investigation centre in Clifden, Co Galway to which seven gardai were assigned on a full time basis for over two years from November 1999 to the summer of 2002.

It was by any standards, a huge operation, in relation both to man-hours and expense. The police force carried out an extensive trawl of all

records, interviewing past residents and local people of Letterfrack who
had any interaction with the school. The gardai also physically dug up
numerous areas in Letterfrack, including those areas where it had been
alleged boys were clandestinely buried. Following an exhaustive search,
in January 2003, Superintendent Tony O'Dowd told *The Irish Catholic*
that "there is no evidence available that would suggest that foul play led
to the deaths of anybody buried inside or outside of the cemetery at the
old Industrial School in Letterfrack." The Superintendent added that
"there was no evidence of a mass grave." Local people who know the
area also concurred in this evaluation.

The high profile set of accusations involving the Christian Brothers
in Letterfrack was comprehensively exposed as a macabre and sinister
fabrication by the gardai whose investigation did not yield a shred of
evidence to support the allegations. Indeed the Garda statement was
unambiguous in rejecting the newspaper accusations. But this news
got just a small amount of space in the national papers and barely made
a ripple on the national radio and TV stations.

Responding to the allegations made by Mannix Flynn, Br Edmund
Garvey, the communications director for the Christian Brothers, wrote
a letter to *The Sunday Independent* on January 12, 2003 refuting his rant.
Garvey contradicted Flynn's interview writing:

"It is certainly not true to state that young boys were murdered in
Letterfrack. The claim that the gardai in Clifden 'uncovered a massive
paedophile ring in Letterfrack is also untrue. This can be checked with
the gardai in Clifden. It follows, therefore, that it is not true to say that
'boys murdered' were 'buried like dogs all over the 5,000 acres of
Letterfrack wilderness. All who died are buried in the cemetery there or
in cemeteries elsewhere. No boy died in Letterfrack while Mannix
Flynn was there in 1968-1969. The last boy to die there was buried in
the cemetery in 1942.

"Surely it is fair to expect that journalists would check the truth of all
claims. Your newspaper was supplied by the Christian Brothers with
clear information concerning the boys who died and were buried at
Letterfrack. The date, place and cause of every death are all fully documented. That information has been supplied to the gardai and is avail-

able for every appropriate authority or person who needs access to it."

A body under every bush scenario as painted by some of the protagonists above turned out to be false. Yet over many months the specious allegations got huge coverage not only in print but on radio as well.

It is now time for people like Bruce Arnold who has written that boys are buried in the woods etc. to produce the hard evidence, ie. the bodies, for these accusations or withdraw and apologise for making them in the first place.

Even more macabre accusations about Letterfrack

Even worse accusations than those of Mannix Flynn, were made in an explosive article in *The News of the World* by journalist Áine de Paor on September 22, 2002. Allegations were made that boys whose death were not officially registered were buried in mass graves. That "Dead boys were simply wrapped in blankets and dropped in lime which quickly dissolved their bodies, wiping out any trace that they ever existed."

Using language, which if used for other faith or ethnic groups could possibly be classed as incitement to hatred, such as "Sinful and pitiless Christian Brothers with blood on their hands wilfully concealed the deaths of boys entrusted to their care. ....UnGodly Brothers who ruled with an iron fist secretly buried ten lads in an unmarked grave."

It is "twisted clerics" who were in charge of "the shameful Letterfrack hellhole."

"To their eternal shame the secretive Brothers only finally owned up to the clandestine cemetery in 1969 when a single headstone was erected IN THE DEAD OF NIGHT!!!" The grave, *The News of the World* said was in use up to 1956. One of its most famous residents, it claims was "Murdered gangster Martin 'The General' Cahill [who] was sent there as a lad and later put his shocking brutality down to what he learned from Brothers he called the mad monks."

But not to be outdone in the same article, farmer Mick Connors (53), is quoted as saying, "ferocious beatings were meted out to pupils and there's no doubt that some boys died as a result. Whenever I hear natural causes given as a reason I immediately think they were kicked to death."

Must have been quite a place: murders, secret burials at the dead of night, wrapped in blankets and buried furtively in quick lime. Hardly a place for an education! The gardai were not quoted in the article. If the newspaper had contacted the gardai prior to this article, it would have heard a completely different story.

And as for the Christian Brothers receiving a retraction of the same allegations made by the persons above, it was a case of dream on. The Brothers refuted the allegations in toto, saying Martin Cahill was never in Letterfrack, a headstone had not been erected at night, all boys had received full Christian burial and most importantly that the deaths of the 17 boys cited had all been recorded. Indeed, the State would have been notified of each boy's death at least twice. Each boy who died in Letterfrack received full medical attention and their death was accounted for.

Mick Connors, goes on to say in the *News of the World* article: "Pupils like myself came back to visit the place and read their friends' names on the headstone. It was a terrible shock."

According to the Christian Brothers: "This man was a pupil at the school from 1959 until 1963. Seventeen years before he arrived in Letterfrack the last boy died and was buried there in 1942. Records show that no boy died while this man was a pupil at the school. No one had, in fact, died there since 1942. The claim made by this same former pupil that 'there's no doubt that some boys died as a result of ferocious beatings' is completely without foundation."

Patsy Flanagan – the boy killed three different ways

Artist and writer Mannix Flynn had appeared in the *States of Fear* series on RTÉ written and directed journalist Mary Raftery. A former engineering student at UCD in the Seventies, who spent a lot of her time heavily involved in extreme Left-wing political causes, Raftery was effusive and proud of *States of Fear* which provoked such huge public response. The three part documentary depicted a certain take on industrial schools run by the religious orders in Ireland as singularly terrible places full of sexual abuse and physical cruelty.

Currently a journalist with *The Irish Times*, she then boasted that, "outrage at the crimes committed against these children was expressed continuously for the three weeks of the series, across acres of newsprint and hours of radio broadcasts all over the country." (second edition *Suffer Little Children* intro page 3) After her series was aired, a national outcry ensued, leading to Taoiseach Bertie Ahern's apology on behalf of the State on the day the third and final episode was shown (May 11, 1999).

She also wrote a book with co-author Dr Eoin O'Sullivan entitled, *Suffer the Little Children: The Inside Story of Ireland's Industrial Schools.* Containing explosive new claims of abuse and punishment, it was published in November 1999. On page 233 of her book, Mary Raftery states the following about the death of a boy, Patsy Flanagan in a Christian Brother Industrial school, Artane, a suburb on Dublin's north side:

"There are a number of accounts from survivors, of deaths of children in mysterious or unexplained circumstances. The *States of Fear* documentaries contained accounts from some of these. One was from Barney O'Connell of the death of a boy in Artane Industrial School. Barney had been detained there during the 1950s, and this child had fallen 40 feet to his death through an internal stairwell. The boy fell past Barney who was on the stairs, almost touching him as he passed.

"It is an image, which he can never forget, he says, and he will not rest until he receives a proper explanation for the boy's death. The Christian Brothers have stated that a boy did indeed die in this manner in Artane during the 1950s, but that it was an accident resulting from the childrens exuberance following a visit to the circus. Once again, no records whatsoever exist on this case in the Department of Education."

The boy falling was an image O'Connell said, he would never forget. However, just after the book was published, Mary Raftery's star witness Barney O'Connell gave a startling interview to *The Sunday Independent* on November 7, 1999. Journalist John Drennan reported O'Conell's story:

"Bernard O'Connell was one of the children in Artane. He was present when a child was thrown over the banisters and fell through an atrium and two 60-foot-high floors. His trauma went beyond the mere witnessing of that event. Bernard was an apprentice carpenter.

"The day after the event, he and between 12 and 15 boys were sent with a workman to repair the hole the boy had made when falling through the atrium. As they brought in the scaffolding they could see a sheet covering something. It was a small pool of blood and guts where the boy had fallen through the atrium. The workman turned and said quietly: 'Barney, go down to the shop, get some sawdust and a bucket and sweep this up.'

"The boy went down to the shop. He swept the blood and guts up into a metal dustpan, placed that into a metal dustbin with the blood-soaked sheet and then put it into the fire. At night he still 'wakes up screaming' at the memory."

Barney O'Connell then went on to make further allegations about the most feared Christian Brother who "didn't just like to f**k you, he liked to beat you within an inch of your life." That gives a flavour, but let's concentrate for a while on the death of Patsy Flanagan.

Soon after this article, a senior Christian Brother, Br M. Reynolds countered with a letter on behalf of the Provincial leadership, stating his desire to point out serious inaccuracies in the account of Patsy Flanagan's death. In *The Sunday Independent* November 21, 1999, Br Reynolds countered:

"The facts, in summary form, are as follows: a boy who was sliding down the banister of the stairs slipped and fell to the ground about 14 feet below. He had external injuries to his mouth and jaw and was taken to the school infirmary. One hour later he was removed to the Mater Hospital, where he died under anaesthetic the following day.

"The external injuries, as described in the coroner's report, consisted of 'a lacerated wound' on the lower lip, 'superficial skin lacerations and bruises on the lower jaw in the region of the chin' and four broken teeth. The matter was reported to the authorities at the time, and an inquest was held. Sworn evidence was taken from eyewitnesses, doctors and a garda sergeant.

"The Coroners verdict was that the boy had died of 'cardiac and respiratory failure, secondary to acute congestion of the lungs following the injuries accelerated by general anaesthesia and probably predisposed to by the presence of an enlarged thymus gland. The garda, in his evidence to the inquest, stated that 'there is no suspicion of foul play.' The Coroner stated that the Brothers had exercised adequate supervision. The truth is that no boy was thrown over the banister."

Br M. Reynolds.

Not to be outdone, Mary Raftery's witness, Barney O'Connell, now living in California, wrote a letter back to the newspaper the following week, in which he stood over his claim about what happened in Artane:

"I hereby reaffirm my statement to John Drennan. I saw a child being physically beaten by an Irish Christian Brother on the stairwell leading to dormitory number one. This child was running away down the metal staircase with a very angry brother hitting the child's back with his leather strap and shouting in anger to 'stop.' The brother pushed the child into the landing wall. The child, literally fleeing for his life now, bounced off this wall, spinning kitty-corner on the metal stairs landing, and both the child and the Christian Brother crashed into me.

"I was knocked backwards and downwards, and I fell down several stairs. The kinetic energy of the child colliding into me slowed the child's speed down; the Christian Brother, trying to hit, slap, grab the child, collided into the child, pushing/shoving/throwing the poor child over the banisters stair-rail. Being about seven feet above the first-floor main landing, the child fell about 40 feet onto the ground floor below. This area was known as the long hall. This happened in the winter of 1956."

Bernard 'Barney' O'Connell, in *The Sunday Independent*, 12 December 1999.

Three versions of boys death

Did you notice anything unusual in the correspondence? Br Reynolds certainly thought he did and pointed it out in his reply the next week:

"Sir, Mr O'Connell stands by his story. Which one? He has now presented the public with no fewer than three different versions of this event. In one version the boy fell 40 feet, brushing past Bernard and almost touching him. In the second version the boy was actually thrown over the banister by a Brother and fell a distance of 120 feet. In this account, Mr O'Connell describes external injuries which are totally at variance with the injuries described by the surgeon in the Mater Hospital and by the pathologist.

"The third version given by Mr O'Connell states that both the boy and a Brother crashed into Bernard, knocking him down several steps. He finishes his third account by stating that the event took place in the winter of 1956. In fact, the sad accident occurred on February 18, 1951. The factual account of what happened is contained in the coroners report, the contents of which were outlined in my original letter. The coroner's report states clearly that no foul play was suspected and that there was adequate supervision in place at the time of the accident. The records show that no other boy resident of Artane died in the 1950s."

Br M Reynolds (*Sunday Independent* 19 December 1999).

When this correspondence started off, Breda O'Brien who was then a *Sunday Business Post* columnist, did some serious research over a weekend and made her finding known on the *Pat Kenny Show* on RTÉ radio. O'Brien had got hold of the coroner's report referring to the boys. The veracity of the account of Patsy Flanagan's death in Mary Raftery's book wasn't just called into question, the account was publicly traduced.

O'Brien pointed out that just like her article, the coroner's report of Patsy Flanagan's death was freely available in the public domain for those willing to look. In the *Sunday Business Post* of November 28, 1999, she wrote: "A simple visit to Artane, where the boy who died is publicly commemorated, combined with a visit to the coroner's office, would have revealed that the coroner's report says that the boy fell 14 feet, had no visible external injuries except facial ones, that sworn testimony was taken and foul play was not suspected. It would have been the author's prerogative to cast doubts on the validity of the coroner's report. But to be unaware of or to omit the existence of a coroner's record is completely unacceptable."

The big guns were wheeled out, other journalists like Colm Toibin and Fintan O'Toole mobilised to defend Raftery, saying she did not have access to the Christian Brother archive. But the coroner's report did not come from their archive anyway.

Raftery responded claiming O'Brien had privileged access to records from the Christian Brothers rather than from the public record. Raftery wrote (in *The Irish Times* 13/1/2000) that, "several former inmates of Artane, eye-witnesses to the tragedy, continue to believe that questions need to be answered with regard to this death."

"It is relevant to note," she added, "that this particular incident now forms part of the extensive Garda investigation into the hundreds of allegations of severe physical and sexual abuse of boys by Christian Brothers at Artane up to the late 1960s."

Raftery was challenged about these statements on Eamon Dunphy's *Last Word* radio programme. It was put to Raftery that the Garda Press Office had confirmed that this incident had been investigated previously, it was no longer the subject of investigation, and would not be in the future unless new evidence were to emerge.

Mary Raftery's response to this information was: "This is complete rubbish. This is rubbish. This is rubbish."

With regard to the coroner's report itself, Br M Reynolds (in a letter to *The Irish Times* on December 22, 1999) wrote pointedly that Raftery's witness in her book, who had already given three different accounts of the same incident describes injuries, "which are totally at variance with the injuries described by the surgeon in the Mater Hospital and by the pathologist.

"The witness states that the event took place in the winter of 1956. In fact the sad event occurred on February 18th, 1951."

The evidence at the inquest which formed the contemporary coroner's verdict, as Reynolds clarified, did not come from the Brothers alone. A garda sergeant, a surgeon, a pathologist and a student who witnessed the accident also gave evidence. This journalist has a copy of all those reports before him as he writes.

A section of the report by sergeant Jeremiah Murphy in Raheny Station dated February 19, 1952 states: "The sergeant interviewed James Timmins, aged 16 years, another inmate of the Institution who informed the sergeant that he was standing on the stairs at about 8.30pm on the 18/2/1951, acting as a steward, he saw all the boys go up the stairs and go into their dormitory. The deceased after entering the dormitory returned again and asked Timmins 'Did you ever see a Circus trick?'

"He then leant his body on the hand rail, slid downwards for a short distance when he seemed to overbalance and fall face forward to the floor below a distance of 14 ft 8 ins. Timmins lifted him up and he saw deceased put his hand to his left side as if he was hurt and then asked Timmins where were his teeth, who on examination found three of the deceased's teeth broken in his front upper jaw. There is no suspicion of foul play by the Gardai...."

At the inquest carried out by the coroner for the City of Dublin, statements were taken from a range of people. One completed by P Mac Auley on 20th February 1950 said that, "An operation for the injury to his lips and gum was deemed necessary, and was performed by me at about 12.30am on 19th February 1951. The anaesthetic was given by Dr Hugh Raftery, resident anaesthetist...."

The further report by Doctor Maurice Hickey came after his post-mortem. The final Inquest report stated that Patsy Flanagan died "from cardiac respiratory failure secondary to an acute congestion of the lungs, accelerated by general anaesthetic, probably predisposed by the presence of an enlarged thymus gland." The City coroner concluded that, "I regard the supervision of the Brothers as adequate."

What can be said about this case? As the lawyers say – *Res ipsa loquitor* – reality speaks for itself. Patsy Flanagan's death was very unfortunate. It happened, according to contemporary evidence, in a very different manner from accounts espoused in Mary Raftery's book and claims made in the national press that a Christian Brother had pushed Patsy Flanagan over the bannister to his death. A blood libel too far? But it wasn't to be the last.

Incidentally, the Christian Brother who was on duty that day in the corridor, has been so traumatised by the allegation and innuendo that he has been receiving psychiatric help since the allegation arose.

Artane: funerals of the undead

Patrick Walsh is a leading member of Survivors of Child Abuse (SOCA Ireland), an active and very vocal group which campaigns on behalf of those who claim to have survived abuse.

In an interview with Patsy McGarry, the religious affairs correspondent for *The Irish Times*, in an article entitled, 'Artane Boys faced the music – and the straps' on 25 September 1999, Mr Walsh tells of his experiences in Artane under the care of the Christian Brothers. He claimed it was very violent. Therefore, part of the article says that, "The man in charge of the infirmary would get extremely agitated when boys came in clutching their stomachs after being punched by Christian Brothers. He was afraid of appendicitis.

"Patrick recalled two funerals of boys who had been rushed to the Mater Hospital with "acute appendicitis."

"Not yet in the band proper," the article continues, "Patrick was also beaten. Records say that between October 1963 and October 1964 he was detained in the infirmary five times. Each followed bad beatings."

None too pleased, the provincial leader of the Christian Brothers in the Northern part of Ireland, Br J. K. Mullan shot back with a brusque letter on October 9, 1999.

Noting with "deep regret and disbelief the seriously misleading article" that the Christian Brothers had read, he said it was outrageous that he had not been contacted for his comment on the allegations, nor had the simple facts been checked before publication.

Br Mullan pointed out: "The implication is that the boys who were beaten and seriously injured by the Brothers were then dispatched to hospital where they died. The use of quotation marks around the words "acute appendicitis" seems to imply that the boys died from some other cause. The fact of the matter is that no boy resident in Artane died while Patrick Walsh was there."

He also revealed that, "the records for Artane Industrial School show that Patrick Walsh was never admitted to the infirmary during that period stated." [in the article]

The Irish Times editor of the day, Mr Connor Brady wrote back to apologise for the "procedural oversight occurred as a result of which Mr. Walsh's allegations were not put to the Christian Brothers in advance of publication." While expressing regret and correcting the errors that had been made, he added that, "A further error took place in citing Mr Walsh's dates of admission to the infirmary. Artane records show that he was admitted four times between October 1964 and October 1965."

Patrick Walsh did not then disappear off the scene, but was even cited as an authority about Artane in a recent *Irish Independent* news article. (24/8/ 2007)

Responding to a letter from Mr Jim Higgins T.D., (a member of the Irish House of Parliament), the Minister for Justice of the day, Mr John O'Donoghue T.D. wrote back on 7 December 1999:

"I have been informed by the Garda authorities that an investigation team has been set up to examine allegations in relation to Artane. All allegations of physical and sexual abuse are being thoroughly investigated, with the files being forwarded to the Director of Public Prosecutions where appropriate. In relation to the suggestion that children died as a result of this abuse, *I understand that the Garda investigation, to date, has no evidence to support this allegation.*"

Concerning Artane there have been many vocal allegations of murder, of educational deprivation, starvation, brutality and child sexual abuse.

Based in Clontarf, the team of 10 gardai along with a detective sergeant were on the case full-time since early 1998. It began with a small number of allegations which soon mushroomed in number. Most allegations related to physical abuse in the late 1940s to late 1960s when Artane closed. Almost 30 Christian Brothers were interviewed during this investigation, many over allegations of horrendous sex acts on minors.

Yet by September 2003, this full-time investigation carried out by ten gardai over a period of three and a half years, resulted in only one criminal prosecution, but no convictions.

Bruce Arnold on the Fr Moore Report

In August 2007 journalist Bruce Arnold had news and opinion articles in *The Irish Independent* revealing (and lauding) the contents of a report done by a Fr Henry Moore of Dublin Archdiocese in 1962. This Moore report was one man's view of what he, as Artane's part-time chaplain for two years, regarded as a tough and deficient regime.

When Fr Moore's report was brought to the attention of the Department of Education at a meeting on December 13th, 1962, that department ordered a snap two day inspection of Artane which was carried out by qualified and competent department officials on the 20th and 21st of December 1962.

At the public hearing on Artane held by the Commission to Enquire into Child Abuse, chaired by Judge Ryan on the 15/9/05, it was pointed out that the Department of Education (DoE) inspectors commented very favourably on the conditions and education given in the Christian Brother institution. They contradicted practically everything that Fr Moore said on specifics in relation to the standard of education, food and health.

Bruce Arnold, however, chose to run down the results of this Department of Education inspection referring to it as a whitewash.

The Moore Report was proffered by institutional campaigners as their exhibit A, their trump card, their incontrovertible evidence that Artane was a cruel, and substandard educational regime run by abusive Christian Brothers.

But who was Fr Henry Moore, whose report was so highly praised and robustly defended by Mr Bruce Arnold?

A public letter from Jim Beresford, a researcher for SOCA Ireland to the head of the Child Abuse Commission (dated July 31, 2007) mentions "the 1962 Report on Artane industrial reformatory written by the then prison chaplain, Fr Harry Moore."

Harry, was the more informal name used by Fr Henry Moore. Here's a few questions - what were Moore's qualifications, what were the personal attributes which would lend weight to his assessment and personal testimony? A quick search of *The Irish Times* online archive quickly brings answers. It is easily backed up by those who knew Fr

Moore at Artane.

Fr Harry Moore (70), is a retired priest of Dublin Archdiocese who on January 21, 2005, pleaded guilty and was convicted on charges of buggery and indecent assault performed on a then 16 year old male youth between July 1984, and March 1985. Fr Moore was described in the court as an alcoholic whose father had died before he was born, meaning that as a child, Harry Moore was placed in an orphanage where he stayed until the age of 17.

During the public hearing on Artane chaired by Judge Ryan, it was made clear that the Department of Education disagreed severely with virtually all of the contents of the Moore report.

The counsel for the Christian Brothers questioned the reliability of the Moore report, pointing out that there are matters within it, particularly what he says about the quality of the education, "which we know already by objective evidence were spectacularly wrong." Mr Hanratty, the Christian Brother's counsel also described as "a well known fact because it's in the public realm that the author of the [Moore] report was himself convicted of sexual abuse of a teenager in the past, in fact he pleaded guilty to the offence." This last fact was reported in the national press the next day.

Interestingly, Bruce Arnold finished his article in *The Irish Independent* (11/8/07) with a very cryptic reference to Fr Moore: "The Department of Education visitors did a white-wash on Artane and ever since, the Father Moore Report has been effectively suppressed. All the exchanges before the Commission confirm this, with the added indignity that Moore, for offences four decades later, has had these brought up at the Commission – without being ruled out of order by the Judge, which he should have done, since they are totally unrelated – in order to further discredit the Moore Report."

At the time of this book going to press, there was nothing in the national media about Fr Moore's conviction for sexual abuse of minors, even though these details were easily discoverable. One would have expected that any journalist writing about Fr Moore would have searched, uncovered and *revealed* his past because the qualifications of Fr Moore and the credibility of his report depends on it. Questions remain why institutional campaigners failed to explicitly reveal important facts about the author of the Moore report to the public:

Qn 1. Did Bruce Arnold know that the author of the Moore report had been convicted of sexual abuse of minors?

Qn 2. If not, why did he not know?

Qn 3. If he did know, why did he fail to reveal this important fact to the public?

The ghost funerals of 'Our Boys'

In October 1999, an hour-long documentary type programme called *Stolen Lives: Our Boys* by presenter Louis Lentin was broadcast on TV3 in Ireland and repeated again in November 12th 2000, not long after the transmission of the *States of Fear* programme. The programme contained a number of very serious allegations against a few Christian brothers by past pupils of the industrial schools.

One of the chief witnesses in the programme was one Gerald Joseph Kelly who entered Artane at the age of nine and remained there from 1966-69. Claiming he was sexually abused by one of the Christian Brothers, he then alleges that he was severely beaten up for hours by the Superior when he complained to him of the alleged abuse. Gerry Kelly from Waterford, goes on to tell Louis Lentin: "I know Louis, I was one of the lucky ones. I got away that evening. Cause I know there were some kids who made complaints who never got away. I attended their funerals."

Again, the Christian Brothers' provincial leader Br J. K. Mullan totally repudiated these allegations in a letter to *The Irish Times* on November 25, 2000.

The Brother commented that, "One particular past pupil claimed that he had attended the funerals of boys who had died while in Artane. It was further implied that these boys had died following beatings administered by the Brothers. This allegation is completely untrue.

"The records show that no boy died in Artane during this person's time there. This is a matter of verifiable fact. In addition, this same past pupil claimed that a particular Brother who allegedly had been abusing him made certain lewd comments during Mass, as a result of which the pupil fainted and had to be transferred to the infirmary. Versions of this story have been repeated elsewhere, to the extent that the Brother is easily identifiable. However, the record shows that the Brother was not teaching in Artane at the time in question. That is also a matter of verifiable fact."

That a national broadcaster would deal with a sensitive issue with a programme containing, "unfounded, uncorroborated allegations" was a matter of great concern to the Christian Brothers, Br Mullan concluded.

It was former Artane resident, Gerry Kelly who physically jostled some of the Irish bishops as they walked into Maynooth College in April 8, 2002 to hold a meeting to discuss the issue of child abuse.

The Bishop of Meath was confronted in his car, and when the Bishop of Killaloe, Willie Walsh, came over for a sympathetic word, Mr Kelly wept. Having to watch the ugly scene of Bishop Martin Drennan, an extremely quiet-spoken gentleman, being tugged by Gerry Kelly as he walked through the main doors of the national seminary and pontifical university was one of the low points in regards to rational discussion of the whole issue.

Mary Raftery and Brother Joseph O'Connor

Mary Raftery's book, *Suffer Little Children*, contains serious allegations of sexual abuse of boys against another Christian Brother, Br Joseph O'Connor, someone who was dead, and unable to defend himself. The report of his death is colourful if totally inaccurate. It would logically raise questions about the rest of the story and the other claims the same witness made.

In the section 'Barney's Story, Artane Industrial School (Christian Brothers), 1949-1958,' it is alleged that Br Joseph O'Connor, who was a nationally known figure because of his leadership of the Artane Boys Band which led out Gaelic games matches in Croke Park Stadium, had sexually abused boys in Artane.

"One of his victims has described how, when he heard that Brother O'Connor was dying in Dublin's Mater Hospital, he went down and waited around the hospital until O'Connor was dead. He then went in to take a look at the body. He describes how he had an overwhelming need to actually see him dead. This man tells of being tied to a bed and raped at the age of eleven. He testifies to having his head pushed into a drawer, and the drawer closed tight on his neck as he was being raped by Brother O'Connor. In account after account from survivors of Artane, Brother O'Connor's name is one of those repeatedly mentioned in the context of sexual abuse. Barney's experiences at his hands have scarred him for life...."

However, journalist Breda O'Brien disputed this description of events entirely. In her article 'Child Abuse Book: the facts and fictions' which appeared in *The Sunday Business Post* (29/11/1999) she wrote:

"....Similarly with regard to a Brother Joseph O'Connor against whom serious charges were levelled after his death, it is alleged that a man abused by him was so distraught by this abuse that he hung around the Mater Hospital for days when he heard that O'Connor was dying. He then went into the hospital mortuary to lift the sheet to confirm that O'Connor was dead. In reality O'Connor died miles away in a Christian Brothers home in Baldoyle. Why was the place of death not independently confirmed?....

"If Br O'Connor did not die in the Mater Hospital as claimed in Raftery's book and she failed to even check basic facts such as this, just how much of the other claims in the book can be trusted?"

One is caught between various possibilities to get the events in line.

Perhaps the Christian Brother in question had the power of bilocation? Or was he sympathetic to Woody Allen's quip that 'I'm not afraid of death, I just don't want to be there when it happens!'

Another important episode in the book is erroneous. Why did Mary Raftery not bother to check the basic facts of this extraordinary story? How about the other allegations about the same man. Are they also false?

What can be deduced from all these events? Say what you like about solicitors and you get sued. Say the most outrageous libel against a religious order in Ireland and it's carry on as normal. Religious orders are easy targets, and soft prey for anyone who wanted to attack their actions and reputation.

The death and exhumation of William Delaney

Among a very small number of influential journalists in Ireland, after the eruption of the abuse scandal, fact was allowed to be obscured. Wild and at times, absolutely outrageous claims were allowed to be proclaimed on the national air waves and repeated in print, achieving bold headlines and very few hard questions. Simple types of questions, such as, 'where is your proof?' were put aside or completely forgotten.

The exhumation of a thirteen year old boy who had died of natural causes over 30 years previously was one of the darker episodes in the last number of years concerning false allegations.

Following complaints made by a number of former residents of Letterfrack, a large and long-running garda investigation commenced in 1999. Among the allegations received was that a young boy was severely beaten with a flagpole and died as a result. In 2001, the high profile spokesman of a victims' support group alleged that the former resident of Letterfrack, William Delaney, had died as a direct result of a blow to the head received during a savage beating by a Christian Brother.

The son of a Traveller family, William Delaney had initially been sent to Letterfrack under a court order in 1967 for stealing a bicycle. On returning home from there on holidays in July 1970, he complained of a headache and was examined by a doctor. Sadly, he collapsed at home and was transferred to St Luke's Hospital, Kilkenny where he died at the age of 13 on July 18th 1970. It was believed by the boy's parents at the time that he had died from meningitis.

Arising from their enquiries into the allegations, the gardai, with the approval of the boy's family obtained permission to exhume the boy's body for forensic examination.

The whole matter was spread across newspapers with large headlines, ranging from the sensible 'Boy's body to be exhumed as part of Letterfrack abuse investigation' (*The Irish Times* 18/4/01) to 'Horror of Letterfrack still lingers' (*The Irish Independent* 18/4/01). The headline in *The Irish Independent* (19/4/01) 'Witness claims boy was kicked to death' was, it seemed, par for the course. On the same day, the paper ran an article about William Delaney's father, reading 'Victim's father doubted explanation of collapse.'

William Delaney, the young boy caught in the centre of these allegations, was buried under the shelter of a weathered granite headstone at
St Kieran's Cemetery on Hebron Road in the city of Kilkenny. In the
presence of the William Delaney's family, the exhumation took place
shielded by boards and a plastic tent from the keen media attention.

At first light, 6am on that dull April morning (18/4/01) gardai began
their grim task of exhuming the body, helped by 12 members of a
Dublin-based forensic team, a garda ballistics expert and local gardai.
By 7.25am, two local gravediggers, helped by a few specially-trained
precise diggers from the gardai had got down to four feet in depth.

Dr Maria Cassidy, the assistant State pathologist arrived at 7.30am.
There she carried out a detailed examination of the remains before they
were removed at 10.25am to St Luke's Hospital for an autopsy. While
the final autopsy results were being waited for, *The Evening Herald*, the
main Dublin evening paper, sold its paper on 19 April 2001 with the
poster headline 'Now it's Murder Enquiry'.

It alleged that the initial results found the boy had died from a blow
to the head, and it looked like murder. A garda enquiry it was going to
be. Not to be outdone BBC Northern Ireland, on the same evening
trumpeted the headline, 'Exhumed boy had skull damage' with the sinister sounding subhead, 'Suspicious circumstances.'

Immediately, the gardai notified the press of the opposite, and RTÉ
that night ran the headline: 'Gardaí reject Letterfrack murder inquiry
claim.' "Gardaí have denied," RTÉ News said, "that a murder inquiry
has been launched into the death of thirteen-year-old William Delaney,
whose body was exhumed in Kilkenny yesterday.

"A newspaper report claimed that detectives were this evening set to
upgrade the investigation into the death of the teenager to a murder
inquiry. However, Gardaí say that a murder inquiry has not been
launched. They indicated that no decision could be taken on the matter
for a number of days."

What the autopsy revealed

The remains of the young boy were so well preserved that the assistant State Pathologist, Dr Marie Cassidy, could tell gardai within an hour of her preliminary examination that William did not die from a blow to the head. Meningitis was also ruled out as a possible cause of death.

Instead, the evidence in the autopsy pointed to the ravages of an infection on one side of the skull suggesting that William Delaney died from a severe ear infection or untreated tooth abscess.

The Deputy State Pathologist, Dr Marie Cassidy carried out her post-mortem on April 18, 2001. Her report, dated August 8, 2001 stated that "there was no evidence of a skull fracture." She summarised her finding as follows in her official report:

"There was no evidence of violence. The skeleton was intact showing no evidence of trauma. There was localised damaged (sic) to the left side of the internal skull and the upper cervical spine, which may be evidence of an antemortem disease process.

"It is possible that he had a middle ear infection, which spread to the brain causing encephalitis or a cerebral abscess, which, if untreated, would have led to his death. This would have been painful and he would have complained of sore neck, earache and headaches. These findings would support that death was most likely due to natural causes and there is no evidence that any violent act caused or contributed to his death."

William Delaney's death certificate recorded that he had died of "acute encephalitis-certified".

What amounted to a build-up towards national hysteria against brutally vicious Christian Brothers fell flat on April 23rd, when the first results came out. *The Irish Independent* ran with 'Reformatory boy died from infection, not a beating.' Self-explanatory to a tee.

After a series of hot headlines, amongst a number of papers, *The Evening Herald* (April 27th) had to admit that the post-mortem on the exhumed body of William Delaney had found that he died of natural causes. The story, perhaps as you would expect went quiet.

However journalist Liam Reid's news article in *The Irish Times*

(27/11/2003) would repeat the same untrue allegation about William Delaney. In an article which signalled that 100 complaints had been made about convicted sexual abuser Br Maurice Tobin in Letterfrack, *The Irish Times* stated: "The Gardaí had received allegations that the boy [William Delaney] had received a beating with a flagpole by a brother before he had been sent home. The post-mortem revealed the boy had died from an untreated infection.

"Investigating Gardaí were told that the infection could have been easily treated with antibiotics, which were widely available at the time. The post-mortem also found evidence that the boy had received a blow to the head."

As revealed above, the autopsy results clearly showed there were no signs that William Delaney had received a blow to the head as alleged, there was no sign of violence or trauma at all, but died of natural causes. A sorry saga for the boy's family, not of their own making was put to rest.

Comment: The high number of sensational claims of murder, secret burial, mass graves, abject violence and sexual abuse by members of Catholic religious communities which later proved to be false in a short space of time is extraordinary. It is this journalist's belief that this climate of giving radio air-time to the most outrageous accusation without checking it for fact, contributed to the zeitgeist or cultural moment which created a space for *Kathy's Story* to resonate with readers and for its sales to flourish.

The lynch mob is rarely a fair means of justice and that is why stable courts and the unbiased application of the law is so important. But in such a culture of hatred towards Catholic religious in modern Ireland, even the steady hands of the judges began to shake, and grave injustice was perpetuated. Here's hoping we all learn from that mistake.

15 A Culture of False Allegations induced by Easy Compensation

'There should be no hiding place for child abusers or false accusers.'
John Fitzpatrick, Kilkenny

I n Ireland, an environment has been formed which provides financial inducement for people to make false allegations of abuse. The Irish Redress Board, was set up by the Irish Government under the Residential Institutions Redress Act, 2002 "to make fair and reasonable awards to persons who, as children, were abused while resident in industrial schools, reformatories and other institutions subject to State regulation or inspection." The Board, which is independent, is currently chaired by Mr Justice Bryan McMahon who was appointed in May 2007.

In February 2003, the then Irish Minister for Justice, Michael McDowell said he was proud that, "the State Redress Scheme won't need strict proof, adversarial justice or courtroom procedures." The normal standard of proof or evidence that is necessary in court proceedings is not required for applications to the Redress Board.

The October 2004 newsletter from the Redress Board, detailed how of the 2,011 cases processed to that date, 71 applications had "been refused as, on the face of the documentation, the application was outside the Boards terms of reference as laid down in the 2002 Act. In other words the applications did not relate to residential institutions as defined in the Act." Jumping on these figures, Florence Horsman-Hogan of the charity L.O.V.E. blasted the Redress Board for paying out compensation too easily.

The L.O.V.E spokeswoman suggested: "If only 71 out of 2,000 people who have applied for an award have had their application refused, then doesn't that indicate you had only to be in one of the institutions to receive money?"

She continued: "What's worse is that most of the 71 were refused simply because they fell outside the remit of the Redress Board, i.e. they were never in one of the institutions to begin with.

"In other words, almost 100 per cent of people who have applied for an award have received one. It's a wonder far more haven't applied so far given how easy it is to get the money." As time ticked on towards the deadline for applications, many more indeed, did apply. And got a financial pay out.

By *July 2005,* The Redress Board noted that, "The rate at which the Board receives applications has increased noticeably in recent months with the Board receiving more than 400 in June and a total of 7046 to date."

In its newsletter of *November 2005* the Redress Board newsletter reported that, "The rate at which the Board receives applications has increased noticeably in recent months with the Board now receiving more than 600 per month and a total of 9551 to date."

According to the newsletter of the Redress Board itself as the closing date approached there was a huge increase in the number of applicants for compensation: By December 16, 2005, by which time the closing date for receipt of applications had passed, the Redress Board had received a total of 14,540 applications. 9,432 of which were received in 2005. 2,255 of these were received in November and *3,700 were received in December.*

To December 2005, "the Board has completed the process in 4267 cases. 3154 offers have been made following settlement talks and 1006 awards have been made following hearings. Five applicants have rejected their awards. Seventeen applications resulted in an award of 0.00 or no award. In applications covering 90 applicants refusals have issued for one reason or another. These applications have been refused as, on the face of the documentation, the application was outside the Board's terms of reference as laid down in the 2002 Act."

The board announced that the average value of awards to date is €76,500, the smallest award being €0.00 and the largest award being €300,000.

The Exponential growth in claims after money was offered

That there was a sharp increase in the number of claims of abuse after the Government announced the compensation scheme did not escape the notice of a number of religious orders and indeed some of the press. A clear example is that of the Christian Brothers.

Speaking before the Commission to Enquire into Child Abuse (chaired by Mr Justice Sean Ryan), in June 2005, the Irish Provincial, Brother David Gibson noted that: "When the Christian Brothers made an apology to all the former residents of their schools, including St Joseph's Industrial School, Letterfrack, on 29th March 1998, there were *three complaints* on the current files relating to St Joseph's, Letterfrack. The message of apology was published on all the major daily papers in Ireland. In the year that followed the apology, and in response to widespread media coverage on radio, television, and the press, a further *nine complaints* relating to Letterfrack reached the Christian Brothers.

"The number of *complaints increased by 449* following the apology made, on behalf of the State, by the Taoiseach, Mr Bertie Ahern, on 11th May 1999. The Taoiseach apologised to former residents of institutions who had been abused and accepted responsibility, on behalf of the State, for those who were abused. In addition, he recommended that the Statute of Limitations be altered and soon after promised to establish some form of compensation scheme."

Br David Gibson added that the Christian Brothers "did not accept some of the newer (post-1999) complaints." That there were instances where they "wondered very seriously about the truth of some complaints."

This was a further advancement on their statement of October 2003 when The Christian Brothers' Communication Office said it did not accept the "now established perception that there was a widespread, systematic sexual abuse in the residential institutions," although it has "openly acknowledged" that some abuse did take place. The Brothers said that over 95% of its members who had been accused of sexual abuse while working in a residential institution had also worked in normal day schools for up to 40 years without any allegation or hint of complaint made about them in that time.

The person in charge of Christian Brother correspondence with the Redress Board, (on behalf of St Mary's – the Northern Province only) told this writer that as of December 2006 that they had received approximately 2,100 applications related to the relevant institutions run by the Northern province of the Christian Brothers. There has been a total of 572 applications made concerning the Southern (St Helen's) Province. That is a total of *2,672 applications* for compensation.

The person in charge of Redress Board correspondence for the Northern Province of the Christian Brothers said, "there had been no cooling off period since the Redress Board was announced," and that there had been what she described as "a constant flow of applications."

Journalist Patsy McGarry of *The Irish Times* wrote in July 6, 2004 that, "A clear pattern to emerge from evidence presented to the Ryan Committee to date is the marked increase in allegations of abuse which followed the Taoiseach's apology in May 1999." The Ryan Committee is another name for The Commission to Inquire into Child Abuse.

The Good Shepherd Sisters told the Ryan Commission in the summer of 2004 that, "before 1996 there were no complaints against the congregation. In 1997 there were five, four more in 1998, and a further three in 1999 before the Taoiseach's apology, giving a total of 12. Between the Taoiseach's apology and June 2000 they had 27 more. Between October 2000 and January 2002, when the indemnity deal was agreed in principle, they had a further 123. There were 105 more by December 2002, and since the establishment of the Redress Board another 220, making a total 467." Other religious orders also noticed that a similar pattern had emerged.

A frightening scenario – courtesy of the Redress Scheme

The Redress Board was set up by the Irish Government under the Residential Institutions Redress Act, 2002 to make fair and reasonable awards to persons who, as children, were abused while resident in industrial schools, reformatories and other institutions subject to state regulation or inspection.

Let's just imagine for a moment, that you are a lay man accused of awful crimes against vulnerable and mentally challenged juveniles. You were spat on in public and regarded as the face of evil. Your name and reputation were made like muck. Your criminal trial takes years to come to court and but it takes the jury just over an hour to return a unanimous vote of not guilty. You are declared innocent of the crimes for which you are accused.

You are sitting there at home one day, relaxing by the fire, and thinking about your previous trauma when a letter drops through the letter box addressed to you from the Irish Redress Board. You open it to read that a certain person is seeking compensation for a certain wrong against them, and that you are the person accused of perpetrating that grave crime. You read on down the Redress Board letter to find that the person who had previously accused you of the crime of which you have already been found not guilty is the one now accusing you of the same misdemeanour but in a different forum. You are given two weeks to respond, although you are told, your response is not necessary.

How would you feel? You have suffered greatly. You have been to court where you have been exonerated. And now this letter from the Redress Board. Your nightmare has not ended, quite the opposite, it is only beginning. Again.

You hold your breath and gaze at the letter in disbelief. The official letter following its standard form, tells you that the whole matter is confidential and it would be illegal for you, in any way to make public the identity of your accuser or what the accusation was now being brought before the Redress Board in an effort to seek compensation.

Would you feel that justice was being done? If you later heard that the Redress Board gave this same accuser compensation for the abuse the person claimed to have suffered. If you are innocent, then why is this person getting money? Would you still feel justice was being done?

Don't worry, because *for you* this scenario painted above is only imaginary. But for another person, an experienced teacher and care worker [not Paul Farrell mentioned in the previous chapter], this scenario was very, very real.

I cannot report the outcome in any case which came before the Redress Board because the law which set up the Redress Scheme makes it a crime for anybody to reveal the identity of those who were either accused or indeed the identity of those who sought and received financial compensation for alleged suffering. (Residential Institutions Redress Act, 2002/ Section 28).

The accusations made by John Prior

John Prior is the moving force behind many horrendous public accusations against the Christian Brothers as well as being co-founder of a memorial Trust to Joseph Pyke, a boy who, he claimed, died as a consequence of being beaten by a Christian Brother. Prior was a complainant who made a statement alleging abuse, which led the gardai to start a criminal case against a Christian Brother at the Circuit Court in Tralee in 1999. He accused Brother X (who is 78 and still alive) of sexual abuse.

This criminal case went for a judicial review at the Dublin High Court before Justice Peter Kelly in April 2001. This judge had stiff words to say about stark conflicts in evidence involving allegations which centred on St Joseph's industrial school in Tralee over 40 years ago.

Judge Kelly told the court, "It is not necessary to rule on aspects of delay etc. In fairness to the Applicant [Brother X] he has been able to take issue with details in the Book of Evidence about location etc. and is in a position to counteract many allegations." The judge also noted that John Prior said in his statement of evidence to An Garda Síochana in 1995 that it was "only in the last twelve months" that he was able to talk about his abuse, yet the Applicant [Brother X] was able to produce correspondence from 1992, showing that the complainant had been in contact with the Christian Brothers in relation to the same problem.

Justice Kelly stated that both the gardai and the DPP acknowledged that the investigating gardai had told Brother X in late 1996 that no prosecution would take place. Due to its concern about the sustainability of a prosecution in the substantive case, the DPP indicated that the State did not oppose the request by Brother X for the order.

Christian Brother X who was accused by John Prior, left the Four Courts as "a free and innocent man."

Justice Peter Kelly ordered the granting of an injunction, restraining the DPP in perpetuity from prosecuting the Applicant (Brother X) on this matter. [cf. Judicial review 497 of 2000, dated 30/4/2001]

He instructed that the criminal case was not to proceed.

But John Prior later told a *News of the World* reporter on August 29, 2004 that he had been awarded 'substantial damages' by the Redress Board. Prior freely chose to put his assertion that that he had been awarded money after he made allegations of "sexual and physical abuse" against three brothers on the public record. Two of the brothers had died and he named them. Only Brother X, who is alive, was not named.

In the *News of the World* article, John Prior is quoted: "I will take [the surviving] Brother X to court.... I want my day in front of Brother X."

Joe Bourke is a 54 year old waiter who lives in Killarney. He attended the same Christian Brother institution in Tralee as John Prior, arriving at St Joseph's Industrial School in 1959 at the age of 7. He would stay there for 9 years. Since leaving the school, he has kept in close contact with a very large number of boys who went through its doors and claims he would be able to name 300 boys off the top of his head. "Everybody knows where I am and I know where everybody is," he said. Mr Bourke also made a formal complaint himself to the police against one Christian Brother.

However, when Mr Bourke heard the accusations against Brother X by John Prior, both he and the large group of former pupils with whom he has regular contact were both "shocked and appalled" about what they heard. One discussion led to another and Mr Bourke asked 10 boys to put in their own words what they thought of Brother X. Within a week, Mr Bourke says, he had in his possession letters from past pupils stating that in their own experience, Brother X was a fair and impeccable gentleman, a man of the highest order, against whom not even the slightest whiff of suspicion could be held. Joe Bourke said these letters show what Brother X was like: "He was a big man, a hard man, but he did not commit any sexual crime. These letters state he was a gentleman, he was fair, he was always helpful to the children and that they had great respect for him."

Although Brother X was never convicted in an Irish court of law, and indeed, is to be regarded as "a free and innocent man," John Prior, the man who accused him, still received compensation for the allegations he made before the Redress Board. And so, of the three Christian Brothers involved, the principle of 'innocent until proven guilty' was effectively thrown aside, allowing their reputations to be attacked. Surely this is a scandal?

Mr Bourke also says he is aware of another past pupil who alleged that he was abused by a Christian Brother; however this man in Ulster was not even at St Joseph's when this Brother was at the school. Despite this, Bourke claims, the man still got a pay out from the Redress Board.

The Irish Government introduced the 1998 Act for Protection of Persons Reporting Child Abuse, section 5, to prosecute anybody for making a false allegation of abuse. But by 2005, the L.O.V.E. group decided to lobby the Irish Government to introduce harsher punishments for false allegations and to examine why the present legislation had not up to that point been utilised to secure a conviction.

They believed the legislation should have been used to deter false allegations thus helping those who suffered from abuse, by deterring others from wasting State agencies' time and resources.

In late 2006, the Garda Press Office in Dublin were able to tell this writer that, "We are not aware of any prosecutions under this act."

However, in June 2007, Paul Anderson was convicted of making a false allegation of sexual abuse against a priest of Dublin Diocese. (See chapter 12).

Solicitors Trawling for claimants

The part of solicitors in this noted increase of compensation claims cannot be overlooked. In the Irish, British and even American press, there has been a rash of advertisements by various solicitors' firms proclaiming the size of financial award available to claimants. Some firms of solicitors even organised meetings in America and Britain to encourage people to make a claim to the Redress Board. In this, on occasion, they were working together with counselling and former resident groups.

In August 2007, the Redress Board revealed that it had paid lawyers representing those alleging abuse in State care €83.5 million. This amounts to 13% of the €648m paid out in total so far. The €83.5M went to 601 individual legal firms representing 6,494 victims. It is estimated that if current trends of pay out continue the final pay out of the Redress Board will be over 1.1 billion euro.

Director of the *One in Four* group, Colm O'Gorman suggested that the total amount of money paid in legal fees could not be properly scrutinised under the current policy of secrecy employed by the Redress Board.

He told *The Irish Examiner* in August 2007, "We would like to see where this money has gone and be able to see how it has helped people to rebuild their lives. "I sometimes wonder," he said, "when we look back at the outcomes has it been worth all the money we have spent. It is very hard to know because it is such a secretive process, even if 10% on legal costs does not seem too unreasonable."

It was revealed in October 2003 that the same Mr O'Gorman, as director of *One in Four,* was being paid a salary of €80k per year.

When this journalist questioned O'Gorman at the time about his remuneration-package, he answered: "I won't justify it. I don't feel I need to justify my salary. Salaries are benchmarked across the sector."

This was at a time when Noel Barry, the director of the *Right Of Place* victim support group in Cork said he was paid €314 per week. Barry was outraged that O'Gorman was getting paid "more that a TD."

At the same time Christine Buckley of *The Aislinn Centre* for abuse survivors in Dublin said her group had helped more than 3,000 people in four years and the three workers, including the director, were paid €32,000 between them in 2003.

The contrast in wages could hardly be any greater. Yet, when asked about his annual wages in February 2007, Mr O'Gorman again refused to disclose his remuneration. His spokeswoman said it was, "Confidential and benchmarked."

Victim Alliance Support: Tom's Story

Tom Hayes has shown himself to be a man of unshakable integrity and great personal bravery. He was put in a convent orphanage run by the Sisters of Mercy at the age of two for a period of six years, and was treated very well there. As a child resident of an Industrial school run by the Christian Brothers in Glin, Co Limerick for eight years, he suffered a great deal of bullying. He has stated that abuse took place by a small number of Christian brothers and that a great deal of peer bullying and sexual abuse was carried out by older boys within these institutions. Mr Hayes is the secretary of a voluntary group called *Alliance Victim Support* with 300 members, and lives in Co Armagh.

The aim of the Alliance, founded in 1999, is "to access all Social, Educational, Counselling, Family Tracing and Legal Services for those who as children were in Institutions. We also assist and support their families." This is to Tom's story:

"In May of 1999 the Taoiseach, Mr. Bertie Ahern, T.D. made an apology on behalf of the State to all those who had been abused while resident in the various Industrial schools and orphanages.

As a direct result of this apology a number of different groups were formally set up to represent the many thousands of former residents. These groups all had their own agendas.

"Once the Commission to Enquire into Child Abuse was established under the then Chairmanship of Ms Justice Laffoy we saw our task as ensuring that all those who were in the Institutions would support this Commission so that a full and honest account of what took place would be published. However, it soon became clear that some other groups wanted separate offices and accommodation in their own areas and they saw the Government's National Office for Victims of Abuse (NOVA) as a threat. Once the Residential Institutions Redress Board was established in December 2000 the places run by these various groups became the madrassas of the support structure.

"The establishment of these so-called victim support units has created a 'cottage industry' for the group leaders themselves while allowing a dependency culture to develop that continues to ensure that these very vulnerable people never become fully integrated into society. These places themselves have now become the present day Institutions but with little accountability.

"Evidence has come to our attention that the passing round of information about schools, the names of Christian Brothers, nuns and lay members of staff openly took place. Many former residents saw the support structure as assisting them with writing their statements and furnishing information that they themselves did not have. There were also people there who would write the statements for them. We at the Victim Alliance Support group, began in 2000, to be asked the names of Christian Brothers, the years that they were in certain schools, what classes they taught, what they were like, and some even asked what uniform the Brothers wore – all to make an application to the Redress Board for compensation.

"All that was needed was the name and year of a known nun or brother that had previously been reported for abuse, and that would be used in their statements. The Alliance Committee reported these cases to the authorities. We publicly complained about false claims and even asked that the Religious Orders themselves take legal action against any person making such false claims against any one of their members.

"I have been saddened by the callous and indiscriminate way that some former residents have behaved towards their former religious teachers. They have lied and perjured themselves for money or status. They did so even when the evidence clearly showed that they were lying. When I heard the names of Christian Brothers and nuns that I knew personally, being accused of abuses I ensured that the Alliance Committee themselves would not be part of assisting with any information or details that would assist these people making false accusations.

"The Industrial Schools and the system within were horrible places to have lived in. Nobody who was there will ever fully forget their experiences. I claim, with personal experience, that those of us who came to the Industrial Schools as orphans from the Convents were the real victims. We were like lambs to the slaughter for the more street-wise children. Many of these had been abused themselves at home. What I and those like me from the Convents, will never forgive the Brothers for, was their failure to protect those of us, who complained about these abuses. Our lives have been ruined as a direct result of these failures.

"I was determined that I and the Alliance Support Group of which I am secretary would always work to support those who came to us for guidance and assistance with integrity. I believe that I have achieved that aim."

The Canadian Experience of Compensation schemes

All this would be understandable perhaps, if Ireland was in the unenviable position of being the first country in which a response to allegations of child abuse was called for. But it wasn't. Not by a long shot.

While the Residential Institutions Redress Bill was still to be implemented, and interested parties were being sounded out for their considered input, a report about the operation of a similar scheme in Nova Scotia, Canada came to light and was publicised in the Irish press.

In the early Nineties a few complaints of abuse were filed against Canadian state employees who had worked in children's residential units. In a bid to seek a less adversarial scheme of sorting the matter out, the Government set up what was known as the Compensation Program, in many respects similar to the Redress scheme later put in place in Ireland. Closely examined by retired judge, Fred Kaufman a report on the compensation program was published in January 2002.

Lashing the Government sponsored compensation scheme at the news conference, launching the report Judge Kaufman said, "In the end, everyone suffered." The $56 million plan was meant to compensate alleged victims of physical and sexual abuse at various state-run homes but the 681 page report called the scheme fundamentally unfair to many employees of the province, saying it did a disservice to true victims of abuse.

"The program was seriously flawed." he said. "So flawed that it has left in its wake true victims of abuse who are now assumed by many to have defrauded the Government, employees who have been branded as abusers without appropriate recourse, and a public confused and unenlightened about the extent to which young people were or were not abused while in the care of the Province of Nova Scotia.

"This report cannot begin to separate out the true and false claims of abuse. One of the by-products of a flawed Government response has been to now make that determination (in the majority of cases) impossible."

Judge Kaufman saw as central to the malaise, the fact that "little or no validation was required for claims (which) was a recipe for disaster." Does this begin to look familiar? The Canadian judge believed that, "A Government response that fails to appropriately balance the interests of complainants and suspects is flawed regardless of whether individual complainants or suspects are in the right or in the wrong."

When the Nova Scotia compensation programme was introduced in 1995, only 25 complaints had been filed accusing just nine government employees. But soon after the Canadian Government set up a redress scheme, roughly 1,500 people filed complaints naming over 400 government employees. Again, similar in so many respects, this is what happened in Ireland, except Irish people were forewarned by the Canadian experiment.

"I was to determine," Kaufman said, "whether the Government response was appropriate, fair and reasonable. The simple answer is that it was not. It was commendable that Government was concerned about the plight of abuse victims and understood its obligation to rectify past wrongs and prevent future wrongs. However it lost sight of its obligation to its own former and current employees. And fairness became yet another victim. And so did the credibility of the Program itself."

Kaufman's thorough review concluded that this particular compensation program introduced in Canada not only smeared the names of innocent employees, but made many true victims of a terrible abuse look like fraud artists. This was a double scandal.

Personal Comment on some aspects of Redress Scheme:
In the Republic of Ireland, the Redress Board can make compensation payments even if accusations are made against a person who was too invalided or sick to make their own defence, as well as those who are dead. How were the dead to defend their good name? Were the

mentally and physically incapacitated allowed the presumption of innocence until proven guilty with valid evidence?

There is no doubt that physical and sexual abuse of children and
minors has been carried out in a very brutal manner by a number of
people in this country, including those who are clergy and professed
religious. However, it has become clear over recent years that the short
step in Ireland between allegation and compensation has had lethal
consequences for the reputation of Catholic religious, the vast majority
of whom were and are innocent of any wrong doing. Indeed, they have
spend their entire lives doing their very best to help out vulnerable people in need, at a time when society in general looked the other way and
the State gave each child an allowance which amounted to a pittance,
for the time, to fund their care.

As it currently stands, many a good man and woman have been
accused in the wrong. To actually be at the receiving end of a false allegation of child abuse must be incredibly destructive for any adult
because it is virtually impossible for a worse fate to befall any person in
the current cultural climate. But the question still stands: Have we now
entered a phase where regarding allegations of child abuse, a person is
innocent until proven religious?

Should every citizen in the state have the right to a presumption of
innocence and due process in a court of law? If so, how is this made
manifest in the workings of the Redress Board? Should Catholic religious accused of abuse be excluded from this right? If so why?

A certain *zeitgeist* prevails in Ireland, a pervasive cultural spirit of
the age, which people live in and act out without even being aware how
prevalent it is. It would appear that an anti-Church sentiment mixed
with an offer of easy compensation have caused innocent people to be
accused without proper cause.

The Irish Government must take a good part of the blame for the
creation of this culture, for it is this Government which chose to provide the taxpayers money to fund the Redress Board, compensating
some who were abused but in addition, creating a financial incentive to
others who were not abused, to make false allegations for the sake of
monetary gain.

It is the Government which substantially funds victim support groups with a large advocacy/campaigning role, such as *One in Four*, which have accompanied some false accusers as they went to make their accusations (which turned out to be fraudulent). It is also the Government which created and perpetuates the legal framework which ensures, in de facto terms, few people are ever charged, never mind convicted for making false claims. On top of this, the Irish Government supports RTÉ, the national broadcaster, which has allowed some of the most outlandish claims to be aired almost uncontested.

A few questions still persist about the whole Redress Board Scheme. Do those accused have a proper opportunity to receive justice? Do those who make the accusation bring credible evidence that would stand up in court? Even though the Irish criminal justice system has refused to countenance certain accusations, an accuser can then go to the Redress Board and seek financial award for the same accusation that was earlier thrown out of court.

Is it fair therefore, that a person, under the present conditions in Ireland, can suffer hardship twice for the same allegation and by the same accuser?

Does the Irish taxpayer have any rights to fair and just treatment?

The Redress Board pays out money to the vast majority of people who were resident in these institutions and apply to it for money. This of course, is not the fault of the members of the Redress Board; they are simply following the law under which the RIRB was set up by the Irish Government. It is the Redress Board who have to weed out and deal with the cockle and the wheat, who are given the unenviable task or sorting out the true claims of abuse from the false.

Dropping the threshold of proof well below the judicial norm has, however, encouraged some chancers who want their mortgage paid off early, to try their luck. It is a sad fact of human nature that if an easy opportunity is there, some people with little scruple will take advantage.

"Why not?" they say. As we know, human nature isn't perfect. And people can be motivated by financial advancement, revenge, false memory and the creation of 'an abuse excuse' to rationalise their problems in later life.

When the State launches a compensation scheme which is estimated will pay out over 1.1 billion euro, surely it is right and proper that people should provide proof that they were abused before they can receive any money. Otherwise, some unscrupulous people will simply make a false allegation to get more money.

The State which provides the honey pot, to provide sustenance for the bees, shouldn't be too surprised when some hungry bears turn up to dip their paws at will. Especially as there are so few safeguards against this happening. Yes, the State, taking money from the Irish taxpayer, provides compensation to people who were resident in certain institutions, some of whom were abused, yet this does not justify allowing those who were not abused or suffered no harm to a bag load of money. Nor should it encourage them to destroy someone's reputation among their religious peers and ensure that they, as innocent persons wrongly accused, are put through the mincer emotionally.

As it stands, the Redress Board has become a State-sponsored ATM machine, where virtually anybody who keys in a claim, gets a pay out. It is the Irish taxpayer who is being abused, it is the Irish taxpayer who is being financially raped by this ill-thought out compensation scheme.

We need to stop. Stop immediately and look at this Frankenstein the State has helped create. Does this Redress scheme do justice to all involved? I think not. There is a lot of collateral damage. Just as one child being abused is one too many, so too is one person being falsely accused of abuse.

A number of people who were in the care of religious institutions suffered cruelty and, at times, quite vile mistreatment by some of those entrusted with their care. Often these institutions were under the ultimate command and inspection of the State who also let them down and for this they deserved an apology, which they have received, as they have rightfully received an apology from the various religious orders. In a number of cases, not before time. People who were abused should receive compensation, just as those who wickedly carried out abuse should be jailed for their criminal offences.

If people who say they were abused receive compensation, surely they should be expected to show that they were abused and are in fact entitled to that financial compensation? The statistics from the Redress Board itself show quite clearly that a very large number of people applied for financial compensation. A number of factors point out that innocent people have been accused in the wrong in order for false accusers to receive money. This is wrong. According to its initiators, the Redress Board was set up to bring about justice but those hopes have not been realised: the Redress scheme has created more injustice.

16 Britain too has its Culture of False Allegation

The range of people who suffer false allegations of abuse is spread right across society. Many lay people have also found themselves in a similar situation, especially in Britain, where teachers and care workers in particular, have been hit hard.

During the late Eighties, the Cleveland Child Abuse Scandal rocked Britain when social workers dawn raided many good homes to take children from their parents, with whom the children were perfectly safe, at the word of one mistaken doctor. With the aid of a controversial diagnostic 'test' for sexual abuse, the rate of abuse referrals doubled virtually overnight. Working class families were left powerless as their children were taken away. It was only when middle class families with the know-how and connections to make their voice heard, created a community rumpus that brought things to a head, with a parental mass march from the local hospital where their children were being kept to the offices of the local newspaper.

A Public Inquiry led by the then High Court judge, Dame Elizabeth Butler-Sloss, examined the 121 cases. The inquiry consequently called on social workers to seek corroborative evidence, to look at the whole family situation, and not to act solely on the basis of medical opinion using the new testing method. It also recommended greater inter-agency cooperation between social workers, police and medical staff.

After a long fight through the courts, 80 per cent (96 out of 121) of the children alleged to have been sexually abuse were returned to their innocent parents. Some of the children caught up in the scandal were those already known to social services for neglect or abuse of some type.

This was not the end of the matter in Britain but more the first downpour of Winter.

During the Orkney Abuse Scandal in 1990, ten children, aged between eight and 15 were alleged by over-zealous and mistaken social workers to have been the victims of ritual abuse, centred on a paedophile ring which, they claimed, was operating on the remote Scottish island.

After a thorough investigation a local sheriff ruled that the evidence was seriously flawed and all the children (except the Willsher children) were sent home to their parents. In September 2006 one of the children taken into care, May Willsher, 24, started legal proceedings against the State for taking her away from her family.

Yet sometimes, it is people in the caring professions like teachers and care workers who themselves can be at the receiving end of false allegations of abuse. An influential support group, called *F.A.C.T. (Falsely Accused Carers and Teachers)* provides support to falsely accused carers and teachers throughout the UK. It also has links with other groups of people who find themselves in a similar position of being falsely accused of abuse:

False Allegations Support Organisation (FASO)
Families Anti Social Services Inquiry Team (FASSIT)
Parents Protecting Children
British False Memory Society

False allegations of abuse have become so troublesome in Britain that official notice has been taken and activities to prevent its reoccurrence have been stepped up.

In a speech on the need to strengthen school discipline, Conservative Party leader, David Cameron told the *Policy Exchange* on the first of August 2007 that: "I want to strengthen the position of teachers further. More must be done to protect teachers from the tiny minority who are bent on undermining authority in schools by making false allegations of abuse against the teacher. A recent survey in SecEd magazine indicated that 20 per cent of teachers had been falsely accused and 55 per cent of teachers knew a colleague in their school who had been.

"The Teacher Support phone line is taking almost twice as many calls about pupil allegations than it did a year ago. Yet in the past ten years only three per cent of serious allegations have resulted in a conviction. We believe teachers must have the protection of full anonymity until the case against them has been dealt with...."

The Conservative Party has in effect condemned the rise of false allegations against teachers. Mr Cameron was at least matching the new provisions of investigation announced in November 2005 by the Education Secretary, Ruth Kelly who said, "The number of allegations made each year is very small as a proportion of the children and staff in our schools.

"But it is vital that they are dealt with properly and fairly. We must protect children. Being abused by a trusted adult can have a devastating effect on a child and their future.

"Equally, I am very much aware of the devastating effect that being wrongly or unfairly accused can have on an individual, their family and career, and how delay and publicity can exacerbate that."

The Education Secretary announced new guidelines for schools, other education establishments, and the Crown Prosecution on arrangements to speed up the process of dealing with allegations of abuse against teachers and support staff. The guidelines made clear that accused teachers should not be automatically suspended from work. This move was hailed as a victory by the National Association of Schoolmasters Union of Women Teachers (NASUWT), which has campaigned for years on this issue.

The general secretary of the NASUWT, Chris Keates, said the new guidance was a significant step forward: "This guidance will not prevent those who abuse children from being identified and dealt with appropriately. Those who abuse children have no place in schools," she said. "It does, however, have the real potential to ensure that those who are falsely accused, and their families, are spared the months and sometimes years of trauma and distress before being exonerated."

In responding to the guidelines which called for greater confidentiality until firm evidence of abuse was found, Secondary Heads Association (SHA) general secretary, Dr John Dunford said: "We know there are cases of wrongly accused teachers experiencing real professional and personal tragedy as a result of unacceptable delays and lack of anonymity."

"The guidance issued today introduces a procedure which will help avoid unnecessary delays and respect anonymity. It is now up to local authorities and the police to take on board the recommendations. We sincerely hope they do."

The Government move was also generally welcomed by teacher unions as well the highly popular education website *SecEd* which has run a campaign "Don't abuse my name" for over a year now. It has fought to gain greater recognition of the impact false allegations can have. Another part of their campaign focuses on "the need for anonymity for accused teachers, until a full investigation is completed and guilt established."

Yet many teachers are not happy with what they regard as the minimal effect of the new guidelines outlined above. The press officer for F.A.C.T. (Falsely Accused Carers and Teachers), Ms Gail Saunders told this journalist that her group is all too aware that frequently historical allegations (many dating back decades and made by people with criminal backgrounds) have caused innocent members of the teaching profession to have their career destroyed.

She welcomed the fact that a number of teacher unions, at the behest of their members, had become more vocal about the treatment of teachers at the receiving end of allegations. Gail said her organisation "sought the maintenance of anonymity of the accused up till the point of conviction." So far, she said, this has been rejected by the Government.

Ms Saunders said that as things stood in Britain, the speed and public nature of procedures to do with investigations still lay at the discretion of the employer. As she spoke in August 2007, she said, "Just this morning, I received a call from the spouse of school principal who had lost his job and had his name emblazoned on local press headlines, even though he claimed complete innocence and was not convicted."

These government guidelines most obviously, she said, "do not happen in practice."

Some observers in this area believe that the situation has actually got worse with untested allegations officially revealed to prospective employers by the police without redress.

One member of F.A.C.T. from near Gwent in South Wales, told this writer of his titanic struggle against false allegations which first arose when he was 66 years of age. Mr James Hepburn (now 74) worked as a gardener all his life and helped instruct boys in gardening in two approved schools in Wales which took in young boys who found themselves in trouble. He said the emotional trauma of being falsely accused was almost unbearable. It was the "first thing I thought about when I got up in the morning, most of the day, and the last thing at night. It was always on my mind. It was torture, it was not fair."

In 1966 he got a job in St Aidans, an approved school in Widnes, on the outskirts of Liverpool. He started as an assistant to the gardening instructor hence he had daily contact with the boys. These boys were all of school age and had been through the courts. He was there from 1966-1978. He later got a job in Ty Mawr school in south Wales as the gardening assistant, and worked there for five years. He was made redundant in 1984 as some of the school departments closed, and for the next 19 years worked as a self-employed gardener.

"I remember the date, it was the 21st of January 1999 at half past eight in the morning that two police officers came knocking on our front door. They asked my name and did I once work at St Aidan's in Widnes? Then, they arrested me, took me to the local police station and questioned me for six hours. I was charged towards the end of March, and it went on from there. It came to trial in May 2001. The charges were four of buggery and nine of indecent assault. There were four accusers.

"I had a good counsel, Lord Carlile of Berriew, to act as my barrister, but even just before going to trial we were getting drip drip disclosures from the police.

"The main problem is corroboration by volume. It is placing quantity over quality of evidence. Some of the accusations didn't even make sense.

"The trial was expected to go on for two weeks but collapsed after two days, after the evidence was heard. The jury were directed by the judge what decision to come to, and the charges were quashed. Statements in my favour by witnesses were held by the police for eleven months before they were released to the defence. Both the judge and prosecutors from previous trials involving the same school knew from what the accusers was saying, that some of my accusers were speaking a load of rubbish. The jury weren't even allowed to decide on this, the prosecution knew it was a load of rubbish. It was a not guilty verdict."

Asked was this type of case common, Jim said, "Oh yes, it is happening all over the country. This is when F.A.C.T. got together. I thought initially, I was on my own, and asked why this was happening to me? But I found out that it was widespread. It turns out that there is a whole generation of carers and teachers being demonised by this."

These carers and teachers were being hurt especially by the practice of police trawling for allegations. An inquiry into abuse in children's homes in North Wales (known as the Waterhouse Report, 2000) highlighted the issue of child abuse in residential institutions but rubber stamped rather than addressed potential investigative flaws in police trawls. However, there was persistent questioning of the validity of both the method of trawling and the convictions which arose from this practice. This in turn, led to an inquiry by the Home Affairs Committee in the British House of Commons which on 30 October 2002 called for new safeguards to cover prosecutions in historical child abuse cases. (An alternative view on this matter can be seen at www.careleavers.com and at the website of the Association of Child Abuse Lawyers).

Committee chairman, Labour MP Chris Mullin said that: "No one wishes to minimise the suffering of victims of abuse or the damage that it can do their lives, but the plain fact is that many police trawls are not generating evidence of sufficient quality to satisfy the burden of proof. A point which is graphically illustrated by the fact that the Crown Prosecution Service rejects a staggering 79 per cent of institutional child abuse cases referred by the police compared to an overall rejection rate of just 13 per cent. I am in no doubt that a number of innocent people have been convicted and that many other innocent people, who have not been convicted, have had their lives ruined."

Incidentally, this same Labour MP became famous in Ireland, for his support of the eventually freed Birmingham Six, six Irish men wrongly convicted for an IRA bombing.

Liberal Democrat member of the Committee, Bob Russell MP said: "As this inquiry progressed I became increasingly alarmed that there are many men in prison who are almost certainly innocent of the serious crimes for which they were convicted. The manner in which evidence was given to the courts, with several people making near identical allegations against one individual, helped create a climate where the truth was difficult to determine. I hope that our Inquiry will assist those who have been wrongly convicted to seek justice through the Court of Appeal or the Criminal Cases Review Commission."

Conservative leader, David Cameron was also on the committee and it remains to be seen what impression this might have made on his intentions if elected to power.

This Home Affairs Committee gave a damning indictment of many of the prosecutions and convictions which resulted from police trawls into historical abuse allegations, which took place during the late 1990s in Britain. Of particular note, the committee called attention to the process of 'corroboration by volume.' In its main recommendations it noted the: "use of similar allegations, as evidence to corroborate a charge, is a particularly sensitive issue. However, given the dangers of prejudice, we believe it is necessary to tighten the rules for excluding such evidence, so that 'similar fact' evidence is only admitted if it bears a striking similarity to the evidence relating to the charged offence. This should, we believe, be accompanied by a presumption in favour of ordering separate trials, in cases where there is no striking similarity between the counts of abuse listed on the indictment."

And once again problems caused by the 'green eyed monster' raised its head – the effect of financial compensation. The Home Affairs Committee concluded that: "The potential for compensation to act as an inducement for giving false or exaggerated evidence during investigations of this kind, is another area of real concern. To minimise this risk, we have recommended that the working relationship between personal injury solicitors and the police be guided by a 'model relationship', to be drawn up by the Home Office."

The problem with trawling was that Police officers were approaching former pupils of these institutions for children in an unregulated fashion, allowing them at times to ask leading questions. The Home Committee report stated that, "The risk that the prospect of compensation might induce some individuals to give untruthful evidence is said to be compounded by a number of factors. First, the almost open invitation, given by the police during a trawl, to make an allegation of past abuse. Secondly, the advertisement by solicitors of civil compensation actions and awards. Thirdly, the working relationship that has been established between certain firms of personal injury solicitors and police forces. Finally, the conduct of group litigation, in civil compensation actions, is said to leave little opportunity for scrutiny in each individual case."

In a climate where public anxiety about possible child abuse is heightened by tabloid headlines, shrill TV programmes, and police asking leading questions to potential witnesses who are attracted by the lure of financial compensation, it almost goes without saying, that miscarriages of justice became more likely.

As a point of regret the Committee added, "We are conscious of the fact that many of these recommendations are simply closing the door after the horse has bolted." As they say in Ireland, 'Now, you're talking!'

As the situation currently stands, police trawl operations have largely trailed off in England and Wales, but continue in Scotland. However, as the recommendations of this Home Affairs Committee were not accepted by the UK Government, it would be fair to say that the cultural and legal shortcomings which led to the highlighted miscarriages of justice remains alive and active. Indeed, the organisation F.A.C.T. UK currently has fifty members who are in jail, many for long periods of time, and all of whom claim to be innocent of the charges for which they were convicted.

17 Literary Frauds and Follies

Mainstream Publishing of Edinburgh have resolutely stood behind their publication of Kathy's book in face of questioning from a number of journalists. The managing director of Mainstream, Bill Campbell told this journalist himself in September 2006 that he still supported the book. However, after the credibility of *Kathy's Story* began to fall apart, I emailed him again in October 2006 with a list of pertinent questions about the book: "Concerning recent developments about the book, *Kathy's Story*, which you publish in Britain with the title *Don't Ever Tell*, may I ask you for your comment on the following questions.

Kathy O'Beirne claims to be 44 whereas her family have produced her birth cert showing she is actually 50 years of age.

Her official school records also show she was in her local national school in Dublin, until the age of 12 and a half years which contradicts the claims in her book.

May I ask you:

1 – Do you still stand behind the veracity of the book?

2 – Do you believe that your company has been duped by the author?

3 – Given the new evidence surrounding the book, shall it be withdrawn by Mainstream Publishing?

4 – Shall a sequel to this book be published? Is it still in the pipeline or shall it be withdrawn?

5 – Can you tell us what documentary evidence you have seen to satisfy your company that the book's claims are wholly true?

6 – Would you have a rough idea how much money that Mainstream Publishing has made from its publication of *Don't Ever Tell*?

7 – Concerning Tom Carew's book *Jihad!*, it purported to be written by

an SAS soldier. This assertion turned out to be false. Can you give
an idea why the book was not withdrawn from print?"

Believe it or not, after a number of phone calls, I still failed to get
any answers. But he did tell *The Bookseller.com* in November 2006 that
he still stands by "the author, the book, and the story," blaming the
furore on a larger family row. "We've seen enough evidence to convince us of its veracity," he said.

However, it is not the first time that questions have been asked
about best-selling books published by Mainstream Publishing.

Publishers declare Jihad!

In Mainstream publicity –Tom Carew, and SAS author.

But in reality – Phil Sessarego, tank-part scrap merchant.

Another bestseller for Mainstream was *Jihad!* by a Tom Carew who
presented himself as "a young ex-SAS soldier," who had fought with the
Mujahideen in Afghanistan. It was published in March 2001 and cata-
pulted him to international stardom. Tom Carew began to appear regularly on TV as an expert on the SAS.

The Mainstream blurb of the time said:

"In 1980, Ronald Reagan and Margaret Thatcher had taken over the
leadership of the West, and the Soviets had invaded Afghanistan – the
most crucial battle of the Cold War was about to begin. In the high
mountain passes of the northwest frontier and the Hindu Kush, the
CIA and Britain's MI6 saw an opportunity to bring the mighty Soviet
army to its knees. Their weapon: the Islamic guerrillas of the Afghan
Mujahideen.

"The first Western agent to link up with the Mujahideen was Tom
Carew, a young SAS soldier with a talent for 'black bag' covert operations. Over a period of a year, Carew led a series of extraordinary recon-
naissance missions inside Afghanistan; in the course of these operations, he became as close to the Mujahideen as any European infidel
could. Set against the backdrop of the last truly wild and lawless country on earth, Carew's edge-of-the-seat narrative sheds new light on the
Cold War and the conduct of special operations in the modern era."

The BBC did an investigative report into this 'Tom Carew' on

November 14, 2001. It turned out that this book was fraudulent in its basic premise. The BBC news web site ran the headline: 'Author lied about SAS membership.'

As it turned out, the author was a certain Philip Sessarego who had never served in the SAS. He had been a soldier who had twice been turned down for entry into the SAS by their rugged selection tests.

In his book, he claimed to have served at least 14 years in 22 SAS, the regular army's elite regiment, but his was exposed as false. His own family dismissed the book as fanciful. However, Mainstream still stands by the book, and five years after it had been 'outed' they still sell it. The author had been in the Army and had served in Afghanistan.

According to *The Sun* newspaper at the time: "Sessarego DID travel to Afghanistan during the 1980s – but was not on a military mission and is understood to have worked salvaging Russian military vehicles."

Sesserego was ripping angry when confronted about this by the BBC interviewer. At the end of a strong barrage of probing questions as he made this way out of the building, he actually punched the cameraman.

The day after the BBC programme, Mainstream issued this press release on their web site: Tom Carew on BBC Newsnight: "Some of you may have seen BBC News last night, which claimed that Tom Carew was never a member of the SAS. They claim that although he trained with the SAS and was part of the Demonstration Troop of non-members who did jobs for them he was never part of the Squadron.

"The BBC does not dispute the fact that Carew fought in Afghanistan, which is what his best selling book *Jihad!* centres on. Ironically Carew did not need to exaggerate his association with the SAS. The book has become an international best seller because it is the first insightful, realistic account of what it was like to live and fight alongside the Afghans and specifically the Mujahideen, not because it has been marketed as an SAS memoir."

More amazing again was the rest of the Mainstream statement, where they were reassured by the world's reaction:

"Mainstream bought the book from a reputable agent and took Carew's credentials in good faith, aware that the ghost-writer had a

splendid military background. The manuscript and cover were scrutinised by the Ministry of Defence who gave the go-ahead with only
minor amendments. Newspaper serialisation was sold to *The Sunday
Times* and *The Sunday People* because of its unique and absorbing
account of fighting with the Mujahideen.

"After the events of September 11th, a whole year after publication of
the hardback, the author was in great demand as a commentator on the
events in Afghanistan. The Guardian bought a further extract and
Carew was called upon for comments by media throughout the world.
We were astonished to receive calls questioning the authenticity of our
author yesterday but have been reassured by the reaction of key book
buyers, foreign publishers and overseas distributors." (News 15
November 2001)

The author at least initially held out: "The BBC have got their wires
crossed. Every word in the book is true." The video of the Carew interview is well worth watching. The BBC confronted him after discovering
he'd never served in the SAS. After being confronted, the author turned
on his heels and stormed towards the exit door. At this point, the BBC
interviewer said:

"Isn't the truth that a real SAS man would stand his ground and
provide an answer and you don't have one?"

(Tom Carew assaults the cameraman – cue noise of breaking glass).
CAREW: "There's your answer."
BBC INTERVIEWER: "That's enough."

(You can watch the whole BBC video on this site. It's highly recommended: http://www.igorboog.com/stories/experts/)

In 2007, the book is still for sale. Why would the truth get in the way
of a good story? Mainstream appear to be happy with the book because
they still sell it. At least Sessarego had been in Afghanistan, Kathy
O'Beirne was never in a Magdalene laundry.

More questions about other Mainstream books

Mainstream published a book called, *The Sheriff* in 2006 by a former garda, Gerry O'Carroll, a Kerryman who joined the Gardai (Irish
Police Force) in the early 1970s.

According to the Mainstream publicity: it was the story of a senior garda officer who had seen "much bloodshed and plenty of controversy." Gerry O'Carroll spent three decades investigating "some of the country's most high-profile crimes and here he explains the motives behind them and reveals the confessions that led to convictions."

This book, the publisher tell us, recounts Gerry's story from his upbringing among a large family in rural Kerry to his professional success as one of Ireland's most well-known policemen. Gerry also worked as a columnist for *The Evening Herald* newspaper in Dublin.

Soon after *The Sheriff* was published in 2006, the family of a woman who died as a result of the Dublin Bombing in 1974 protested at the major inaccuracy of the episode which dealt with her death. The woman killed in this horrific bombing was Josie Bradley, and it was her twin sister, Marian Bradley who protested at its false portrayal. Marian Bradley sent a letter to *The Sunday Times* in Dublin:

"Dear Sir,

I wish to point out that on page 103 in Gerry O'Carroll's book 'The Sheriff' there is incorrect information concerning my twin sister, Josephine Bradley. Mr. O'Carroll states that 'We witnessed images that day that would haunt us for the rest of our lives. It seems strange, but I remember just one of the victims that I helped to coffin and lay out. She was a beautiful young girl. Her name was Josephine Bradley. She was from Kilcormac, Birr, County Offaly. She was only 21 years of age.'

"The facts are that Josie lived for three days after this atrocity and was found by me in Jervis St. Hospital the following day, Saturday, after calling all the city hospitals and searching the city morgue for her. She finally passed away from her horrific injuries on the following Monday night. Therefore it was impossible for Mr O'Carroll to have 'put her in the coffin' as he states in his book. Mr. O'Carroll should not use untruths to sensationalise his book. Nor did he have the common decency to seek permission from me or my family to publish her name and address."

Marian Bradley, (Sister Of Josie Bradley)

Blackrock, Co Dublin.

Marian told this author that she was appalled that someone would, as she put it, "attempt to make money on the back of a wrongful description of the death of my twin sister. When I first became aware that Mr O'Carroll was writing a story on this, before the book was even published, I tried to contact him via *The Evening Herald* newspaper. I e-mailed him, but did not even receive the courtesy of a reply. That episode in the book is the only one that I read. I am so angry I refuse read the rest of the book. But I can assure you, the one episode that I read about my twin sister is completely inaccurate."

Founded in Edinburgh in 1978, Mainstream Publishing is one of the leading non-fiction publishing companies in Scotland. It has grown prodigiously in recent years. So much so, that in 2005 it entered into partnership with Random House, the publishing powerhouse.

In September 2006, the month that *Kathy's Story* was exposed Mainstream was awarded the title of publisher of the month on a very important web site www.booksfromscotland.com which is majority owned by the Scottish Publishers Association (SPA).

It seems ironic that the book listed between *Jihad!* and *Don't ever Tell* on the SPA web site is a book entitled *Fakes, Forgers And Phoneys: Famous Scams and Scamps* by the well-known and highly respected Magnus Magnusson. In the book, Magnusson explores "...literary forgeries, archaeological frauds, impostors, and hoaxers in the world." But let's face it, it's not the first time this has happened in the world of publishing. Anyone can be taken for a ride if they don't watch out. Take Oprah Winfrey for instance.

Ireland having its own James Frey moment

On October 26, 2005, Oprah Winfrey announced that the book *A Million Little Pieces*, by author James Frey, was her latest choice for her TV book club. The sales of this non-fiction memoir of his violent and reprobate years as an alcoholic, drug addict, and criminal racketeer, reached over 3.5 million copies, enough to make Frey a very rich man indeed. But by January 8, 2006, The Smoking Gun investigation team in the USA, a team which frequently uses police files and contacts had shown that the book was greatly exaggerated. Its appeal to women, it seemed, was that Frey, a grand reclamation project, needed to be loved out of his lunge towards oblivion. According to The Smoking Gun team:

"Police reports, court records, interviews with law enforcement personnel, and other sources have put the lie to many key sections of Frey's book. The 36-year-old author, these documents and interviews show, wholly fabricated or wildly embellished details of his purported criminal career, jail terms, and status as an outlaw 'wanted in three states.'"

When *The Smoking Gun* (TSG) confronted him on Friday afternoon (January 6th, 2006) with their findings, "Frey refused to address the significant conflicts we discovered between his published accounts and those contained in various police reports. When we suggested that he might owe millions of readers and Winfrey fans an explanation for these discrepancies, Frey, now a publishing powerhouse, replied, 'There's nothing at this point can come out of this conversation that is good for me.'

"The author, James Frey alleges that he first submitted a transcript to literary agents as a work of fiction, but one of the agents, said it would only work if presented as fact. So the initial manuscript was jazzed up and made ready for publication as a memoir. This was later disputed by his publisher, Doubleday who have said they received the manuscript as a work of non-fiction.

"In the book, Frey presents himself in an overwhelmingly negative light. Eight times he says in the book: 'I am an Alcoholic and I am a drug addict and I am a criminal.'"

Some episodes of the book were so preposterous and far-fetched that early on some journalists did cast doubt on its authenticity. One book episode recounts Frey undergoing brutal root-canal surgery without the aid of anaesthesia. In another episode we encounter, an aeroplane trip during which the incapacitated protagonist Frey is bleeding, has a hole in his cheek, and is wearing clothes covered with "a colourful mixture of spit, snot, urine, vomit and blood."

Curiously, what is now a stock literary character, the molesting / rapist priest also has a walk on part. Perhaps he appeared from central casting at *The Da Vinci Code*.

Frey "recounts" walking into a church in Paris. What was he doing in Paris? He had made for Europe after jumping bail in Ohio. And what was he doing in the church? Making a detour as he was on his way to commit suicide by throwing himself into the River Seine of course. While in the church, and pouring out his heartache about his troubled life to a priest, the priest makes a lunge for Frey's crotch, exclaiming, "You must not resist God's will, my son."

That any man including a Catholic priest would try to say that sexually molesting somebody is doing God's will is beyond me. Anyway, a vicious punch-up ensues, with Frey possibly killing the groping cleric, our intrepid author, James Frey kicked him in the balls 15 times. *Mon Dieu!* I bet that was sore.

Frey spoke quite openly to the investigating team first. But then, as he gradually realised that he had been rumbled, he began to clam up. Following this *The Smoking Gun* team received a very strong letter from Frey's solicitor, in which TSG were told:

"As you are undoubtedly aware, my client has lucrative book and movie deals in place, as well as having an expectation of prospective economic benefits. It is certainly foreseeable that your publication of a false story about Mr Frey – particularly one falsely attacking his credibility – will imperil both his existing and anticipated economic benefits, resulting in substantial damages to my client.

"If litigation were to ensue to seek redress for any such defamatory publication, my client's recoverable damages would be in the range of millions of dollars.....

"If you publish a story which directly states or insinuates that my client is a liar, and that his book about certain aspects of his life has been falsified, you will be exposed to substantial liability."

So there we go. Publish your findings and take the consequences.

After The Smoking Gun exposé, Oprah invited the author back on the show (on January 26, 2006) to answer a few pertinent questions that she had. The second interview is very interesting, and Frey is very open:

Oprah: "James Frey is here and I have to say it is difficult for me to talk to you because I feel really duped. But more importantly, I feel that you betrayed millions of readers. I think it's such a gift to have millions of people to read your work and that bothers me greatly. So now, as I sit here today I don't know what is true and I don't know what isn't. So first of all, I wanted to start with *The Smoking Gun* report titled, 'The Man Who Conned Oprah' and I want to know—were they right?"

James: "I think most of what they wrote was pretty accurate. Absolutely."

Oprah: "Okay."

James: "I think they did a good job detailing some of the discrepancies between some of the actual facts of the events..."

Oprah: "What [*The Smoking Gun*] said was that you lied about the length of time that you spent in jail. How long were you in jail?"

James: [*The Smoking Gun* was] right about that. I was in [jail] for a few hours."

Oprah: "Not 87 days?"

James: "Correct."

As the interview progressed, Frey responded to questions on different pivotal episodes in the book. In bringing their talk to an end, Oprah said she realised it had been a difficult time for the author.

James: "I think you're absolutely right. I mean, I think this is obvious, this hasn't been a great day for me. It certainly hasn't been a great couple of weeks for me. But I think I come out of it better. I mean, I feel like I came here and I have been honest with you. I have, you know, essentially admitted to...to lying."

At the end he said he thought he had learned from his mistake and thought it would make him a better person.

According to a press release from Doubleday & Anchor Books, a publisher's note and an author's note to the readers will be included in future editions of *A Million Little Pieces* and available on the www.randomhouse.com at a later date.

Of course, all the while, the publishers were counting their money. Perhaps in this case there was no victims singled out. But people had been conned and betrayed. Millions of people, some of whom read the book to gain hope and a steer to tackle addiction felt that they had been betrayed.

Interestingly, a pertinent point that Oprah puts to the publisher is also a very important one in the case of *Kathy's Story*. Oprah suggested to Nan Talese, publisher and editor-in-chief of *A Million Little Pieces* and the senior vice president of Doubleday, a division of Random House:

"But if you're publishing it as a memoir, I think the publisher has a responsibility because as the consumer, the reader, I am trusting you. I'm trusting you, the publisher, to categorise this book whether as fiction or autobiographical or memoir."

The bottom line is, a memoir is an account of the author's experiences. James Frey did not have many of those experiences in his book. Indeed, he admitted that he made them up. He admitted that he lied. The book therefore is not a memoir and should not have been sold or promoted by the publisher as a non-fiction book.

On September 12, 2006, Frey and publisher Random House, Inc. reached a tentative legal settlement, where readers who felt that they had been defrauded by Frey's *A Million Little Pieces* would be offered a refund. To get the refund as tentatively agreed they would almost be asked to jump through hoops, and upside down to get their money. Customers may have to submit a proof of purchase, a page from the book, and make a sworn statement that they purchased the book under the assumption that it was a memoir. This is still unfinalised at time of writing. The publisher stated in September 2006 that the possible agreement would first have to seek court approval.

First described by the *Denver Post* as a "A brutal, beautifully written memoir." The book turned out to be embellished beyond repair. But people still agreed that the author, James Frey had great talent as a writer.

One journalist, John Dolan put it well: "The key to understanding Frey is that he realised you can't lay it on too thick for an audience addicted to silly fantasies."

Other types of literary frauds abound, and some of them were highlighted shortly after *Kathy's Story* was publicly called into question by her family.

Whereas Kathy was always the person she claimed to be, but invented a life story, other authors have invented themselves totally.

Other Interesting Literary Frauds around the World

James Tiptree Jr was a very successful science-fiction writer in the 1970s and '80s. The author's most famous books are collections of short stories such as *Smoke Rose Up Forever* but he also wrote two novels as well. In 1975, a respected editor of science fiction introduced James Tiptree's work to the world in the following terms:

"there is to me something ineluctably masculine about Tiptree's writing.... his work is analogous to that of Hemingway.... that prevailing masculinity about both of them – that preoccupation with questions of courage, with absolute values, with the mysteries and passions of life and death as revealed by extreme physical tests."

The books themselves portray a fascination with and description of male preoccupations. In an introduction to Tiptree's story in his *Again, Dangerous Visions* anthology, Harlan Ellison gave his opinion that "[writer, Kate] Wilhelm is the woman to beat this year, but Tiptree is the man."

But James Tiptree, had a secret. In 1970 he wrote: "I have what every child wants, a real secret life.... not a bite-the-capsule-when-they-get-you secret, nobody else's damn secret but mine."

And the little secret was that James Tiptree Jr was a woman. The author's real name was Alice B. Sheldon. She was born in 1915, had been brought up in Chicago by well-to-do parents who were big cheeses on the social circuit. At an early age she was taken to Africa on a hunting expedition and learned there to use a gun. As an adult, she became successively a painter, a military intelligence officer, a CIA agent, and an experimental psychologist who earned a Phd for her studies.

Only in later life, in 1967, at the age of 51 did Alice Bradley Sheldon take to science-fiction writing; which she did with great success. The only thing was that people never saw the author James Tiptree, and began to ask questions.

Alice Sheldon first married at 19 but got a divorce when her drunken husband began to shoot at her too frequently. She later married Huntington Sheldon.

The revelation of the true identity of James Tiptree seems to have upset Alice B. Sheldon so much that she had to go on medication, suffering from severe depression. She was so shaken, it was said that she never recovered. In 1987, when it was discovered that both she and her husband were suffering from debilitating diseases, she shot him and then killed herself.

And it wasn't some mutual suicide pact either. Seemingly, they discussed it and the husband didn't wish to enter any such pact. So she killed him, before committing suicide herself. Writer Julie Phillips has completed a biography of her: *James Tiptree, Jr.: The Double Life of Alice B. Sheldon*. One reviewer describing the biography said it: "starts with cannibals, ends in a murder-suicide and thrills all the way through."

Fun and Games in Australia and Switzerland

Prior to Frey's literary bout of creativity, a Holocaust-memoir *Fragments: Memories of a Wartime Childhood* by Benjamin Wilkomirski turned out in 1997 to be another fabrication. This time it was written by a Swiss man, Bruno Doesseker, who only knew Auschwitz and Madjanek camps as a tourist.

He had used the holocaust as an anchoring instrument with which he could haul himself into a position of profit and prestige. But not before the author had won many literary prizes, and was invited to give lectures on his experience all over America. He even had a very public and emotional 'reunion' with another holocaust survivor, (a soul mate whom he had known from his time in Auschwitz) in an American synagogue.

This woman, Laura Grabowski also claimed to be a "fellow survivor" who corroborated his story. She turned out to occupy the same class of literary truthfulness and be a serial fibber who had previously written of being a victim of satanic abuse, a story that had been debunked over ten years earlier.

Wilkomirski narrates his book from the perspective of a frightened child in a series of disjointed flashbacks in which he describes the horrible life in the Nazi camps. He draws a harrowing picture of a cruel regime: there are episodes were bloodied rats crawl from dead bodies; of a kind woman giving the poor boy her very last scrap of hardened bread; of young babies who chew their fingers to the bone before they pass away; and of the protagonist learning the necessary survival techniques from an older boy, who taught him out of kindness.

First published in German in 1995, *Fragments*, has since then been translated into twelve different languages. It went on to become a best-seller in Switzerland and two documentary films were based on it. The American edition of the book was published in 1996 by Schocken, an imprint of Random House. The publishers made great efforts to promote the book, going so far as to print teachers' study guides and other supplementary materials.

The publisher of the book's hardback edition, Jewish-interest publishing imprint, Jüdischer Verlag promptly and honourably withdrew their edition from print upon discovering the truth about it. According to the New York Times: "We are very disappointed to make this decision," said Nadine Meyer, the editor of Jüdischer. "We are sad about it and we feel sorry about it, but also have a responsibility as a publisher."

Another Swiss writer, Daniel Ganzfried, investigated the *Fragments* book: "I found some of what he wrote about and the whole repressed memory thing unbelievable," Mr Ganzfried said. "I found a birth certificate for him dated February 12, 1941. He never suffered in these terrible places set up by the Nazis."

To back up his Jewish identity, Wilkomirski told the investigating Ganzfried that he was circumcised. However, Wilkomirski's ex-wife and an old girlfriend quickly rebutted this claim. The book's credibility continued on a sharp downhill movement from then on.

Commentators are divided on their reason for the book's appearance from the hands of the author. Some think it was just for money, while others think that the book is a genuine result of faulty 'recovered memory therapy.'

Deborah Lipstadt is an Emory University lecturer who had assigned *Fragments* for her class on Holocaust memoirs. When confronted with evidence that it was a fraud, she is reported to have commented that the new revelations "might complicate matters somewhat, but [the work] is still powerful." She subsequently disavowed the book completely. In a later interview with Robert Birnbaum in *The Morning News* she said: "First of all, I used the *Fragments* book early on, shortly after it appeared. Then some suspicions arose that it might not be accurate. I was asked, on the run, literally on the fly, by Blake Eskin: 'What if it weren't quite true?' So I said, 'Then it will be a powerful novel.' When I found out the degree to which Wilkomirski falsified that story, I immediately stopped using it. But my throwaway line continues to be cited. "

Another author, this time highly praised Australian, Helen Demidenko wrote a book *The Hand That Signed The Paper* which was presented as a fictional novel drawing on the terrible experiences that her family went through in Ukraine before and during the Second World War.

The 1995 dust jacket synopsis read: "*The Hand that Signed the Paper* tells the story of Vitaly, a Ukrainian peasant, who endures the destruction of his village and family by Stalin's communists. He welcomes the Nazi invasion in 1941 and willingly enlists in the SS Death Squads to take a horrifying revenge against those he perceives to be his persecutors.... "This remarkable novel, a shocking story of the hatred that gives evil life, is also an eloquent plea for peace and justice."

Critic Jil Kitson described it as: "A searingly truthful account of terrible wartime deeds that is also an imaginative work of extraordinary redemptive power."

The author, a six foot tall lady with blonde hair down to her waist, who used to turn up to literary events in Ukrainian national dress was in her early twenties at the time. Would you believe that she turned out to be someone called Helen Darville, whose family hailed from Scunthorpe, England. 'Eh by gum, lad' – not quite mystery from the East, but perhaps she played orchestral works by Sergei Prokofiev on her iPod while she worked.

The Catholic Horror Fiction of Maria Monk

In the early 19th century, a great number of Irish and German immigrants began to emigrate to America, and as the majority of these were of the Catholic faith, this fact began to cause great unease among the 'Nativists'. (So-called here, because the Indians were the true nativists). The confluence of both economic protectionism and religious intolerance caused many 'nativists' who where White, Anglo-Saxon and Protestant to resent this great influx. Added to this mix was a strong anti-Catholicism which baulked at the slightest scent of 'popery' and Catholic religious.

As a political expression of this sentiment, the 'Know Nothing' political group was set up to defend a way of life that was strictly white and Protestant. Many take the Klu Klux Klan to be its contemporary American continuation.

It was into this world that a book by Maria Monk dropped like a bombshell. *The Awful Disclosures of Maria Monk: the Hidden Secrets of a Nun's Life in a Convent Exposed* was first published in New York in 1836.

The book centred on the Hôtel Dieu convent and hospital in Montreal, Canada. Maria Monk's central accusation was that convent nuns were having sexual relations with priests from the neighbouring seminary who supposedly entered the convent without any noise or commotion through a secret tunnel.

After taking her vows, she alleges: "Nothing important occurred till late in the afternoon, when, as I was sitting in the community-room, Father Dufresne called me out, saying, he wished to speak to me. I feared what was his intention; but I dared not disobey. In a private apartment, he treated me in a brutal manner; and, from two other priests, I afterwards received similar usage that evening. Father Dufresne afterwards appeared again; and I was compelled to remain in company with him until morning."

From these encounters, babies were born within the convent. However, to hide their illicit beginnings, soon after birth, these babies were baptised, then strangled, and hurriedly dumped in a quicklime pit in the basement of the convent. She herself claimed to have lived in the convent for a total of seven years before becoming pregnant by a priest, but unable to bear the thought of having her child destroyed, she had finally fled.

Murder most horrid – not only that but uncooperative nuns disappeared. In another episode, she alleges that a certain nun, 'Sr Frances,' who refused to take part in the alleged criminal acts with the rest of the nuns, is brought before the five priests and the Bishop for being disobedient, sentenced to death, and immediately bound and gagged, tied face upwards on a bed, other beds are then thrown on top of her, and the five priests along with the nuns jump upon the bed and literally crush the 'poor victim' to death.

She is then unbound and buried in quicklime (what else) in a cellar, where all vestiges of this existence and murder are destroyed. Murdered, buried in quicklime and then classed as disappeared. Will we ever hear the like of it again?

The endpoint of the book was reached with Maria Monk discovering that she was pregnant by a 'Father Phelan,' and not desiring to see her baby killed she decided to finally flee the convent. After a great struggle she finally escaped to New York, all the time pursued by agents of the Church until she was finally rescued by brave Protestant ministers.

But did it sell?

The printing of the book was anticipated, by announcements some months prior to it in the nativist newspaper, the *American Protestant Vindicator*. As a sensational attack on the practices of Catholic religious it soon became a rallying point for the nativist cause. Needless to say it sold very well. According to the *Protestant Vindicator*, by the end of July, 1836 it had already sold over 26,000 copies. By the start of the Civil War, it would have sold 300,000 copies. Since that time it has sold millions of copies. *Awful Disclosures* remained in print for years afterwards in various formats and has been revived intermittently.

Who really wrote and published the book?

After being found to be pregnant in the Magdalene Asylum in Montreal, Monk was asked to leave, and quickly took up with a Mr William K. Hoyte, head of the Canadian Benevolent Society, an organisation that combined Protestant missionary work with a very strident anti-Catholic activism. Hoyte took Monk as his mistress, and together they travelled to New York. Here, taking advantage of her fantastical imagination, Hoyte introduced her to fellow nativist activists, namely the Rev. J. J. Slocum, Rev. George Bourne, and Theodore Dwight.

Between them they wrote the book. But shortly after the book was published and real profits began to roll, law suits between the various parties began to ricochet around New York courtrooms. It turned out that Slocum was the principal author, while Hoyte and Bourne were major contributors. Maria herself changed sides and eventually, because she was underage at 18, Mr Slocum was made her guardian.

The first edition of the *Awful Disclosures* carries the imprint of Howe and Bates. This was not a publishing house because Howe and Bates were employees of Harper and Brothers. But because those at Harper were worried about the reaction of their Catholic customers should they publish Maria Monk's book, they created this new imprint. It seems there was no way that Harper and Brother would deny themselves such a moneymaking venture.

A 1997 paperback edition, for example, was released in England by Senate, an imprint of Random House in the United Kingdom. (Random House currently owns 50% of Mainstream Publishing, publisher of *Kathy's Story*).

How did it all fall apart?

The Protestants of New York and Montreal demanded an immediate independent investigation which took place and confirmed that the allegations were untrue but some still believed the story and said the Protestant investigators were just Jesuits in disguise.

In October 1836 the New York City newspaper editor and Protestant, Col. William Leete Stone went to Montreal and had obtained permission to inspect the Hôtel Dieu thoroughly with Maria Monk's book in hand. He was first of all searching for the secret passageways between the convent and nearby seminary. Looking at the layout and architecture of the convent and after questioning her he acknowledged:

"After 10 minutes the imposture had become as plain as day. I now declare more openly and boldly than ever that neither Maria Monk nor Francis Partridge have ever set foot in the convent of the Hôtel Dieu."

On top of this a large number of respected citizens from New York and Montreal made statements under oath. A respected doctor Robertson gave a sworn affidavit of having been approached by this Maria Monk and heard her change her story in a contradictory fashion four times as he questioned her. Mr Hoyte was in her presence as she was interviewed.

A Mrs McDonnell, who was in charge of a Magdalene Asylum in Montreal testified that Maria Monk had been a prostitute placed in her charge. As time went on, the mother of Maria Monk and her own daughter testified that the allegations contained in the book were false.

Her daughter, Mrs St. John Eckel, was told by her sister that her mother admitted the book was a lie. Mrs Eckel later wrote in her own autobiography, "My mother did not write her book; in fact, the book itself admits that she did not. She only gave certain facts which were dressed up by the men who afterwards helped to cheat her out of the proceeds of her crime."

Once her claims were discredited, Maria Monk fell from public view. It soon emerged that she had been a prostitute in Montreal, and that the years she claimed to have spent in a convent were actually spent in a Magdalene Asylum for wayward girls. She had never been a nun. She wasn't even a Catholic. Her own mother testified that she was mentally unstable, prone to fantasies and easily influenced.

How was it so popular, how was it believed?

When Maria Monk's book was first published, it's audience was already predisposed to accept the fantastical story that she presented for the readers. Already at that stage, America had a long history of anti-Catholic sentiment and even government policy.

The book played on nativist fears, ignorance and misunderstandings. And without ever lapsing into pornographic language it had lashings of religion, sex and violence. An unbeatable combination it turned out.

There were literary precedents to the book. In 1835 Rebecca Reed wrote a book, *Six months in a Convent* whose false and inflammatory description led local nativist activists to burn the convent to the ground. This book also became a best seller. Both the book by Reed and the handlers of Maria Monk obviously saw a market for this anti-Catholic horror fiction.

The book by Maria Monk is modelled on the gothic novels so popular in the early 19th century. The genre-defining elements of this gothic novel was that of 'a young, innocent woman being trapped in a remote, old, and gloomy estate where she learns the dark secrets the place contains, and after harrowing adventures makes her escape.' Does this sound familiar?

Where was she talking about?

The Hôtel Dieu that she attacked in her book was, at the time, one of the most highly respected institutions in Canada, by Catholics and Protestants alike. A charity hospital founded by a lay nurse, in 1642, Catholic nuns were asked to help and a convent began beside it in 1659. Just before the book was published, the workers in the hospital had distinguished themselves by their zeal in treating victims of a recent cholera epidemic. Many people in Montreal were outraged by the salacious attack on the convent.

The editorial in *The Montreal Herald* (October 20, 1835) was appalled by the action of *The Vindicator* newspaper which supported the book and gave its judgement thus:

"The Sisters of Charity [who were in charge of the Hôtel Dieu Convent] are equally respected and are the means of effecting important services to the community. They practice Christianity by feeding the hungry, clothing the naked, protecting the orphan, and ministering to the sick, the afflicted, and the dying—'pursuing the noiseless tenor of their way,' courting no popular applause, and seeking their sole reward in 'conscience void of offence toward God and man.'

"We do not pretend," the newspaper said, "to be defenders of the Roman Catholic religion or of any of its particular institutions. We are Protestants and glory in being so, but we will not so far forget the precepts of Our Divine Master as to connive at traducing the character of individuals who are exemplary members of society, although they are of a different religious persuasion from ourselves."

Who was Maria Monk and how did she die?

Maria Monk was born to a Protestant family in St Johns, Quebec. In 1816, her own mother signed an affidavit describing Maria as an uncontrollable child, a fact she attributed to a brain injury suffered when Maria was very young: a slate pencil was rammed into her ear, penetrating her skull. From that time on, according to her mother's testimony, Maria was uncontrollable and subject to wild fantasies.

An account of Maria Monk's death at the age of 33 may be found in 'Dolman's Register' of October 9, 1849. "Two months ago or more, the police book recorded the arrest of the notorious but unfortunate Maria Monk, whose book of *Awful Disclosures* created such excitement in the religious world some years since.

"She was charged with picking the pocket of a paramour in a den near the Five Points. She was tried, found guilty, and sent to prison [to Welfare Island, New York City], where she lived up to Friday last, when death removed her from the scene of her sufferings and disgrace. What a moral is here, indeed!"

The book's continuing after-effects

Maria Monk's literary fraud helped to popularise and lodge in the public imagination a raft of anti-Catholic stereotypes which continue into our own time and place. These stock characters of prejudiced fantasy, the strict authoritarian Catholic priest preaching chastity and practising sexual assault in private, ideas of crafty manipulation by the Jesuits, young girls duped and held against their will in isolated convents.

Yale professor Peter Viereck once described Catholic baiting as "the anti-Semitism of the liberals," while Episcopalian historian, Philip Jenkins could even author a recent book entitled *The New Anti-Catholicism: The Last Acceptable Prejudice* (Oxford University Press 2005). It's clear that Catholic horror fiction obviously finds a welcome reception.

These characters continue not just in the backwaters of uneducated Alabama but also in the consciousness of cultural elites who hold sway, in America, across western Europe and Australia as well.

Kathy's Story is simply Maria Monk for the 21st century

Kathy O'Beirne's description of her dreary life is filled with such a constant flow of horror and misfortune that it strains to breaking point the credulity of a reader to believe that such uniform misfortune fell on one person in a single lifetime. Looking at the statistical probability of it happening to Kathy, would make it unlikely to begin with.

In short, it's too bad to be true. But that an event didn't occur never stopped a good book being published. As a person once said of Ronald

Reagan, when a man is this lucky, it isn't just luck. When a woman like Kathy O'Beirne is this unlucky, it's not just bad luck, it's simply lies.

Whereas she seeks to portray herself as a victim in her book, she in fact, is not a victim but the the perpetrator of life-destroying false allegations against perfectly innocent people.

Kathy can be accused of a lot of things, but lack of imagination is not one them. And it is this imagination which had provided the main meat for this supper of deprivation. There is something in people that wants to feed that horrid, carnal nasty side of them.

Kathy O'Beirne would not have sold her book unless there was an appetite and receptive audience for that sort of literature, and a publisher saw a market for it. The current spate of miserable literature (mis. lit.) books which weigh down bookshelves across the Western world is like an outbreak of emotional pornography. Do people feel better in comparison after reading about someone who has had an awful life? I don't know, but the current phenomenon of "Mis. Lit." should provide subject matter for a large number of books for some time to come.

Appendix 1 Nora Wall– case declared a miscarriage of Justice

After her release and the apology from the DPP, Nora Wall, the former Mercy sister, applied for a grant of miscarriage of justice. This was heard by the three judge Court of Criminal appeal who gave the judgement below. Their finding of new evidence in the case of a man and woman who had been convicted and jailed is quite shocking:

> D.P.P.-v- Nora Wall
> [2005] IE CCA 140
> Court of Criminal Appeal Record Number: 147/99
> Date of Delivery: 16/12/2005
> Court: Court of Criminal Appeal
> Composition of Court: Kearns J., Herbert J., Butler J.
>
> Judgment by: Kearns J.
> Status of Judgment: Approved
>
> Grant application for miscarriage of justice
> Outcome: Grant application

THE COURT OF CRIMINAL APPEAL

On 10 June, 1999, the applicant was convicted by the Central Criminal Court of rape contrary to common law and of indecent assault contrary to common law as punishable by s.10 of the Criminal Law (Rape) Act, 1981. On 23 July, 1999, the applicant was sentenced by the Central Criminal Court to imprisonment for life for the offence of rape and to 5 years imprisonment for indecent assault.

On 27 July, 1999, the applicant brought a bail application before the Court of Criminal Appeal, at which point senior counsel on behalf of the respondent conveyed to that court the respondent's consent to the granting of leave to appeal, and further consented that the appeal be allowed and that a retrial be directed. This startling turn of events was referable to (a) the inadvertent calling as a witness on behalf of the prosecution, Patricia Phelan, a person whom the respondent had specifically directed should not be so called at the trial and (b) matters regarding the complainant, Regina

Walsh, which had not been disclosed to the lawyers representing the applicant prior to trial.

On 22 November, 1999, counsel for the respondent indicated to the court of criminal appeal that the respondent was not proceeding with an application for a retrial. Counsel for the respondent further indicated that the respondent "fully and ungrudgingly" accepted that the applicant was entitled to be presumed innocent of all charges preferred against her. The court accordingly quashed the conviction of the applicant and the sentences imposed in respect thereof. ....

The Newly-Discovered Facts

Without demur from the respondent, Mr. Rogers, senior counsel for the applicant, outlined the following facts, which fall into three broad categories, as constituting "newly-discovered facts" within the meaning of s.9 of the Act:-

(1) Regina Walsh – history of previous allegations, her psychiatric history immediately prior to the making of the complaints against the applicant and her reliance on 'flashbacks', so described by her, to retrieve these alleged incidents from her past

(a) That the complainant, Regina Walsh, had previously alleged that she was raped in London by a black man, in respect of which allegation she had made no complaint to the police.

(b) That the complainant, Regina Walsh, had previously had a violent relationship with her then boyfriend Tommy Mulcahy, in the course of which she was beaten and abused, as a consequence of which she was twice admitted to hospital, but in respect of which she made no complaint to the police.

(c) That the complainant, Regina Walsh, had made a complaint of assault against her aunt June O'Brien to the Garda Siochana in Waterford in 1996, which complaint was withdrawn by her some days after making same.

(d) That the complainant, Regina Walsh, had made three complaints to the Garda Siochana of assaults upon her by one Carol Tracey, who was never traced and in respect of which complaints no proceedings took place.

(e) That the complainant, Regina Walsh, had taken an overdose of tablets in 1996, as a consequence of which she was admitted to St. Declan's

Ward, Ardkeen Hospital, Waterford, under the care of one Dr. Sheppard, for psychiatric assessment and treatment immediately prior to her making the complaints the subject matter of the prosecution of the applicant.

(f) That had the direction of the respondent been followed the only evidence in the case against the applicant would have been that of the complainant, Regina Walsh, whose recollection of events was admitted to be solely the product of 'flashbacks' and who had no full memory or recall in the matter.

(2) Patricia Phelan – the calling of a witness deemed to be unreliable despite the respondent's specific direction not to do so – non-disclosure of the unreliability of the witness.

(g) That on the 24 April, 1997, the respondent had directed, for reasons as yet undisclosed, that one Patricia Phelan ought not to be called as a witness for the prosecution upon the trial of the applicant. Patricia Phelan had, on the 10 January, 1997, made a statement to Garda Sinead Connolly, then of Kilkenny Garda Station, purporting to corroborate the complaints made by Regina Walsh, by giving an eye-witness account of the alleged participation by the applicant in the alleged rape of the complainant.

(h) That the said Patricia Phelan had made prior complaints involving indecent assault and/or rape to the Garda Siochana against Harry Phelan, her late uncle, and also against one Michael Fitzpatrick.

(i) That the prosecution by the respondent of the said Michael Fitzpatrick for rape and indecent assault upon the sister of the said Patricia Phelan and for indecent assault upon the said Patricia Phelan was restrained on the grounds of delay in judicial review proceedings heard in the High Court before McCracken J., in the course of whose judgment, doubts were expressed concerning the credibility of the evidence offered by the said Patricia Phelan.

(j) That the said Patricia Phelan had made prior complaints to the Garda Siochana against one Joe Maguire that he had ripped off her shirt and assaulted her, and these complaints were later withdrawn by her.

(k) That Garda Sinead Connolly, then of Kilkenny Garda Station, who was responsible for taking the aforementioned statement of Patricia Phelan on 10 January, 1997, in pursuance of the investigation of the complaints made by Regina Walsh against the applicant, was also a member of the Garda Siochana responsible for investigating the foregoing complaints by Patricia Phelan against Harry Phelan and Michael Fitzpatrick.

(l) That the respondent herein was a party to the aforementioned judicial review proceedings in *Fitzpatrick v DPP*, of which the Chief State Solicitor had carriage on behalf of the respondent and in which the prosecution of Michael Fitzpatrick on foot of complaints by Patricia Phelan had been restrained by McCracken J.

(3) Regina Walsh and Patricia Phelan - false statements in evidence

(m) That the said Patricia Phelan after the trial, conviction and sentence of the applicant, had voluntarily made contact with Sr. Mona Killeen, who had been a lifelong friend and supporter, and admitted to her and subsequently to members of An Garda Síochána also, that she had lied in her statement and in her evidence upon the trial of the applicant, in saying that she had witnessed the involvement of the applicant in the alleged rape and sexual assault of the complainant, Regina Walsh, when she had not.

(n) That the complainant, Regina Walsh, had connived in the said deception by the said Patricia Phelan.

Form of the Hearing

.... Patricia Phelan wished only to confirm that the outline of facts was accurate and to further confirm her statement made to the gardaí on 2 April 2001. In the course of that statement, Patricia Phelan had stated :-

● *"In the trial, held at the Central Criminal Court in Dublin, I gave evidence on oath in the complaint against Nora Wall and Paul McCabe. In evidence, I told the judge and jury that I saw Paul McCabe rape Regina and that Nora Wall was present holding Regina's legs down. I gave other evidence but I cannot remember what. At the time I gave this evidence in court, I knew it was wrong and against the law but I just wanted to get back at Dominic (i.e. Nora Wall). I was also afraid to pull back on my evidence because I thought that once I had made a statement I had to give evidence in court. The reason why I wanted to get back at Dominic was because she used to physically beat me when I was living the Group Homes. She gave me a terrible life and I hated her. I remember ringing Sr. Mona Kilkeen. She was a good friend of mine for many years. It was during the trial, but I cannot remember much of the details. Some months after the trial, I rang Sr. Mona again. I was very distressed at the time. It was bothering me at this stage about the false evidence I had given in the trial."*

Needless to remark, the fact that a corroborative witness is shown to be unreliable would not of itself amount to a miscarriage of justice. However the evidence went a great deal further in the present case to the point where it is now established that Patricia Phelan on 10 January 1997 made a statement to the Garda Siochana which was untrue and at the trial gave entirely fabricated evidence in circumstances which give rise to a compelling inference of collusion between her and the complainant resulting in the fabrication of evidence which in the judgment of this court would render it unsafe to leave any of the evidence of either girl to a jury. The present case was almost equally noteworthy for the significant failures of communication between the various offices and persons concerned in the prosecution. In recommending that a prosecution against the applicant be brought, the officer charged with responsibility for the file within the respondent's office had noted as follows:-

"Evidence of Patricia Phelan

● *Local gardaí who have dealings with her during previous investigations have found her most unreliable. She never mentioned to the members anything about a rape at any time. Therefore her evidence should not be accepted as accurate."*

Following receipt of this recommendation, a decision to prosecute the applicant was made on 24 April, 1997. In so directing, an instruction was given that the defence solicitors be given copies of the statements made by Patricia Phelan and that they be further informed that the prosecution did not intend to call her as a witness. Owing to an oversight, the Office of the Chief State Solicitor omitted to inform the legal advisers of the applicant that it was not intended to call Patricia Phelan as a witness at the trial. While her statements were not included in the book of evidence served on the defendants, senior counsel in advising proofs on 28 April, 1998, directed that Patricia Phelan be called as a prosecution witness. In a letter dated 1 October, 1999, written by the respondent to the Attorney General, the respondent stated that:-

● *"Senior counsel is satisfied that at the time of advising he failed to advert to the direction which was not then present to his mind. He believes that he failed to realise that the statement of Patricia Phelan had previously been seen by him when submitted with the original file, and, for the reasons set out above, treated the statement as though it was new material which had only come to hand."*

Unfortunately neither junior counsel or the solicitor in attendance at the trial from the office of the Chief State Solicitor reminded senior counsel of the direction from the respondent and accordingly Patricia Phelan gave evidence at the trial. The importance of that evidence may be gauged from the fact that the jury only convicted the applicant in respect of one incident, that being the incident in respect of which Patricia Phelan gave corroborative evidence. In respect of the other offence, which depended exclusively upon the evidence of the complainant, the jury acquitted the applicant. Further, the learned trial judge had seen fit in his summing up at the conclusion of the trial to decide, in exercising the discretion vested in him so to do by statute, to warn the jury about the dangers of acting without corroboration on the evidence of the complainant alone.

In the course of his outline of the facts to this court, Mr. Rogers also drew the court's attention to similarities in detail which emerged in the statements furnished by the complainant and Patricia Phelan, suggesting connivance to a significant degree between the two girls. He further adverted to the fact that Garda Sinead Connolly was a garda officer common to both this particular prosecution, and the prosecution of Michael Fitzpatrick, wherein McCracken J. had expressed doubts of his own about the credibility of Patricia Phelan as a witness.

Conclusion of this Court

In acceding to the application of the applicant herein, the court does not find it necessary to distinguish in terms of gravity between the various newly-discovered facts which the court is satisfied show that there has been a miscarriage of justice in this case. The prosecution which did take place inasmuch as it involved the tendering of corroborative evidence by a witness known to be unreliable was thus, in that format, a prosecution that should not have been brought. There was further a most unfortunate breakdown in communications or systems failure between the respondent's office, that of the Chief State Solicitor, the Garda Siochana and prosecuting counsel which the court is satisfied constituted a serious defect in the administration of justice brought about however unintentionally in this instance by agents of the State. It is now also accepted by the respondent that there had been significant non-disclosure in this case, including

(a) the information that Regina Walsh had made, but not pursued, an allegation of being raped in England and

(b) the non-disclosure of Regina Walsh's very proximate and material psychiatric history. It seems to this court that the applicant was further prejudiced during the course of her trial by evidence of which the defence had no prior notification, namely, that Regina Walsh recalled the alleged episodes of rape by reference to 'flashbacks and/or retrieved memory'. There was no scientific evidence of any sort adduced to explain the phenomenon of 'flashbacks' and/or 'retrieved memory', nor was the applicant in any position to meet such a case in the absence of prior notification thereof.

As previously indicated, this court does not find it necessary on the agreed facts of this case to elaborate a hierarchy of the newly-discovered facts which either singly or cumulatively amount to a miscarriage of justice. Virtually all of the newly-discovered facts are facts of significance which confirm the court in its view that there has been a miscarriage of justice in this instance.

The court will therefore grant the certificate sought in this case.

Judgement printed above is an excerpt from Courts Service website.

Appendix 11 : Final Questions to Kathy O'Beirne

On Friday 7th September, 2007 this author wrote this letter to Kathy O'Beirne asking her to send the relevant documents and answer pertinent questions on her book.

"Dear Kathy,

I am writing a book, part of which deals with accusations made in your book, Kathy's Story / Don't Ever Tell.

Can you answer the following questions, and send me the documents listed below, within 7 days of your receiving this letter.

I would appreciate if you could send the answers to the following questions to the address above.

Thank you for your time and help,

Yours respectfully,

Hermann Kelly

1. During an interview on RTÉ radio's Tonight with Vincent Browne Show on Wednesday June 22, 2005 you stated during the interview that, "I got my daughter's Birth Certificate after 30 years on Friday."
   Can you send me a copy of this child's birth certificate

2. In an interview with Hermann Kelly on the last Friday of June 2005 you claimed that she had all her files showing that you were in a Magdalene Laundry.
   Can you send me copies of these files, and show this evidence.

3. According to the publicity material in the 2005 catalogue of Mainstream Publishing which published her book: "At 13, back in another Magdalene Laundry, Kathy was raped and became pregnant. Poorly from birth, her baby Kelly Anne, spent the rest of her short life in a home run by nuns and when she died she was interred in a mass grave. Kathy still doesn't know where her baby is buried."
   I asked you about the burial of her child and you flatly contradicted the publishers publicity: "Who was buried in a mass grave? Who told you that? You want to get your facts right." When I pointed out it was in the publishers press release, you said they had "got their facts wrong. There is nothing about her being buried in a mass grave in the book." You added that her daughter, "was very well looked after by the nuns."
   Why did you fail to mention this important matter to the publishers before the book catalogue went to print?

Do you have any documentation to show where your daughter was looked after?

4. During an interview with Niall Donald of the Sunday Mirror the second Friday in August 2006:
You said of Eamonn, Oliver, Margaret and Mary O'Beirne:
"We are related, but I am not their sister."…. "I didn't grow up in the same house, because I was taken out of the house…. I am not even related to them. I am distant related to them. But that is about all. We are not blood. We are not blood related at all. And feel free to ring my solicitor to confirm what I have just told you. And you can write that as well."
You're family have produced your birth certificate showing you are a child of the same parents.
Do you withdraw this claim that you were adopted and you are not the sister of Eamonn, Mary, Margaret etc O'Beirne?

5. You also told the same journalist:
"Well I can guarantee you that I have a letter stating from the nuns that I was in the Magdalene laundries and their care, which I received on Thursday. I received it on Thursday with my legal team."
Can you send me a copy of this letter from the nuns showing that you were in a Magdalene laundry?

6. You also told the same journalist: "I have my facts, my proof and every-thing else…. I have just received a psychiatrist's file that handed me over to the Magdalene laundries. Isn't that strange?"
Can you please send me a copy of this file that handed you over the Magdalene laundry?

7. In 2005/2006, you told journalists that you were 45 years of age. Can you produce evidence of this?

8. Your sister Mary, applied under Freedom of Information Act to learn of the length of stay you had at St Loman's Psychiatric Hospital in Dublin. The FoI office told her that you had already applied and been sent a copy of your St Loman's files?
a Do they show that you were there for 2 years?
b Do these files provide evidence that you suffered any of the hardships portrayed in your book?
c Can you send me a copy of your files from St Loman's?

9. Friends of Fr Fergal O'Connor OP, founder of Sherrard House hostel

have told this journalist that he said that you claimed that he raped you, physically beat you up and was emotionally abusive to you?

a   Did Fr O'Connor rape you, beat you up or emotionally abuse you?

b   Did you make any claims against or concerning Fr Fergal O'Connor OP to Dublin Diocese?

c   Have you ever claimed that members of a male religious order were raping or sexually abusing young girls in Sherrard House ?

d   Please state what these these claims were?

e   Did you make any claims against Fr O'Connor to either the Health Board and/ or the Gardai?

f   What were these claims?

g   What was the outcome of these investigations?

10. A friend of yours, Margaret Power has made a statement to Gardai that you asked her to lie and say falsely, that she had seen you being raped by a priest in the late 1960's in Clondalkin.

a   Where you ever raped by a priest in the late 1960's in Clondalkin?

b   Did you ask Margaret Power to say she had witnessed this happening?

c   Have you given any witness statements to either Dublin Diocese or the Gardai that you were raped at this time?

d   Or that Margaret Power was your witness?
Margaret Power said that you offered to buy her a house if she perjured herself and gave false witness that she had witnessed you being raped.

f   Have you ever offered to buy her a half share in a house if she said this for you?

11. How many criminal convictions do you have?

12. How many and for what crimes?

13. Have you ever been charged with making false allegations?

14. To the best of your knowledge, how many copies of Kathy's Story / Don't Ever Tell have been sold so far?

15. How much money have you made from the book so far?

16. Have you ever made a false allegation against anyone or against any institution which you have attended?"

And the reply? The publication of this book was delayed in order to wait for Kathy's reply, which was as follows: No response.
Reader, draw your own conclusions.

Glossary

An Garda Síochána – The state police force of The Irish Republic. (means 'guardians of the peace')

Dáil – The Irish Parliament which meets in Leinster House, Dublin.

DPP – The Director of Public Prosecutions – initiates criminal prosecutions on behalf of the State.

Magdalene Laundry – Frequently referred to as asylums, these institutions began as part of the rescue movement in 19th century Britain and Ireland to help women who wished to escape a life of prostitution.

As time went on, they changed from short-term to long-term care. The reasons for the women being admitted also increased – for poverty, for the abused, for unmarried mothers etc. The women usually worked in a laundry, washing and pressing clothes.

Redress Board – was set up by the Irish Government under the Residential Institutions Redress Act, 2002 to make fair and reasonable awards to persons who, as children, were abused while resident in industrial schools, reformatories and other institutions subject to state regulation or inspection.

Sherrard House Hostel – run by the Homeless Girls' Society, set up by concerned members of Dublin society, mainly committed Catholics, to help and house young woman and older girls who where in difficulty. It provides a stable home-like environment. A priest of the Dominican Order, Fr Fergal O'Connor OP was a leading light in its work. It has helped many vulnerable young women for over 40 years. It continues this work today. Kathy stayed there for some time in her mid to late teens.

St Anne's, Kilmacud – reformatory convent boarding school run by the Sisters of Our Lady of Charity. The Order say she was there for 6 weeks, Kathy claims she was there for two years.

St Loman's Hospital – A state run psychiatric hospital situated in west Dublin, which catered for youths and adults. While Kathy's family say she went there for about 6 months, Kathy claims she was abused there for a period of two years.

Taoiseach – The Irish Prime Minister (from the Irish – leader)